HOROSCOPE
—2000—

Your Personal HOROSCOPE
— 2000 —

Yearly Horoscopes and
Month-by-month Forecasts
for Every Sign

Joseph Polansky

Thorsons
An Imprint of HarperCollins*Publishers*

Thorsons
An Imprint of HarperCollins*Publishers*
77–85 Fulham Palace Road,
Hammersmith, London W6 8JB

Published by Thorsons 1999
1 3 5 7 9 10 8 6 4 2

Joseph Polansky asserts the moral right to
be identified as the author of this work

A catalogue record for this book
is available from the British Library

ISBN 0 7225 3789 1

www.stardata-online.com
info@stardata-online.com

Printed and bound in Great Britain by
Caledonian International Book Manufacturing Ltd, Glasgow

Contents

ACKNOWLEDGEMENTS

The author is grateful to the people
of STAR ★ DATA, who truly fathered
this book and without whom it
could not have been written.

Introduction

Welcome to the fascinating and intricate world of astrology!

For thousands of years the movements of the planets and other heavenly bodies have intrigued the best minds of every generation. Life holds no greater challenge or joy than this: knowledge of ourselves and the universe we live in. Astrology is one of the keys to this knowledge.

Your Personal Horoscope 2000 gives you the fruits of astrological wisdom. In addition to general guidance on your character and the basic trends of your life, it shows you how to take advantage of planetary influences so you can make the most of the year ahead.

The section on each Sign includes a Personality Profile, a look at general trends for 2000, and in-depth month-by-month forecasts. The Glossary (*page 11*) explains some of the astrological terms you may be unfamiliar with.

One of the many helpful features of this book is the 'Best' and 'Most Stressful' days listed at the beginning of each monthly forecast. Read these sections to learn which days in each month will be good overall, good for money, and good for love. Mark them on your calendar – these will be your best days. Similarly, make a note of the days that will be most stressful for you. It is best to avoid taking important meetings or major decisions on these days, as well as on those days when important planets in your Horoscope are *retrograde* (moving backwards through the Zodiac).

The Major Trends section for your Sign lists those days when your vitality is strong or weak, or when relationships with your co-workers or loved ones may need a bit more effort on your part. If you are going through a difficult time, take a look at the colour, metal, gem and scent listed in the 'At a Glance' section of your Personality Profile. Wearing a piece of jewellery that contains your metal and/or gem will strengthen your vitality; just as wearing clothes or decorating your room or office in the colour ruled by your Sign, drinking teas made from the herbs ruled by your Sign, or wearing the scents associated with your Sign will sustain you.

Another important virtue of this book is that it will help you to know not only yourself but those around you: your friends, co-workers, partners and/or children. Reading the Personality Profile and forecasts for their Signs will provide you with an insight into their behaviour that you won't get anywhere else. You will know when to be more tolerant of them and when they are liable to be difficult or irritable.

I consider you – the reader – my personal client. By studying your Solar Horoscope I gain an awareness of what is going on in your life – what you are feeling and striving for and the challenges you face. I then do my best to address these concerns. Consider this book the next best thing to having your own personal astrologer!

It is my sincere hope that *Your Personal Horoscope 2000* will enhance the quality of your life, make things easier, illuminate the way forward, banish obscurities and make you more aware of your personal connection to the universe. Understood properly and used wisely, astrology is a great guide to knowing yourself, the people around you and the events in your life – but remember that what you do with these insights – the final result – is up to you.

Glossary of Astrological Terms

Ascendant

We experience day and night because the Earth rotates on its axis once every 24 hours. It is because of this rotation that the Sun, Moon and planets seem to rise and set. The Zodiac is a fixed belt (imaginary, but very real in spiritual terms) around the Earth. As the Earth rotates, the different Signs of the Zodiac seem to the observer to rise on the horizon. During a 24-hour period every Sign of the Zodiac will pass this horizon point at some time or another. The Sign that is at the horizon point at any given time is called the Ascendant, or Rising Sign. The Ascendant is the Sign denoting a person's self-image, body and self-concept – the personal ego, as opposed to the spiritual ego indicated by a person's Sun Sign.

Aspects

Aspects are the angular relationships between planets, the way in which one planet stimulates or influences another. If a planet makes a harmonious aspect (connection) to another, it tends to stimulate that planet in a positive and helpful way. If it makes a stressful aspect to another planet, this disrupts the planet's normal influence.

Astrological Qualities

There are three astrological qualities: *cardinal*, *fixed* and *mutable*. Each of the 12 Signs of the Zodiac falls into one of these three categories.

Cardinal Signs   Aries, Cancer, Libra and Capricorn
The cardinal quality is the active, initi-ating principle. Those born under these four Signs are good at starting new projects.

Fixed Signs   Taurus, Leo, Scorpio and Aquarius
Fixed qualities include stability, persistence, endurance and perfectionism. People born under these four Signs are good at seeing things through.

Mutable Signs   Gemini, Virgo, Sagittarius and Pisces
Mutable qualities are adaptability, changeability and balance. Those born under these four Signs are creative, if not always practical.

Direct Motion

When the planets move forward through the Zodiac – as they normally do – they are said to be going 'direct'.

Houses

There are 12 Signs of the Zodiac and 12 Houses of experience. The 12 Signs are personality types and ways in which a given planet expresses itself; the 12 Houses show 'where' in your life this expression takes place. Each House has a different area of interest. A House can become potent and important – a House of Power – in different ways: if it contains the Sun, the Moon or the Ruler of your chart, if it contains more than one planet, or if the Ruler of that House is receiving unusual stimulation from other planets.

1st House	Personal Image and Sensual Delights
2nd House	Money/Finance
3rd House	Communication and Intellectual Interests
4th House	Home and Family
5th House	Children, Fun, Games, Creativity, Speculations and Love Affairs
6th House	Health and Work
7th House	Love, Marriage and Social Activities
8th House	Transformation and Regeneration
9th House	Religion, Foreign Travel, Higher Education and Philosophy
10th House	Career
11th House	Friends, Group Activities and Fondest Wishes
12th House	Spirituality

Karma

Karma is the law of cause and effect which governs all phenomena. We are all where we find ourselves because of
karma – because of actions we have performed in the past.
The universe is such a balanced instrument that any act
immediately sets corrective forces into motion – karma.

Long-term Planets

The planets that take a long time to move through a Sign
show the long-term trends in a given area of life. They are
important for forecasting the prolonged view of things.
Because these planets stay in one Sign for so long, there are
periods in the year when the faster-moving (short-term)
planets will join them, further activating and enhancing the
importance of a given House.

Jupiter	stays in a Sign for about 1 year
Saturn	2½ years
Uranus	7 years
Neptune	14 years
Pluto	15 to 30 years

Lunar

Relating to the Moon.

Natal

Literally means 'birth'. In astrology this term is used to distinguish between planetary positions that occurred at the time of a person's birth (natal) and those that are current (transiting). For example, Natal Sun refers to where the Sun was when you were born; transiting Sun refers to where the Sun's position is currently at any given moment – which usually doesn't coincide with your birth, or Natal, Sun.

Out of Bounds

The planets move through the Zodiac at various angles relative to the celestial equator (if you were to draw an imaginary extension of the Earth's equator out into the universe, you would have an illustration of this celestial equator). The Sun – being the most dominant and powerful influence in the Solar system – is the measure astrologers use as a standard. The Sun never goes more than approximately 23 degrees north or south of the celestial equator. At the winter solstice the Sun reaches its maximum southern angle of orbit (declination); at the summer solstice it reaches its maximum northern angle. Any time a planet exceeds this Solar boundary – and occasionally planets do – it is said to be 'out of bounds'. This means that the planet exceeds or trespasses into strange territory – beyond the limits allowed by the Sun, the Ruler of the Solar system. The planet in this condition becomes more emphasized and exceeds its authority, becoming an important influence in the forecast.

Phases of the Moon

After the full Moon, the Moon seems to shrink in size (as perceived from the Earth), gradually growing smaller until it is virtually invisible to the naked eye – at the time of the next new Moon. This is called the *waning* Moon phase, or the waning Moon.

After the new Moon, the Moon gradually gets bigger in size (as perceived from the Earth) until it reaches its maximum size at the time of the full Moon. This period is called the *waxing* Moon phase, or waxing Moon.

Retrogrades

The planets move around the Sun at different speeds. Mercury and Venus move much faster than the Earth, while Mars, Jupiter, Saturn, Uranus, Neptune and Pluto move more slowly. Thus there are times when, relative to the Earth, the planets appear to be going backwards. In reality they are always going forward, but relative to our vantage point on Earth they seem to go backwards through the Zodiac for a period of time. This is called 'retrograde' motion and tends to weaken the normal influence of a given planet.

Short-term Planets

The fast-moving planets move so quickly through a Sign that their effects are generally of a short-term nature. They reflect the immediate, day-to-day trends in a Horoscope.

Moon	stays in a Sign for only 2½ days
Mercury	20 to 30 days
Sun	30 days
Venus	approximately 1 month
Mars	approximately 2 months

Transits

This refers to the movements or motions of the planets at any given time. Astrologers use the word 'transit' to make the distinction between a birth or Natal planet (*see 'Natal', above*) and the planet's current movement in the heavens. For example, if at your birth Saturn was in the Sign of Cancer in your 8th House, but is now moving through your 3rd House, it is said to be 'transiting' your 3rd House. Transits are one of the main tools with which astrologers forecast trends.

Aries

♈

THE RAM
Birthdays from
21st March
to 20th April

Personality Profile

ARIES AT A GLANCE

Element – Fire

Ruling Planet – Mars
   Career Planet – Saturn
   Love Planet – Venus
   Money Planet – Venus
   Planet of Fun, Entertainment, Creativity
   and Speculations – Sun
   Planet of Health and Work – Mercury
   Planet of Home and Family Life – Moon
   Planet of Spirituality – Neptune
   Planet of Travel, Education, Religion and
   Philosophy – Jupiter

Colours – carmine, red, scarlet

ARIES

Colours that promote love, romance and social harmony – green, jade green

Colour that promotes earning power – green

Gem – amethyst

Metals – iron, steel

Scent – honeysuckle

Quality – cardinal (= activity)

Quality most needed for balance – caution

Strongest virtues – abundant physical energy, courage, honesty, independence, self-reliance

Deepest need – action

Characteristics to avoid – haste, impetuousness, over-aggression, rashness

Signs of greatest overall compatibility – Leo, Sagittarius

Signs of greatest overall incompatibility – Cancer, Libra, Capricorn

Sign most helpful to career – Capricorn

Sign most helpful for emotional support – Cancer

Sign most helpful financially – Taurus

Sign best for marriage and/or partnerships – Libra

Sign most helpful for creative projects – Leo

Best Sign to have fun with – Leo

Signs most helpful in spiritual matters – Sagittarius, Pisces

Best day of the week – Tuesday

Understanding the Aries Personality

Aries is the activist *par excellence* of the Zodiac. The Arien need for action is almost an addiction, and those who do not really understand the Arien personality would probably use this hard word to describe it. In reality 'action' is the essence of the Arien psychology – the more direct, blunt and to-the-point the action, the better. When you think about it, this is the ideal psychological makeup for the warrior, the pioneer, the athlete or the manager.

Ariens like to get things done, and in their passion and zeal often lose sight of the consequences for themselves and others. Yes, they often *try* to be diplomatic and tactful, but it is hard for them. When they do so they feel that they are being dishonest and phony. It is hard for them even to understand the mind-set of the diplomat, the consensus builder, the front office executive. These people are involved in endless meetings, discussions, talks and negotiations – all of which seem a great waste of time when there is so much work to be done, so many real achievements to be gained. An Aries can understand, once it is explained, that talks and negotiations – the social graces – lead ultimately to better, more effective actions. The interesting thing is that an Aries is rarely malicious or spiteful – even when waging war. Aries people fight without hate for their opponents. To them it is all good-natured fun, a grand adventure, a game.

When confronted with a problem many people will say 'Well, let's think about it, let's analyse the situation.' But not an Aries. An Aries will think 'Something must be done. Let's get on with it.' Of course neither response is the total answer. Sometimes action is called for, sometimes cool thought. But an Aries tends to err on the side of action.

Action and thought are radically different principles. Physical activity is the use of brute force. Thinking and deliberating require one not to use force – to be still. It is not good for the athlete to be deliberating the next move; this will only slow down his or her reaction time. The athlete must act instinctively and instantly. This is how Aries people tend to behave in life. They are quick, instinctive decision-makers and their decisions tend to be translated into action almost immediately. When their intuition is sharp and well tuned, their actions are powerful and successful. When their intuition is off, their actions can be disastrous.

Do not think this will scare an Aries. Just as a good warrior knows that in the course of combat he or she might acquire a few wounds, so too does an Aries realize – somewhere deep down – that in the course of being true to yourself you might get embroiled in a disaster or two. It is all part of the game. An Aries feels strong enough to weather any storm.

There are many Aries people who are intellectual: Ariens make powerful and creative thinkers. But even in this realm they tend to be pioneers – outspoken and blunt. These types of Ariens tend to elevate (or sublimate) their desire for physical combat in favour of intellectual, mental combat. And they are indeed powerful.

In general, Aries people have a faith in themselves that others could learn from. This basic, rock-bottom faith carries them through the most tumultuous situations of life. Their courage and self-confidence make them natural leaders. Their leadership is more by way of example than by actually controlling others.

Finance

Arien people often excel as builders or estate agents. Money in and of itself is not as important as are other things – action, adventure, sport, etc. They are motivated by the need to support and be well-thought-of by their partners. Money as a way of attaining pleasure is another important motivation. Ariens function best in their own businesses or as managers of their own departments within a large business or corporation. The fewer orders they have to take from higher up, the better. They also function better out in the field rather than behind a desk.

Aries people are hard workers with a lot of endurance; they can earn large sums of money due to the strength of their sheer physical energy.

Venus is their Money Planet, which means that Ariens need to develop more of the social graces in order to realize their full earning potential. Just getting the job done – which is what an Aries excels at – is not enough to create financial success. The co-operation of others needs to be attained. Customers, clients and co-workers need to be made to feel comfortable; many people need to be treated properly in order for success to happen. When Aries people develop these abilities – or hire someone to do this for them – their financial potential is unlimited.

Career and Public Image

One would think that a pioneering type would want to break with the social and political conventions of society. But this is not so with the Aries-born. They are pioneers within conventional limits, in the sense that they like to start their own businesses within an established industry.

Capricorn is on the 10th House (Career) cusp of Aries' Solar Horoscope. Saturn is the planet that rules their life's work and professional aspirations. This tells us some interesting things about the Arien character. First off, it shows that in order for Aries people to reach their full career potential they need to develop some qualities that are a bit alien to their basic nature: They need to become better administrators and organizers; they need to be able to handle details better and to take a long-range view of their projects and their careers in general. No one can beat an Aries when it comes to achieving short-range objectives, but a career is long term, built over time. You cannot take a 'quickie' approach to it.

Some Aries people find it difficult to stick with a project until the end. Since they get bored quickly and are in constant pursuit of new adventures, they prefer to pass an old project or task on to somebody else in order to start something new. Those Ariens who learn how to put off the search for something new until the old is completed will achieve great success in their careers and professional lives.

In general, Aries people like society to judge them on their own merits, on their real and actual achievements. A reputation acquired by 'hype' feels false to them.

Love and Relationships

In marriage and partnerships Ariens like those who are more passive, gentle, tactful and diplomatic – people who have the social grace and skills they sometimes lack. Our partners always represent a hidden part of ourselves – a self that we cannot express personally.

An Aries tends to go after what he or she likes aggressively. The tendency is to jump into relationships and marriages. This is especially true if Venus is in Aries as well as the Sun. If an Aries likes you, he or she will have a hard time taking no for an answer; many attempts will be made to sweep you off your feet.

Though Ariens can be exasperating in relationships – especially if they are not understood by their partners – they are never consciously or wilfully cruel or malicious. It is just that they are so independent and sure of themselves that they find it almost impossible to see somebody else's viewpoint or position. This is why an Aries needs as a partner someone with lots of social grace.

On the plus side, an Aries is honest, someone you can lean on, someone with whom you will always know where you stand. What he or she lacks in diplomacy is made up for in integrity.

Home and Domestic Life

An Aries is of course the ruler at home – the Boss. The male will tend to delegate domestic matters to the female. The female Aries will want to rule the roost. Both tend to be handy round the house. Both like large families and both believe in the sanctity and importance of the family. An Aries is a good family person, although he or she does not especially like being at home a lot, preferring instead to be roaming about.

Considering that they are by nature are so combative and wilful, Aries people can be surprisingly soft, gentle and even vulnerable with their children and partners. The Sign of Cancer, ruled by the Moon, is on the cusp of their Solar 4th House (Home and Family). When the Moon is well aspected – under favourable influences – in the birth chart an Aries will be tender towards the family and want a family life that is nurturing and supportive. Ariens like to come home after a hard day on the battlefield of life to the understanding arms of their partner and the unconditional love and support of their family. An Aries feels that there is enough 'war' out in the world – and he or she enjoys participating in that. But when Aries comes home, comfort and nurturing are what's needed.

Horoscope for 2000

Major Trends

1999 was a happy year: a year of great personal and career expansion; a year of catching the lucky breaks; a year of personal pleasure and sensual fulfilment; a year of learning how precious you are in the scheme of things. Always an optimist, 1999 heightened your optimism even further. There was nothing you couldn't be, do or have. Many of these trends are continuing in the year 2000.

The important areas of interest this year will be the body and personal image, personal pleasure, money and finance, religion, philosophy and foreign travel, and friends and group activities.

Pluto in your 9th House this year and for many years to come shows the total transformation that is happening in your personal philosophy of life, religious beliefs and general world view. Spiritual and religious concepts will be deepened and widened. False beliefs or truths that have been misinterpreted will be uprooted and consumed. Pluto is a genius at this sort of thing, and knows what to do. These changes are much more significant than mere psychological changes – for in the final analysis, philosophy creates psychology.

Power in your 11th House shows much involvement with astrology, high-tech pursuits, science and group activities. Your understanding of all these things is broadened.

Paths of greatest fulfilment this year are children, creativity, home and family issues, psychological progress, finance and communication.

Health

Your 6th House of Health is not a House of Power this year, showing that you rather take good health for granted and that there is no need to be overly concerned about these issues. With *all* the long-term planets either making wonderful aspects to you or leaving you alone you are well justified in taking health for granted.

Your vitality is fabulous this year. Those of you who have had health problems in the past should be hearing good news on this front. Healing proceeds much more easily.

The health of your spouse or partner also looks good. Their health is enhanced through metaphysical and spiritual techniques. They are open to new and experimental systems of healing.

Health of children has been delicate the past year or so, but when Jupiter moves into Taurus (from 15th February onwards) you should hear good news here.

If a parent has been ailing, good news comes in the summer.

Three Eclipses occur in stressful places for you. Two occur in July and one at Christmas. These could induce short-term cleansings of the physical body. But since these things take place in a context of strong vitality, the effect of these Eclipses will be minor.

Mercury is your Health Ruler. Its movements and positions are an important factor in your health. But since it moves so quickly, these effects – for good or ill – are short term. Be aware of Mercury's retrogrades, as these can be periods of lowered vitality or lack of confidence in terms of your health: they will occur from 21st February to 14th March, 23rd June to 17th July, and 18th October to 8th November. It would not be wise to start a new health regime, abruptly change doctors or otherwise make important health decisions during these periods.

Though your health is excellent this year there will be periods where the short-term planets can stress you out. These periods don't bring sickness but tend to lower your overall vitality. Be sure to rest and relax more during these periods: 1st to 20th January, 21st June to 22nd July, and 23rd September to 23rd October.

Home and Domestic Life

The 4th House of Home and Family Issues is not a House of Power for this year, Aries. Thus the Cosmos is giving you free will in this area. It does not push you one way or the other. Under these conditions the status quo tends to prevail.

But the three Eclipses effect the domestic and family life, and these could create long-term change in this area. The Solar Eclipse of 1st July occurs in the 4th House. Thus, hidden flaws in the home, with family members or in the overall family relationship come up so that they can be dealt with. The Eclipse doesn't always bring a move, but often a major renovation or repair in the home. The Lunar Eclipse of 16th July reinforces what is said here. Also, since it occurs in the House of Career, it signals a career change. This could be the cause of a move or change in your family pattern. The same is true for the Solar Eclipse of 25th December (also occurring in your 10th House of Career.)

There are six Eclipses in all in the year 2000 – an unusual number. Usually there are only four in any given year. Out of these six, five affect the family relationships – either children, parents or the day-to-day domestic situation. So there are going to be disruptive changes going on – only remember that 'disruptive' is not necessarily bad. Often it is good, but takes up much of your time and energy. Parents may move house, children may go off to out-of-town universities, you could be promoted at work and relocated elsewhere, singles may fall in love and move in with their beloved.

One thing is certain – your family and domestic pattern will be radically different by the time the year is over.

If you are planning major renovations or repair work to the home, 16th June to 1st August is a good time for these. If you are planning to redecorate, buy furnishings or otherwise enhance the home, 18th June to 13th July is a good time – though with Mercury retrograde then, you should do more advance planning that you might normally. The 18th June to 13th July is also a good time for family gatherings and entertaining from the home.

Love and Social Life

Your 7th House of Love and Marriage is not a House of Power this year, Aries. The status quo will tend to prevail. Singles will tend to remain single and married people will remain in their existing relationships. The Cosmos gives you a lot of latitude in this area. It pushes you neither one way nor another. You can make what you will of your love life. The issue is more lack of interest than lack of opportunity. You seem more interested in love affairs, or uncommitted friendships rather than serious romance. With Jupiter still in your own Sign until mid-February, you are feeling your oats, glowing in the knowledge that there are many fish in the sea and a superabundance of opportunities.

Those of you involved in love affairs outside of marriage will experience disruptions in these things – perhaps crises – as the Lunar Eclipse of 21st January and Solar Eclipse of 30th July bring up hidden flaws, fallacies and misconceptions in these areas. Strong, stable affairs will get better, but weak ones will disintegrate. For singles uninvolved in a love affair, the Eclipses can bring opportunity – and shake up your life while they're at it. Love can be *very* disruptive.

Of all your social Houses, it is the 11th House of Friendship and Group Activities that is the strongest. New and interesting friends come into the picture. These are not 'run of the mill' types either. They are brilliant, some even geniuses, spiritual and creative. They will stimulate areas of yourself that you didn't know you had. More importantly, this change emphasizes an area that many of you are weak in. Aries is a sign of independence, action and doing. But the 11th House is an area that deals with group activities and communion of the mind rather than physical activity. Thus you are in a cycle where you can learn the joys of associating with people of like mind, and of working as part of a team rather than solo.

Children of marriageable age are experiencing stormy love lives this year. Married people can get divorced and singles can marry. The highs and lows of love are unusually extreme. There are wedding bells in store for grandchildren of marriageable age – but love needs first to be tested.

The marriage and social lives of your parents are undergoing radical and long-term changes. Crisis will only make strong relationships stronger.

The marriage of a sibling – the eldest – gets severely tested this year.

Career and Finance

This is by far the most important and interesting area in the coming year. The year 2000 may not be much romantically, but it is certainly a major financial year.

The financial tide turned in 1999 when Jupiter entered your own Sign, expanding your horizons, bringing the lucky breaks, teaching you the laws of opulence and prosperity. This year Jupiter will enter your Money House on 15th February and stay there until 1st July.

Jupiter makes a whirlwind tour of your Money House this year – an uncharacteristically speedy movement. Financial objectives will be met quickly and speedily. Good happens in overwhelming ways. Assets you own increase in value. New and incredible earnings opportunities come to you. The financial discipline you've cultivated for the past two years is rewarded.

In July, Jupiter will move into your 3rd House of Short-term Travel and Communication. Thus you will be travelling more and spending more on communication equipment. Many of you will get new (and nice) cars during this period. New computers, faxes, phones, etc. will come to you. Your ability to reach other people is greatly increased.

But because you strike it rich now doesn't mean that you ignore financial discipline. Saturn is still very much in your Money House, though it will leave briefly from 11th August to 16th October. Enjoy your prosperity by all means, but invest a percentage of it for the long term. Investing in your career is a wise choice now.

Saturn in your Money House shows that finances are very important to you. They are high on your agenda this year – perhaps the highest. You measure success in pounds and pence. Your public and professional prestige – your professional reputation – is a big factor in earnings. The fact that finance is important helps you to overcome many obstructions that the faint of heart would not overcome, and this enhances earnings even further.

Saturn is your Career Planet. Thus its move from Taurus to Gemini on 11th August is signalling a career change. The Lunar Eclipse of 16th July and Solar Eclipse of 25th December also signal career change. It would be quite normal for you to feel 'antsy' in your job situation at these times. Change – good change – is happening.

Many of you have been stuck in a position that has kept you tied to a desk, or bound to one function. You've felt a lack of freedom and flexibility. This was necessary for the past two years, as you needed to develop some focus and perseverance. But this lesson is about over and will change either this year or next year. There will be more travelling related to career and more communication with other people. Many of you will move to sales and marketing positions. Others will be involved in teaching and training. Your communication skills will be a factor in your career success.

Paths to financial success this year are property, building your professional reputation, agriculture and agricultural products, copper and sugar. Later on in the year there are opportunities in communications, telecommunications companies, transportation, newspapers and media companies. (Bear in mind that your full horoscope based on your exact date and time of birth could modify this.)

ARIES

Self-improvement

Many of the self-improvement trends that we've written about in past years are still valid now – for these are long-term trends, not things you can develop in a year or so. Pluto in your 9th House for many years to come shows a complete revamping of your religious and philosophical beliefs. Your view of the world and your perspective on life are changing dramatically. Beliefs that held you back are being uprooted, neutralized and cast into the Heavenly fires. 'Every Tree not planted by the Heavenly Father' is being uprooted.

Saturn has been in your Money House for the past two years, enforcing order and discipline – realism – on finance. You needed to take responsibility for money. You needed to learn about money and its uses. You needed to learn how to manage money. These lessons are about over and Saturn is going to teach you about thinking and communication. Do you talk too fast? Do you make snap judgements? Are your words harming yourself or others? Do you sow disorder and dis-harmony with your speech? Saturn is going to adjust all of this in the coming years. You will learn the Power of the Word and its right use.

Uranus and Neptune are now firmly established in your 11th House of Friends and Group Activities. We have written of this earlier. The main lesson here is how to be an individual while being a part of a group. Many people lose their individuality while being in a group – it's as if they don't exist, only the group. There is little danger of this happening to you, Aries. The greater danger for you is being too individualistic. You feel that your perception, your perspective is so true that the group must automatically follow it. This can create tensions. You must think of the group interest while not ignoring your own. This can be a delicate balancing act, but you're up to it.

Month-by-month Forecasts

January

Best Days Overall: 3rd, 4th, 13th, 14th, 21st, 22nd, 30th, 31st

Most Stressful Days Overall: 5th, 6th, 7th, 19th, 20th, 25th, 26th

Best Days for Love: 3rd, 4th, 13th, 14th, 22nd, 25th, 26th

Best Days for Money: 3rd, 4th, 13th, 14th, 15th, 16th, 21st, 22nd, 30th, 31st

The planetary movements this month are overwhelmingly forward. By the 12th, 100 per cent of them will be in forward motion. This is a fast-paced month of progress and achievement – just the way you like things!

Between 70 and 80 per cent of the planets are above the Horizon of your chart, and your 10th House of Career is a major House of Power – thus this is a period of great and positive career progress. Pay rises, promotions, bonuses and increased professional status are likely now. Various career issues that were blocked or stalled by Saturn's retrograde for the past few months, now move forward. Even the new Moon of the 5th is helping your career by clarifying all the confusion and bringing you all the information you need to make the next move.

Family and domestic issues can take a back seat for a while – for even the family seems to support your career objectives.

Usually when the career is this demanding there is little time for personal pleasure and self-fulfilment. But with Jupiter still in your own Sign, you are managing to have some fun too. Sensual fantasies are fulfilled. Only remember not to burn the candle at both ends.

ARIES

Though the Lunar Eclipse of the 21st is basically kind to you, it is still advisable to take a reduced schedule that day – it may not be so kind to the people you rely on. This Eclipse occurs in your 5th House, showing long-term changes in a love affair or with children. Flaws in a present love affair come out in the open for you to deal with. Things you might not have known about the beloved are now revealed, and you have to decide whether you want to continue.

This Eclipse affects Neptune, your Planet of Spirituality – thus the dreams that you have during this period are probably not reliable, and no important decisions should be based on them. There could be a change in a spiritual organization you belong to, or in your meditation regime or with your teachers.

Health and overall vitality improves dramatically after the 20th. The focus shifts to friends, organizations and group activities.

Both love and finances are happy, though there could be a brief blow-up around the 9th. Be patient with your lover during this time, and be careful to avoid getting into debt.

February

Best Days Overall: 9th, 10th, 17th, 18th, 26th, 27th, 28th

Most Stressful Days Overall: 2nd, 3rd, 15th, 16th, 22nd, 23rd, 29th

Best Days for Love: 2nd, 3rd, 11th, 12th, 22nd, 23rd

Best Days for Money: 2nd, 3rd, 9th, 10th, 11th, 12th, 19th, 22nd, 29th

A very eventful, fast-paced but happy month, Aries – both for you and for the world in general.

Most of the planetary power is still above the Horizon for a while. This will start shifting in a month or so, but for now it is safe to let go of family and domestic concerns and focus on your career and 'outer' life.

Between 80 and 90 per cent of the planets are in the Eastern sector of the Self – your favourite sector. Always wilful and independent, during this period you are more so. Always a person to make things happen, this month you are more so – and 90 per cent of the Cosmos is backing you up. Move forward towards your dreams. Create your life as you want it to be. Let the world adapt to you. Your personal happiness is dear to the heart of a Higher Power.

Your most important interests this month are friends, groups, organizations, science and technology, spirituality and charity, and finance.

The Solar Eclipse of the 5th deals kindly with you. Disruptions and sudden changes are working in your favour. This Eclipse occurs in your 11th House of Friends and Group Activities, showing long-term changes in these areas. Relations with a professional organization to which you belong could change drastically. Perhaps there is an internal shake-up in the organization that is the cause. Happily, all the information you need to make good decisions will come to you as the month progresses. High-tech issues or purchases of high-tech equipment will clarify as the month progresses. New information about astrology is also coming to you.

Jupiter makes an important move from your own Sign of Aries into Taurus on the 15th. This is a very significant and happy financial indicator. Wealth and wealth opportunities are going to increase. Assets you own will increase dramatically in value, and the know-how – the exact methodology – of achieving your financial dreams will be revealed in the coming months. But don't spend all your money at once on high living. Saturn is still in your Money House and is counselling wise money management. You're turning an important corner in the financial realm.

Health is excellent all month. Mars in your own Sign after the 12th is giving you the energy of 10 people. You excel at sport and exercise regimes. You get things done in a hurry. You are brash and confident. Be more gentle with others, as you have no idea of your power – what you think is a little love tap can be devastating to another.

Your love life is very happy, especially after the 18th. Be careful of addictive relationships. But really, it's your lover who needs to be careful of addiction – you are one hot number this month!

March

Best Days Overall: 7th, 8th, 16th, 17th, 25th, 26th

Most Stressful Days Overall: 1st, 14th, 15th, 20th, 21st, 27th, 28th, 29th

Best Days for Love: 3rd, 4th, 12th, 13th, 20th, 21st, 22nd, 23rd

Best Days for Money: 1st, 3rd, 4th, 9th, 10th, 12th, 13th, 18th, 19th, 22nd, 23rd, 27th, 28th

With two hot and fiery planets (Mars and the Sun) playing tag in your own Sign, and with 90 to 100 per cent of the planets moving forward all month, things are just the way you like them. The world moves fast. Changes and progress happen quickly. The pace of life quickens, and you revel in every moment.

Add to this an overwhelming percentage of planets in your Eastern sector, and you have a 'Goldilocks month' for Aries – barging in where others fear to tread. Always self-assertive, now you are even more so. Always independent and willing to go it alone, now you are more so – moreover, the entire Cosmos is supporting you.

The main dangers this month are the classic ones for the Aries personality: a tendency to rashness and impetuosity; a tendency not to see or understand another's perspective – or to dismiss it cavalierly. Normally this would make you most unpopular, but interestingly it actually makes you *more* attractive and more appealing right now. People admire your 'can do' attitude and rugged individualism. Love is pursuing you ardently, and is right now behind the scenes. Your lover can't do enough for you and is eager to please. You get your own way in most areas of life now.

Since getting your way is going to be very easy right now, it would not be a bad idea to take some time in seclusion and think about what you really want – not what you *think* you want, or what other people think you should want – but what you, in your heart of hearts, really want. Once this is decided, then go for it – the force is with you. But if you ignore this inner work, you are likely to set patterns into motion which are really not satisfactory and which will not please you when they come to fruition. What a waste of such splendid energy!

Your main areas of interest this month are friends, group activities, organizations, spirituality and charitable activities, the body, the image and personal pleasure, and finance.

Finances are really spectacular now. And though you still need to manage your money strictly, we get a sense of financial freedom. Wealth is increasing and you know what to do with it and how to handle it. Earnings are a source of pleasure to you – especially after the 23rd. Your financial intuition is super after the 13th and you can take it to the bank.

Your health shines all month. Those among you who are athletes are breaking all previous records.

April

Best Days Overall: 12th, 13th, 21st, 22nd

Most Stressful Days Overall: 10th, 11th, 16th, 17th, 18th, 24th, 25th

Best Days for Love: 1st, 2nd, 12th, 13th, 16th, 17th, 18th, 21st, 22nd

36

ARIES

Best Days for Money: 1st, 2nd, 6th, 7th, 12th, 13th, 14th, 15th, 21st, 22nd, 24th, 25th

Another very happy, active and fast-paced month, Aries – just the way you like things.

With 80 to 90 per cent of the planetary power in the Eastern hemisphere of your chart – and with the short-term planets playing tag in your own Sign – your hormones are working overtime. Under normal circumstances this much power in Aries and in the Eastern hemisphere would cause you to bowl over the opposition – to overcome by sheer, brute force. Happily, Venus' move into your Sign on the 6th is restraining you – giving you more charm and grace. You will be less heavy-handed.

Nevertheless, push forward boldly towards your goals now. Create the life that you dream about. Live your dream. The Omnipotent Powers of the Cosmos are behind you and are granting your lawful desires. Hopefully, you used last month to clarify your goals and desires, so you can now focus on what you really want.

By the 13th there will be a decisive shift of planetary power from the top half to the bottom half of your Horoscope. Thus, though career will still be important, you can safely de-emphasize it and focus on getting your family, domestic and emotional life in order.

There are other important shifts happening this month. The North Node of the Moon moves from Leo into Cancer. This reinforces what we said above – there is great personal fulfilment now from family values and inner, psychological progress.

Mars, your Ruling Planet, makes two *very* important conjunctions this month. The first occurs from the 5th to the 7th and brings you in contact with an important teacher or mentor. This is very significant. Many of you will hear good news about university applications or from foreign lands. Important spiritual and philosophical illumination comes to you. There is a financial windfall and the sudden manifestation of a long-held sensual desire. An opportunity for foreign travel comes your way.

The second conjunction is with Saturn on the 16th to 17th. This can have many scenarios. Some of you will be presented with an important career opportunity; some with a promotion. It indicates the taking on of executive power and responsibility. Perhaps there is the fortunate resolution of a government or bureaucratic issue. A financial opportunity comes from an elder or parent figure.

Health and finances are strong all month. Love and money are pursuing you ardently and there is nothing special that you need to do. You are getting your way in both areas this period.

May

Best Days Overall: 1st, 2nd, 9th, 10th, 18th, 19th, 20th, 28th, 29th

Most Stressful Days Overall: 7th, 8th, 14th, 15th, 21st, 22nd

Best Days for Love: 3rd, 4th, 12th, 13th, 14th, 15th, 22nd, 23rd

Best Days for Money: 3rd, 4th, 12th, 13th, 21st, 22nd, 23rd, 31st

Though retrograde activity increases during this period, most of the planets are still moving forward. Add to this a dominance of the Earth element and you get a sense of progress and achievement, albeit more slowly and at a more cautious pace than over the past few months. You might chomp at the bit at all the slow coaches around you – who seem to have no vision of possibilities but can see only what's in front of them. They are concerned with practical, bottom-line issues – in many cases, irrelevant details – which only slow you down. Be patient, this is the astrological weather.

If you are selling to people make sure you emphasize bottom-line values. Appeal to their pocket rather than their imagination.

The planets are firmly in the East, Aries, so continue to create the life that you dream about – only do it more slowly.

Most of the planets are still below the Horizon of your chart, showing that inner growth is more important than overt, outer growth. Inner progress always manifests outwardly in due course. This is the nature of the universe.

Your important areas of interest this month are friends, groups, organizations, networking, science and technology, finance, local travel, sales, marketing, communication, and neighbours and siblings.

Health is still super this month, though you are less hot-blooded than you were last month. You are a much more mellow person these days. Health can be enhanced even further through happy relations with neighbours, siblings and family members. Proper attention to the nervous system and stomach will also enhance your health.

Love tends to be practical and materialistic most of the month. Love is expressed physically and sensuously. Material gifts are romantic turn-ons. Friends and your lover or spouse can be treated as material things – possessions – which you move around and control. But later, after the 25th, love is more intellectual and fraternal. Communication and the sharing of ideas with the beloved becomes unusually important. You want to fall in love with your lover's mind as well as his or her body and material status.

This is a banner financial month. Many important changes are going on – some perhaps like earthquakes. But the end result is good. Major wealth and major earnings opportunities are coming. The new Moon of the 4th is going to clarify your next steps and teach you how to deal with upheavals. A major new business cycle is being born and you are right in synch with it. Prosperity is yours for years to come.

June

Best Days Overall: 6th, 7th, 15th, 16th, 25th, 26th

Most Stressful Days Overall: 4th, 10th, 11th, 17th, 18th, 19th

Best Days for Love: 2nd, 10th, 11th, 22nd, 23rd

Best Days for Money: 2nd, 8th, 9th, 10th, 11th, 17th, 18th, 19th, 22nd, 23rd, 27th, 28th

Your native Fire element is weaker this month, and retrograde activity is increasing compared with last month. The pace of change slows down. Be patient and try not to chafe at the bit. More internal development needs to happen if your goals are to manifest.

The planetary power is below the Horizon of your chart and your 4th House of Home and Family is an important House of Power. Let go of career issues and focus on psychological growth and creating a stable home base. Family obligations are more important than the career now.

The planets make an important shift to the West this month, thus you are less able to go it alone than usual. You will always be independent and self-reliant, but sometimes this is more difficult – this is one of those periods. A good idea now would be to cultivate the social graces – to put other people's interests ahead of your own and appreciate other perspectives. Adapt to situations rather than try to have things your way. Your way might not be the best way.

Your important areas of interest this month are friends, groups and group activities, organizations, science and astrology, finance, neighbours, siblings, sales, marketing, communication and intellectual interests, and home and family.

With many planets in Gemini this period many of you will be involved with the media, mass mailshots, advertising and communication projects. Try to wind these up before the 23rd, as Mercury starts to go retrograde then. After the 23rd be more cautious in your communications and take extra time and effort to ensure that the other person has really understood your message. Don't take things for granted. Much heartache can be spared by doing this. It's also a good idea to have your car, computers and phone equipment checked out before the 23rd. These things are more likely to act up when Mercury is retrograde. Local journeys – especially if they are unnecessary – are better off minimized or rescheduled for when Mercury goes forward again next month.

A great month – especially after the 21st – to move if necessary, redecorate, renovate, buy objects of beauty for the home and for family gatherings.

Finances are strong all month but you can't spend freely and promiscuously. Money management is still very important.

Health is excellent all month, but rest and relax more after the 21st.

After the 21st there are many planets in the Water Signs. People are more sensitive and easily hurt. Be extra careful how you tread.

July

Best Days Overall: 3rd, 4th, 12th, 13th, 22nd, 23rd, 31st

Most Stressful Days Overall: 1st, 2nd, 7th, 8th, 15th, 16th, 29th

Best Days for Love: 1st, 2nd, 7th, 8th, 10th, 11th, 22nd, 23rd, 30th, 31st

Best Days for Money: 1st, 2nd, 6th, 7th, 10th, 11th, 14th, 15th, 22nd, 23rd, 24th, 25th, 26th, 30th, 31st

Jupiter's move into Gemini, your 3rd House, and three Eclipses this month ensure that this will be an eventful, long-remembered month. Two out of three of the Eclipses are stressful for you, so please take a reduced schedule on the 1st (Solar Eclipse) and the 16th (Lunar Eclipse). Since the short-term planets are stressing you until the 22nd, it would not be a bad idea to take a reduced schedule – to rest and relax more – throughout this period.

Many changes and disruptions are happening in the world at large, as Eclipses are always signals for long-term change. But disruptions can come from good things as well as bad things.

The Solar Eclipse of the 1st occurs in your 4th House of Home and Family. Thus there can a be a move or major renovations of the home. Flaws in the present home will be revealed so you can take corrective actions. It would be a good idea to stay close to home during this period, so that future damage and repair bills can be minimized.

The Lunar Eclipse of the 16th occurs in your 10th House of Career – signalling a career or job change. This could be related to moving house. Often these kinds of Eclipses lead to career progress – promotions and the like – but through disruptive activity.

The Solar Eclipse of the 30th is kinder to you – less stressful than the previous two. It shows long-term changes in the creative life, or in relations with your children. Avoid speculations during this period. A love affair comes to a head one way or another.

Health and vitality improve dramatically after the 22nd.

Jupiter moves into your 3rd House this month and will be there for the rest of the year. Your ability to communicate – to teach and learn, to reach more people via marketing programmes – is increasing dramatically. There is more travel in your life but of a domestic rather than a foreign nature. Happy educational opportunities are coming and you should take hold of them.

Jupiter's move out of your 2nd House begins to de-emphasize financial matters. By now Jupiter has bestowed its financial gifts and things are quite the way you want them. You are looking to expand your horizons elsewhere.

Love is happy but you are more interested in fun and games types of situations than commitment.

August

Best Days Overall: 8th, 9th, 18th, 19th, 27th, 28th

Most Stressful Days Overall: 4th, 5th, 11th, 12th, 25th, 26th, 31st

Best Days for Love: 4th, 5th, 11th, 12th, 20th, 21st, 29th, 30th, 31st

Best Days for Money: 3rd, 4th, 11th, 12th, 13th, 14th, 20th, 21st, 22nd, 23rd, 24th, 29th, 30th

Saturn makes a major move out of your Money House, bringing financial relief and respite from a major financial burden. Presumably the lessons of financial management have been learned and you can coast for a while.

With some of the dust settling from last month's Eclipses, you are in a party mood now – wanting to have fun and enjoy life. The Cosmos supports this.

Most of the planets are still below the Horizon of your chart, so the focus is still on family, domestic and psychological issues. Emotional harmony is still where it's at for you.

Saturn's move into Gemini does signal a career shift – or perhaps a change in the guard in your corporate hierarchy. Career success is no longer measured in mere pounds and pence, but in terms of growth and educational value. Your ability to communicate will boost your professional status for the next few years or so.

Having most of the planets in the West – including Mars, your Ruler – show that your normal independence and self-will need to be muted for a while. Social skills need to be developed now.

Health is super all month. Mars in the Sign of Leo all month makes you even peppier than usual. Libido is strong.

Finances are strong this period too. Your Money Planet in Leo brings income through speculations and in happy ways. Money, financial connections and ideas come at parties, sporting events or while you are indulging in sport. Be careful of overspending during this period – until the 6th. After the 6th your Money Planet moves into Virgo. This is a much better period for shopping and investing, as you will be more careful and value-conscious. Money comes from work or through co-workers then.

Love is happier until the 6th. The Love Planet in Virgo doesn't stop love, but makes you oh so critical and perfectionist. It's as if you've forgotten your heart and have related to your loved one only with your mind. Be careful of destructive criticism as it is a sure turn-off. Love is expressed through service during this period. The lover who does for you, who serves your interests, wins your heart.

Much power in the 6th House after the 22nd is good news for job-seekers and employers. Both jobs and employees are easier to find. Health issues also go better then – and if you need to schedule a yearly physical or dental appointment, this is the period to do it.

September

Best Days Overall: 5th, 6th, 14th, 15th, 16th, 23rd, 24th

Most Stressful Days Overall: 1st, 7th, 8th, 21st, 22nd, 27th, 28th

Best Days for Love: 1st, 10th, 11th, 19th, 20th, 27th, 28th, 30th

Best Days for Money: 1st, 10th, 11th, 17th, 18th, 19th, 20th, 27th, 28th, 30th

Retrograde activity is increasing and most of the planets are in the Western sector; this indicates that the pace of life slows down this month. Work to develop your social skills and to attain your ends by negotiation and compromise. Though there are some power struggles this month – one with a boss, parent or elder, another with a teacher or mentor – undue self-assertion is still not wise.

This month is important as there is a major shift of planetary power from the bottom half of your Horoscope to the top half. This occurs in stages and you will feel it strongly by the 22nd. Career and outward ambitions are becoming ever more important and ever more urgent. By now you should have found your emotional comfort zone and be ready to carry this feeling of harmony into the world.

The retrograde of Saturn, your Career Planet, on the 12th complicates your ambitions but doesn't thwart them. Your boss can have an important change of opinion during this period. Career offers may not be what they seem and need more study. In spite of Saturn's retrograde, keep focused on your worldly goals.

Your most important areas of interest this month are local travel, communication, sales, marketing, advertising, neighbours and siblings, parties, love affairs, creativity, children, health and work, love and romance, and friendships, groups and organizations.

Paths to financial increase this month are (until the 24th) sales, marketing, communication, telecommunications, and transportation. After the 24th wealth is increased through property, restaurants, and industries that cater to the home and family connections.

The Money Planet is in the 7th House of Love and Romance until the 24th, and then moves into the 8th House. This shows that earnings are coming through your spouse or partner, social connections and fashion trends. Social grace and skills (as we mentioned earlier) boost your income. After the 24th, earnings come from investors, borrowing or through helping others to prosper. After the 24th you need to put other people's financial interests ahead of your own. You prosper as you understand their financial needs and cater to them.

Love is happy and active all month, and singles might not remain single for long. This is one of the most powerful social periods of your year.

Health is excellent, but rest and relax more after the 22nd.

October

Best Days Overall: 2nd, 3rd, 12th, 13th, 20th, 21st, 29th, 30th

Most Stressful Days Overall: 4th, 5th, 6th, 18th, 19th, 25th, 26th

Best Days for Love: 1st, 9th, 10th, 11th, 20th, 21st, 23rd, 24th, 29th, 30th

Best Days for Money: 1st, 7th, 8th, 9th, 10th, 11th, 14th, 15th, 16th, 17th, 20th, 21st, 25th, 26th, 29th, 30th

Retrograde activity increases this month, making it a good period to develop patience and to work inwardly to perfect your future plans and projects. Having many planets in the Western sector, including Mars, your Ruler, reinforces this slowing-down effect. This is a period where you allow things to happen rather than trying to *make* things happen. When a fruit is ripe it falls from the tree of its own accord and you don't have to forcibly pick it. If you are adapting, compromising and in the good graces of others you will be in the right position to catch the fruit when it falls.

With most of the planets now above the Horizon of your chart your career is important these days. The only problem here is the retrograde of Saturn. Study career changes and offers more carefully and plan your dream career.

ARIES

Your important areas of interest this month are finance, communication and intellectual interests, local travel, neighbours and siblings, health and work, personal transformation, the deeper things of life, debt and its repayment, helping others prosper, religion, higher education, foreign travel, and friends and group organizations.

The full Moon of the 13th occurs in your own Sign, giving you extra energy to handle personal issues, the body and the enhancement of your image. This would be a good day to have some fun.

The new Moon of the 27th occurs in your 8th House of Personal Transformation and Other People's Money. This will bring clarity and illumination on these issues as the month progresses.

Health is still excellent, though you should rest and relax more until the 23rd.

Love is happy and honeymoonish. Sexual expression is unusually passionate and strong. Your lover is focused on financial issues and is prospering. Jealousy and possessiveness can be a problem. Singles meet a significant other this month; married people are more romantic with their partners. Romantic opportunities occur in the usual places – parties, the theatre, nightclubs or sporting events. After the 19th it occurs at a school or religious function.

Finances are strong all month. Until the 19th pay off debt. Afterwards be careful of overspending. Saturn retrograding back into your Money House on the 16th shows a renewed need for financial management.

November

Best Days Overall: 8th, 9th, 17th, 18th, 26th, 27th

Most Stressful Days Overall: 1st, 2nd, 15th, 21st, 22nd, 28th, 29th

Best Days for Love: 8th, 9th, 19th, 20th, 21st, 22nd, 28th, 29th

Best Days for Money: 3rd, 4th, 8th, 9th, 10th, 11th, 12th, 13th, 19th, 20th, 21st, 22nd, 28th, 29th, 30th

You are entering one of the happiest months of your year, Aries – enjoy.

Most of the planets are still in the West, and Mars, your Ruler, enters the Sign of Libra on the 4th. Social issues, the grace of other people, gaining the co-operation and acceptance of others are still very important. With Mars in your 7th House of Love and Romance you are down-playing your personality and reaching out to others. Popularity is strong this month.

Love will be happy as you are going way out of your way to please the beloved. Venus, the Love Planet, is 'out of bounds' all month, indicating that you are going outside your normal orbit in search of love. The search for love takes you to places – both physical and psychological – that you've never been before. Relationships can be addictive during this period – especially towards the end of the month. Yet there is strong passion and instinctual, gut-level behaviour. Sexual encounters can happen suddenly and out of the blue towards the end of the month.

Venus is also your Money Planet. So this going 'out of bounds' is also affecting your financial life. You are experimenting with financial ways and techniques that are new to you – or that are perhaps outside the established norm. Perhaps you are sent travelling to some new and unknown land – developing contacts or business in a new and untried area. Perhaps you are shifted to an area of your company which is outside your normal orbit – or get a promotion to an area in which you have no experience. You seem eager to break financial barriers during this period. With Saturn back in your Money House you still need to manage your resources better and think of the long haul. Spend proportionately. Avoid speculations on the 8th and 9th.

By the 4th, 70 to 80 per cent of the planets will be above the Horizon of your chart. Thus this is a period for pursuing career objectives and focusing on worldly ambitions. Let home and family issues slide for a while.

Health is excellent all month. Avoid over-exercising and rushing about too much from the 20th to the 23rd.

December

Best Days Overall: 6th, 7th, 14th, 15th, 23rd, 24th

Most Stressful Days Overall: 12th, 13th, 18th, 19th, 25th, 26th, 27th

Best Days for Love: 10th, 11th, 18th, 19th, 28th, 29th

Best Days for Money: 1st, 8th, 9th, 10th, 11th, 18th, 19th, 28th, 29th

The pace of change quickens this month as 80 per cent of the planets are moving forwards and there is a Solar Eclipse on Christmas Day. A month of progress and achievement.

Most of the planets are in the East – and the trend strengthens even further after the 21st. You are feeling like your normal independent and self-reliant self again. You can have things your way. You create your own destiny and happiness now. With Mars still in Libra and in your 7th House you are socializing more, but you do so as your own person, on your own terms.

Most of the planets are above the Horizon of your chart, and your 10th House of Career becomes powerful after the

21st. Let go of home and domestic issues for a while and pursue your outer ambitions. Doing right will lead to feeling right.

Career is important in other ways as well. The Solar Eclipse of the 25th takes place in your Career House, showing long-term changes in this area. Probably a career change – either within your present company or to another company. The change, although good, will be disruptive and swallow up much time and energy. Those of you with adult children – or university-age children – will see changes in their career and aspirations as well.

There will be changes in the corporate hierarchy. Your company can be taken over and you will have a new set of bosses with a new set of rules to deal with. This Eclipse is personally stressful for you, so take a reduced schedule – two days before and a day after. Do what needs to be done, but reschedule inessentials. Many of you will be travelling around during this period. Schedule travel days around the Eclipse.

Health is good most of the month, but rest and relax more after the 21st.

You are unusually aggressive in love most of the month. You go after what you want with great courage. Those you pursue have mixed emotions about your aggressiveness. On the one hand they are turned on by your confidence, and on the other they are a little fearful of your power. Moderate things. Until the 8th there could be a clash of wills between you and the beloved – but this is short term. After the 8th harmony is restored. Jealousy and over-intensity in love can create new problems after the 23rd. Err on the side of freedom.

Taurus

ℇ

THE BULL

Birthdays from
21st April to
20th May

Personality Profile

TAURUS AT A GLANCE

Element – Earth

Ruling Planet – Venus
   Career Planet – Uranus
   Love Planet – Pluto
   Money Planet – Mercury
   Planet of Health and Work – Venus
   Planet of Home and Family Life – Sun
   Planet of Spirituality – Mars
   Planet of Travel, Education, Religion and
   Philosophy – Saturn

Colours – earth tones, green, orange, yellow

Colours that promote love, romance and social
harmony – red-violet, violet

Colours that promote earning power – yellow, yellow-orange

Gems – coral, emerald

Metal – copper

Scents – bitter almond, rose, vanilla, violet

Quality – fixed (= stability)

Quality most needed for balance – flexibility

Strongest virtues – endurance, loyalty, patience, stability, a harmonious disposition

Deepest needs – comfort, material ease, wealth

Characteristics to avoid – rigidity, stubbornness, tendency to be overly possessive and materialistic

Signs of greatest overall compatibility – Virgo, Capricorn

Signs of greatest overall incompatibility – Leo, Scorpio, Aquarius

Sign most helpful to career – Aquarius

Sign most helpful for emotional support – Leo

Sign most helpful financially – Gemini

Sign best for marriage and/or partnerships – Scorpio

Sign most helpful for creative projects – Virgo

Best Sign to have fun with – Virgo

Signs most helpful in spiritual matters – Aries, Capricorn

Best day of the week – Friday

TAURUS

Understanding the Taurus Personality

Taurus is the most earthy of all the Earth Signs. If you understand that Earth is more than just a physical element, that it is a psychological attitude as well, you will get a better understanding of the Taurus personality.

A Taurus has all the power of action that an Aries has. But Taureans are not satisfied with action for its own sake. Their actions must be productive, practical and wealth-producing. If Taureans cannot see a practical value in an action they will not bother taking it.

Taureans' forte lies in their power to make real their own or other people's ideas. They are generally not very inventive but they can take another's invention and perfect it, making it more practical and useful. The same is true for all projects. Taureans are not especially keen on starting new projects, but once they get involved they bring things to completion. A Taurus carries everything through. Their finishers and will go the distance so long as no unavoidable calamity intervenes.

Many people find Taureans too stubborn, conservative, fixed and immovable. This is understandable, because Taureans dislike change – in their environment or in their routine. Taureans even dislike changing their minds! On the other hand, this is their virtue. It is not good for a wheel's axle to waver. The axle must be fixed, stable and unmovable. Taureans are the axle of society and the heavens. Without their stability and so-called stubbornness, the wheels of the world (and especially the wheels of commerce) would not turn.

Taureans love routine. A routine, if it is good, has many virtues. It is a fixed – and, ideally, perfect – way of taking care of things. Mistakes can happen when spontaneity comes into the equation, and mistakes cause discomfort and uneasiness – something almost unacceptable to a Taurus. Meddling with Taureans' comfort and security is a sure way to irritate and anger them.

While an Aries loves speed, a Taurus likes things slow. They are slow thinkers – but do not make the mistake of assuming they lack intelligence. On the contrary, Taureans are very intelligent. It is just that they like to chew on ideas, to deliberate and weigh them up. Only after due deliberation is an idea accepted or a decision taken. Taureans are slow to anger – but once aroused, take care!

Finance

Taureans are very money-conscious. Wealth is more important to them than to many other Signs. Wealth to a Taurus means comfort and security. Wealth means stability. Where some Zodiac Signs feel that they are spiritually rich if they have ideas, talents or skills, Taureans only feel their wealth when they can see and touch it. Taurus' way of thinking is 'What good is a talent if it has not been translated into a home, furniture, car and holidays?'

These are all reasons why Taureans excel in estate agency and agricultural industries. Usually a Taurus will end up owning land. They love to feel their connection to the Earth. Material wealth began with agriculture, the tilling of the soil. Owning a piece of land was humanity's earliest form of wealth: Taureans still feel that primeval connection.

It is in the pursuit of wealth that Taureans develop their intellectual and communication abilities. Also, in this pursuit Taureans are forced to develop some flexibility. It is in the quest for wealth that they learn the practical value of the intellect and come to admire it. If it were not for the search for wealth and material things, Taureans might not try to reach a higher intellect.

Some Taureans are 'born-lucky' – the type of people who win any gamble or speculation. This luck is due to other factors in their Horoscope; it is not part of their essential nature. By nature they are not gamblers. They are hard workers and like to earn what they get. Taureans' innate conservatism makes them abhor unnecessary risks in finance and in other areas of their lives.

Career and Public Image

Being essentially down-to-earth people, simple and uncomplicated, Taureans tend to look up to those who are original, unconventional and inventive. Taureans like their bosses to be creative and original – since they themselves are content to perfect their superiors' brain-waves. They admire people who have a wider social or political consciousness and they feel that someday (when they have all the comfort and security they need) they too would like to be involved in these big issues.

In business affairs Taureans can be very shrewd – and that makes them valuable to their employers. They are never lazy; they enjoy working and getting good results. Taureans do not like taking unnecessary risks and do well in positions of authority, which makes them good managers and supervisors. Their managerial skills are reinforced by their natural talents for organization and handling details, their patience and thoroughness. As mentioned, through their connection with the earth Taureans also do well in farming and agriculture.

In general a Taurus will choose money and earning power over public esteem and prestige. A position that pays more – though it has less prestige – is preferred to a position with a lot of prestige but fewer earnings. Many other Signs do not feel this way, but a Taurus does, especially if there is nothing in his or her personal birth chart that modifies this. Taureans will pursue glory and prestige only if it can be shown that these things have a direct and immediate impact on their wallet.

Love and Relationships

In love, the Taurus-born likes to have and to hold. They are the marrying kind. They like commitment and they like the terms of a relationship to be clearly defined. More importantly, Taureans like to be faithful to one lover, and they expect that lover to reciprocate this fidelity. When this does not happen their whole world comes crashing down. When they are in love Taureans are loyal, but they are also very possessive. They are capable of great fits of jealousy if they are hurt in love.

Taureans are satisfied with the simple things in a relationship. If you are involved romantically with a Taurus there is no need for lavish entertainments and constant courtship. Give them enough love, food and comfortable shelter and they will be quite content to stay home and enjoy your company. They will be loyal to you for life. Make a Taurus feel comfortable and – above all – secure in the relationship, and you will rarely have a problem.

In love, Taureans can sometimes make the mistake of trying to control their partners, which can cause great pain on both sides. The reasoning behind their actions is basically simple: Taureans feel a sense of ownership over their partners and will want to make changes that will increase their own general comfort and security. This attitude is OK when it comes to inanimate, material things – but is dangerous when applied to people. Taureans need to be careful and attentive to this possible trait within themselves.

Home and Domestic Life

Home and family are vitally important to Taureans. They like children. They also like a comfortable and perhaps glamorous home – something they can show off. They tend to buy heavy, ponderous furniture – usually of the best quality. This is because Taureans like a feeling of substance in their environment. Their house is not only their home but their place of creativity and entertainment. The Taureans' home tends to be truly their castle. If they could choose, Taureans would prefer living in the countryside to being city-dwellers. If they cannot do so during their working lives, many Taureans like to holiday in or even retire to the country, away from the city and closer to the land.

At home a Taurus is like a country squire – lord (or lady) of the manor. They love to entertain lavishly, to make others feel secure in their home and to encourage others to derive the same sense of satisfaction as they do from it. If you are invited for dinner at the home of a Taurus you can expect the best food and best entertainment. Be prepared for a tour of the house and expect to see your Taurus friend exhibit a lot of pride and satisfaction in his or her possessions.

Taureans like children but they are usually strict with them. The reason for this is they tend to treat their children – as they do most things in life – as their possessions. The positive side to this is that their children will be well cared for and well supervised. They will get every material thing they need to grow up properly. On the down side, Taureans can get too repressive with their children. If a child dares to upset the daily routine – which Taureans love to follow – he or she will have a problem with a Taurus parent.

Horoscope for 2000

Major Trends

1999 was an important work and career year, Taurus. You took on more responsibility, worked harder than usual, assumed more authority, but progressed all the while. Your physical limits were tested and many of you were forced to delegate authority and become more efficient. There was much success but little fun. This is about to change.

Though many of the above trends are continuing this year, it will not be *all* work, work, work. Jupiter, moving through your own Sign beginning 15th February, is going to send you travelling, fulfil your fondest sensual and physical desires, bring you the good life and increase earnings. A sense of optimism and fun enters your life. Good comes to you in 'unearned' and unlooked-for ways. The journeys that Jupiter sends you on will be more pleasurable (not so business-orientated) as the travelling you did last year.

The important areas of interest in the coming year will be the personal image, the body, personal pleasures, finance and career.

Your paths to greatest fulfilment will be spirituality, charity, the body, image and personal pleasures, finance, home and family issues, and the pursuit of intellectual interests.

Health

If you got through last year with your health intact, the year 2000 should be easier. The health aspects are still not what they should be or what you are used to, but the stresses are easing up a bit. Still, you need to rest and relax more, delegate authority where possible, and work smarter – not harder.

Many of the cautions and precautions that we advised last year still apply now. Wear the colours, gems, metal and scents of your Sign. Drink teas or take flower essences made from the herbs of your Sign. Learn to work in a rhythm, alternating between work and relaxation, and between one type of activity with another. Rest when tired. Avoid scheduling activities when the aspects are difficult – see the month-by-month forecasts. Give special attention to your voice, throat and kidneys, as these can be particularly vulnerable in a Taurus. You can strengthen them in drugless ways through chiropractic, kinesiology, foot and hand reflexology, acupressure or acupuncture. The thumbs (between the base and knuckle area) should be massaged regularly. The big toes – above the base – likewise.

Three Eclipses this year could be stressful to you – these are the Lunar Eclipse of 21st January and the Solar Eclipses of 5th February and 30th July. Be sure to rest and relax more during these periods. They will be discussed in more detail in the month-by-month forecasts.

There are also three periods of greatest vulnerability this year. These are 20th January to 18th February, 23rd July to 23rd August, and 23rd October to 22nd November. Be sure to rest and relax more during these periods as well.

If you take adequate precautions and listen to your body, you should come through the coming year with flying colours. You were given enough energy to handle your true needs and responsibilities, but not to handle 'imposed' or frivolous ones.

The fact that your 6th House is not a House of Power is a positive health signal. Most of you will take the necessary precautions and avoid problems.

Home and Domestic Life

Though your 4th House of Home and Family is not a House of Power this year, and you seem satisfied with your domestic arrangements, three Eclipses guarantee that there will be shake-ups and changes.

Since the Sun is your Family Planet, every Solar Eclipse has family/domestic ramifications. But when the Solar Eclipse also occurs in the 4th House, as on 30th July, the effect is magnified.

The Eclipses bring good, but disruptive, changes in the domestic scene. Perhaps there is a sudden move, and you must pack, put your old home up for sale or rent, negotiate with bankers and estate agents, sell your old furniture and otherwise interrupt your normal routine. The end result is good, but the path to it is very hectic. Perhaps you get an inspiration to remodel the home. The end result will be good, but for a few months your home will be a shambles and your routine will be disrupted. Very often, a hidden flaw is discovered during an Eclipse period, which it can take weeks to correct.

There are other possible scenarios as well. Your career is very active and experimental – filled with changes. This could impact on your domestic situation. You are offered the 'job of your dreams' but it requires re-location. Thus you move house even though you are happy with your present residence. Singles could meet the man or woman of their dreams and this person may move in, necessitating remodelling or re-organizing the home. Alternatively a period of adjustment may be needed when the loved one moves in. University students may change flatmates during these periods – or take the decision to change flatmates.

The significant Eclipses impacting on the home this year are the Lunar Eclipse of 21st January, the Solar Eclipse of 5th February (career change) and the Solar Eclipse of 30th – this last is the strongest in this department. The other two Solar Eclipses of 1st July and 25th December are also noteworthy but less dramatic.

On a psychological level, these Eclipses will also bring out old, hidden mood and feeling patterns that you never knew you had. Once they have surfaced you can correct them.

These Eclipses could also change the family pattern. A child goes off to an out-of-town university; a parent retires and moves away; or a parent moves for career reasons.

Love and Social Life

None of your Social Houses is powerful this year, Taurus, so social issues are not high on your agenda. The Cosmos pushes you neither one way nor another. You have freedom to make of your love and social life what you will it to be.

In spite of this freedom, you seem satisfied with the status quo – and this is what will probably prevail. Singles will remain single and married people will remain married.

This lack of interest in social matters doesn't mean that you don't have opportunities, or that you are not attracting the interest of others. You are, and how! But you seem more interested in career and financial issues. Some years are like that.

Saturn has been moving through your Sign since 1999. It has had many effects. One of them is that it has made you conscious of your 'separateness' from others. You feel strongly about your 'natural boundaries' and are perhaps strict in enforcing them. People could see you as cold or aloof – snobbish – even though, at heart, you are not like this. You are serious about yourself, and even chance or minor remarks you can interpret as 'put downs'. Many of you have created 'walls' to protect you from frivolous advances. But these walls deter even the good relationships. You need to work harder to project warmth and love to others this year.

Jupiter moving through your own Sign from 15th February to 1st July should help your social life. It makes you more joyful, jovial, happy and optimistic. As Lord of your 8th House it enhances your sex appeal and personal magnetism. So you are attracting others – the issue is, can you accept the opportunities when they come?

Jupiter's move through your Sign also brings personal and sensual pleasure. Thus there could be 'play and amusement' types of relationships rather than committed, serious ones. Physical cravings get satisfied, but little else. For the coming year this arrangement seems to satisfy you.

The marriage of a parent still seems in turmoil and is very unstable. If the parent is single a remarriage is likely. If you have single children of marriageable age, they are likely to remain single this year. If they are married they are likely to remain married. The marital status of siblings is likely to change, as the many Eclipses bring long-term changes to this area.

Your most active social period will be from 6th August to 22nd November.

Career and Finance

This is the most important and highlighted area for you in the coming year. It will be a banner financial and career year.

Two powerful long-term planets occupy your 10th House of Career, for many years to come. Uranus, which has been there for a few years now, is still causing change, experimentalism and career excitement. Job changes are the norm now as you continue to upgrade and improve your status. Promotions are likely to happen suddenly and out of the blue – when you least expect them. You seem willing to venture into unknown career paths – starting up companies, or working at jobs for which you have no previous experience. Many of you are going off on your own – creating your own companies and businesses. Both of the planets in your 10th House are related to networking and the media – so these areas are important to your career. Many of you will land jobs at these types of companies. Others will make extensive use of the media in your work. Still others will be making use of technology – and perhaps the Internet – as you pursue your career dreams. It is an exciting time to be a Taurus.

Jupiter in your own Sign from 15th February to 1st July is increasing earnings, bringing pay rises and promotions at work. Your self-esteem is higher this year than it has been in the past, and as a result you command higher wages. After 1st July Jupiter moves into your Money House, again increasing earnings and making the assets you own (your house, or stocks and bonds, furniture or art, etc.) worth more. Jupiter is going to teach you the 'how' of wealth this coming year.

Though you will be earning more in the year 2000, Saturn also moving through your own Sign, and then into your Money House, counsels the wise use of resources and prevents you from squandering them in riotous living. Jupiter's impact on you can make you more risk-taking and speculative. Saturn will reinforce your natural conservatism. You will need to balance between the two. Well-hedged bets – calculated risks – will be rewarded.

Jupiter and the Lord of the 9th House in your own Sign shows increased business travel this year. You probably travelled (to foreign parts) last year too, but this year it is more pleasurable. You seem more able to combine business with pleasure.

There is a Jupiter–Saturn conjunction this year – something that happens only once in 20 years. And it occurs in your own Sign. Thus a new business and financial cycle is beginning for you and for the world at large – and it will be a good one. It shows that the universal business cycle will be harmonious to you – will play to your strengths – will be comfortable for you over the next 20 years. You will shine in the coming business environment.

Pluto is still in your 8th House of Other People's Money and will be there for many years to come. Thus you are learning more about debt – its constructive and destructive sides. You have more access to other people's money – but also more responsibility. Your spouse or partner is very focused on finances and earnings – and is also prospering this year.

Self-improvement

There is tremendous focus on the career and 'outer' success this year. This is all well and good and part of the plan for your life. Only remember to carve out some space for yourself – to do things that you really *like* to do. Work, by all means, but also have some fun.

Pluto's move through your 8th House is doing many things. On a financial level it will teach you some of the deeper mysteries of money and investment. Outside capital will come easily to you and the temptations to get into debt will be great. It is wonderful to have access to outside capital, but you must use this money wisely – to invest in things that will go up in value and not in things that go down. Investors will invest in you or your projects very willingly in the coming years, only remember that they are not doing this out of the goodness of their hearts but because they expect a reasonable return on their investments. Thus you have a responsibility to deliver this. In a sense, you will be working for them and not for yourself.

You Taureans have many virtues, but being a visionary is generally not one of them (your unique personal horoscope based on the exact day and time of your birth can modify this). Yet, these days (and for years to come) you *are* visionary when it comes to your career. You see things that others don't see. You see future trends. You dream dreams and they happen. On the one hand this is wonderful, on the other it can subject you to criticism and ridicule if you discuss these with the wrong people. Learn to keep your counsel. Believe in your vision, act on it, but be silent about it. This will be a great protection for you.

Month-by-month Forecasts

January

Best Days Overall: 5th, 6th, 7th, 15th, 16th, 23rd, 24th

Most Stressful Days Overall: 1st, 2nd, 8th, 9th, 21st, 22nd, 28th, 29th

TAURUS

Best Days for Love: 1st, 2nd, 3rd, 4th, 13th, 14th, 21st, 22nd, 28th, 29th, 30th, 31st

Best Days for Money: 3rd, 4th, 5th, 6th, 7th, 13th, 14th, 15th, 16th, 17th, 18th, 21st, 22nd, 25th, 26th, 30th, 31st

Between 80 and 90 per cent of the planets are above the Horizon of your chart and your 10th House of Career becomes a major House of Power after the 20th. This is a month of outer achievement and progress – a month for achieving career goals. With 90 to 100 per cent of the planets moving forward there is much forward movement in your career, and in your life in general.

With so many planets above the Horizon it is usually safe to ignore domestic and emotional concerns. But the Lunar Eclipse of the 21st won't let you. It shows a move, or the uprooting of the normal domestic and family pattern. A career change could be the cause of it. Perhaps your career forces you to relocate – or forces a family member to relocate. Hidden flaws in your home are likely to surface now so that you can correct them. And while all this is happening you have the intense demands of your career – rest and relax more after the 20th. In particular, reduce your schedule around the time of the Eclipse. Handle essentials and let lesser things go.

With Saturn still in your own Sign this is a great period for dieting, exercising and taking on a disciplined health regime. This is especially called for now, since the urges to the good life are very strong until the 20th.

Love is passionate and tempestuous this month – especially around the 9th. Jealousy and possessiveness can cause problems – even though you are going way out of your way to please the beloved, and doing yeoman work for their finances. Singles have abundant love opportunities.

Finances are happy this month. There is great financial optimism. Mercury in Capricorn shows earnings from property, lumber, office equipment and from conservative, long-term investments. Your financial judgement is especially sharp and keen until the 19th. This is a good time to make important purchases as you have an eye for quality and value. A sudden financial windfall comes around the 27th—28th. Elders, bosses and people above you in status are supporting your financial goals. Your good reputation is like money in the bank.

February

Best Days Overall: 2nd, 3rd, 11th, 12th, 19th, 20th, 29th

Most Stressful Days Overall: 4th, 5th, 17th, 18th, 24th, 25th

Best Days for Love: 2nd, 3rd, 9th, 10th, 11th, 12th, 17th, 18th, 22nd, 24th, 25th, 26th, 27th, 28th

Best Days for Money: 6th, 9th, 10th, 13th, 14th, 15th, 16th, 19th, 24th, 25th, 29th

An important and significant month for you, Taurus – major changes for the good are happening – but first the Cosmos might need to blast away some obstructions and stubbornness.

The most important headline this month is Jupiter's move from Aries into your own Sign on the 15th. This is not only important in a physical way – in terms of the material gifts that Jupiter brings – but in a psychological and spiritual way. For Jupiter is bringing you optimism, happiness, self-esteem, honours, recognition, sex appeal and the good life. You are going to start catching the lucky breaks and redefining yourself as 'blessed and fortunate'. On the material level, earnings will skyrocket, there will be more foreign travel, more access to outside capital – either through increased lines of credit or through investors – and an ease to paying off debt. Debts will melt away in the coming months. Many of you will inherit money or be remembered in someone's will. Substantial sums of money are coming to you.

TAURUS

The Solar Eclipse of the 5th is going to clear the path for all this good. When the Sky Dragon swallows the Sun, it is also going to swallow stubborn mental and physical patterns that were holding you back. While it is happening events can be disruptive – but remember, you are one strong and persistent person. When you hold on to a pattern, you really hold it. Major force is necessary to make you let go. Co-operate with the changes and you'll be on the high road to your heart's desire. You are not losing anything except some problems.

This Solar Eclipse is particularly strong on you, Taurus, so take a reduced schedule – the two days before and a day after will be sufficient. Discernment is necessary during this period. Things that absolutely *must* be done should be done – but things that are elective should be rescheduled.

This Eclipse is bringing important career changes. Obstructions to your career goals are blasted away – either through a shake-up of the management of your present firm, or through another job offer, or through a shake-up of your competitors. Let patience do its perfect work – all the information you need to make good career decisions is coming.

Your health is not what it should be until the 20th, so rest and relax more. Remember the discussion in the Health section, above.

Love is more spiritual and idealistic this month, and your spouse or partner is supportive financially.

Mercury's retrograde from the 21st onwards doesn't stop earnings but throws more complications into the picture. Do more research about all financial dealings and commitments.

March

Best Days Overall: 1st, 9th, 10th, 18th, 19th, 27th, 28th, 29th

Most Stressful Days Overall: 3rd, 4th, 16th, 17th, 22nd, 23rd, 24th, 30th, 31st

Best Days for Love: 3rd, 4th, 7th, 8th, 12th, 13th, 16th, 17th, 22nd, 23rd, 24th, 25th, 26th

Best Days for Money: 1st, 5th, 6th, 9th, 10th, 12th, 14th, 15th, 18th, 19th, 22nd, 23rd, 24th, 27th, 28th

Between 90 and 100 per cent of the planets are moving forward, and the Sun and Mars in Aries are speeding things along. There is much happening in both in your personal life and in the world. Everyone is rushing and there is pressure on you to do the same. Be careful, though, that you don't succumb to the demon of speed when it comes to finances and important financial decisions – not until the 14th, while Mercury is retrograde. It is going to be difficult, but resist the urge to invest, buy or make serious financial commitments without doing the necessary research. All the fine print in a contract needs to be understood by all parties. Don't make a move until you are clear on everything. Financial opportunities will come to you all year long – don't worry about passing up on something that you don't understand.

The planetary power is overwhelmingly in the Eastern hemisphere of your chart. Thus this is a time for making things happen – a time for action and self-assertion – for demanding from life what you want of it. It is a time for thinking of your own needs and desires and creating conditions for your personal happiness. The Cosmos wants this and is supporting your efforts.

Most of the planets are still in the upper half of your chart, and your 10th House of Career is still very powerful. You can safely let go of – or de-emphasize – home and family issues and focus on your outer, worldly-type ambitions. Though your career is a lot calmer than it was last month, it is still quite active. Venus' move through this House is bringing personal satisfaction and the favour of those above you. A basically successful career month.

Your most important areas of interest are the career,

friends, groups, organizations, spirituality and charitable activities, personal pleasure, and the body and the image.

Health and vitality are much improved over last month. Mars moving into your own Sign gives you much energy, passion and enthusiasm. There is a new zest for athletics and daredevil manoeuvres. Don't overdo it. Mars in Taurus increases your libido and personal magnetism. You get your way in most things, only be careful of bulldozing the opposition. Try charm first before you use force.

Finances improve once Mercury moves forward on the 14th. Sales, marketing and media activities – as well as your financial intuition – are good sources of income. After the 14th many stalled deals, payments and projects start moving forward again.

Love is active and passionate. The tendency is to love at first sight – but Pluto's retrograde on the 14th cautions you to slow down. Let love develop and grow.

April

Best Days Overall: 6th, 7th, 14th, 15th, 24th, 25th

Most Stressful Days Overall: 12th, 13th, 19th, 20th, 26th, 27th

Best Days for Love: 1st, 2nd, 4th, 5th, 12th, 13th, 19th, 20th, 21st, 22nd

Best Days for Money: 1st, 2nd, 6th, 7th, 8th, 9th, 10th, 11th, 14th, 15th, 21st, 22nd, 24th, 25th

Between 80 and 90 per cent of the planets are in the Eastern sector of your chart, and 40 per cent of them will be in your own Sign. This is a period where you can have things your own way. And though there will be some opposition, you have the power and will to cut through it with ease. A hundred-mile journey seems daunting when you are riding a bicycle, but in a Mercedes it is not so daunting – it is fun –

a jaunt. The opposition and obstacles in your life have not disappeared, but you have more energy to deal with them. And that makes all the difference in the world.

Spend the early part of the month clarifying your goals and objectives. When the Sun moves into Taurus on the 19th, move into action. Create conditions as you desire them to be. With 90 per cent of the planets in forward motion, this indicates great progress and achievement.

The majority of the planets are still above the Horizon of your Horoscope, though this will soon change. In the meantime, focus on your outer, worldly life and let go of domestic, family issues. With your Family Planet moving into your own Sign, there is a feeling of great family support for your true desires.

Your important areas of interest this month are the career, spirituality and charity, friends, groups and organizations, and personal pleasure, the body and self-image.

Until the 19th the element of Fire is very strong in the world. Mars, the planet of action and speed, will be in your own Sign as well. Thus there will be great pressure on you to make hasty decisions, to leap into action without adequate forethought. The world is awash with a great optimism – and thoughts become actions very quickly. It will be difficult to resist these tendencies. People are acting as if they can have anything, do anything, be anything without regard for cost or consequences. But if you delay important decisions until after the 19th you will be happier with them. They will be more practical.

Shopping for big-ticket items will also go better after the 19th. Many planets in your own Sign will ensure that you get the best deal and don't overpay.

Your health is vastly improved over how it has been for the past few months. But good health habits now will come in handy in the future.

Love is strong all month, though a marriage should not be rushed into.

TAURUS

May

Best Days Overall: 3rd, 4th, 12th, 13th, 21st, 22nd, 31st

Most Stressful Days Overall: 9th, 10th, 16th, 17th, 24th, 25th

Best Days for Love: 1st, 2nd, 3rd, 4th, 9th, 10th, 12th, 13th, 16th, 17th, 18th, 19th, 22nd, 23rd, 28th, 29th

Best Days for Money: 3rd, 4th, 5th, 6th, 12th, 13th, 14th, 21st, 22nd, 24th, 25th, 31st

A very happy, powerful and ultra-prosperous month, Taurus. Enjoy.

Most of the planets are in the East now, and your own Sign of Taurus contains most of them. Also, 60 per cent of the planetary power is moving through your Sign – at one time or another – this month. You are certainly feeling your oats. You have the strength of 10 and achieve your goals very easily. Even the increase in retrograde activity will have little impact on you now. You can have things your own way and create the life you desire to create.

All this power in your own Sign is certainly improving your health. Exercise regimes and sport activities go very well. You look and feel great. Sensual pleasures – some you might not have known about or thought about – are coming to you in great abundance. People are catering to you. You are very much in synch with the universe and it is a heady feeling. Health problems of the past will tend to disappear now.

The planets have now shifted to the bottom half of your Horoscope, so that career activities, though important, are becoming temporarily less so. There is a need for emotional harmony and inner growth to match the tremendous outer growth going on in your life.

Your important areas of interest this month are the body, the image and personal pleasures, finance and career.

The main challenge this month is balancing your desires for the good life – your personal desires – with your career obligations and ambitions. I reckon that personal desires will win out this month.

Earnings are soaring this month. Whatever you touch turns to gold. The Jupiter—Saturn conjunction – which denotes a major business cycle in the world – occurs in your own Sign. I read this as your being in synch with the important trends in global business for the next 20 years. This is an important long-term prosperity signal. Over the next 20 years or so you will certainly have your financial ups and downs, but the trend will always be towards greater personal prosperity. You have a unique ability to align yourself with global business and market trends – often unconsciously. In fact, I would advise those who study these things to observe the Taureans in their midst – what are they thinking and feeling? How do they size up a business proposition? This will be a powerful indicator of the trends of the times.

Love is stormy towards the end of the month – your focus on money and perhaps financial issues is the problem. This is short term.

June

Best Days Overall: 8th, 9th, 17th, 18th, 19th, 27th, 28th

Most Stressful Days Overall: 6th, 7th, 12th, 13th, 14th, 20th, 21st

Best Days for Love: 2nd, 6th, 7th, 10th, 11th, 12th, 13th, 14th, 15th, 16th, 22nd, 23rd, 25th, 26th

Best Days for Money: 1st, 2nd, 4th, 5th, 8th, 9th, 12th, 13th, 14th, 17th, 18th, 19th, 22nd, 23rd, 27th, 28th, 29th, 30th

The planetary power is still in the East and your own Sign of Taurus is still strong. Push forward boldly towards your goals. Personal fulfilment and happiness are yours. You can and will have things your way.

Your Career Planet is retrograde all month and most of the planets are below the Horizon: Continue to give more attention to home and domestic issues and let your career coast.

Retrograde activity increases this month and affects some important areas of your life. The retrograde of Uranus (your Career Planet) and of Neptune in your 10th House (which affects the career) suggests caution in all career changes, job offers and the like. Ambitions might seem like they are going backwards instead of forwards, but this is only appearances – change and progress are happening on deeper levels. You must let time do its perfect work.

Mercury, your Financial Planet, goes retrograde on the 23rd. Try to wrap up major purchases, investments and major financial commitments before then. Since your Money House is powerful this month, Mercury's retrograde is unlikely to stop earnings, only delay things and cause some unnecessary complications. Happily, the new Moon of the 2nd occurs in your Money House and will do much to clarify financial confusion as the month progresses. Sales, marketing, trading, buying, selling and family connections are the road to earnings this period. There are interesting opportunities in property and restaurants during this period as well.

The retrograde of Pluto causes love complications. And, though you are unusually attractive and are enjoying high self-esteem, love needs time to develop. Your social confidence and judgement are not up to its usually high standards. Neither marriages nor divorces should be scheduled now. Aside from Pluto's retrograde, it is receiving stressful aspects early in the month showing upheavals and conflicts in love – ride them out and don't rush to judgement or action.

Health is good this month. The ebbing of career demands is helping matters. Both Jupiter and Saturn in your own

Sign shows a need to balance the good life with a stern diet. The desire to binge and the desire to overeat co-exist in an uneasy relationship. Don't allow the ups and downs of finance to affect your health.

July

Best Days Overall: 5th, 6th, 15th, 16th, 24th, 25th, 31st

Most Stressful Days Overall: 3rd, 4th, 10th, 11th, 17th, 18th

Best Days for Love: 1st, 2nd, 3rd, 4th, 10th, 11th, 12th, 13th, 22nd, 23rd, 30th, 31st

Best Days for Money: 1st, 2nd, 6th, 7th, 10th, 11th, 14th, 15th, 20th, 21st, 25th, 26th, 27th, 29th, 30th

This is a major eventful month with much disruption going on, both personally and in the world around you – take a reduced schedule especially after the 22nd.

Three Eclipses happen in July, which is an unusual number. Eclipses always signal long-term change in the world. The Sky Dragon needs to blast away obstructions to the Heavenly Plan. Periods of chaos are normal around Eclipse periods.

Two out of three of these Eclipses are stressful to you, so take a reduced schedule. The Solar Eclipse of the 1st occurs in Cancer, your 3rd House. It is a stressful one since it impacts on the home, family and domestic condition – the eclipsed Planet, the Sun, is your Family Planet. Thus moves, renovations, repairs and family upheavals are likely now. Since the Eclipse impacts on Venus, your Ruling Planet, we can see a redefinition of the personality and an image change happening over the next month or so. But the family and domestic issues seem the strongest. The next Solar Eclipse on the 31st will affect the Sun (your Family Planet) and occurs in your 4th House of Home and Family. This reinforces the tendency towards moves, repairs and renovation.

TAURUS

The Lunar Eclipse of the 16th occurs in your 9th House and is much kinder to you. This Eclipse will be powerful for those of you who are students, or involved in academia. It shows a change in your educational status – probably a good one – a graduation, an acceptance to a university or to a graduate school, etc. Perhaps there are upheavals in your church or place of worship – the vicar, priest or other religious leader may change or retire. Long-term changes are going on in your religious beliefs and philosophy of life as well.

Jupiter's move into Gemini coincides with the Solar Eclipse of the 1st. Thus, the redefinition of your image and personality probably involves wealth – you are taking on a wealthier image, dressing more expensively, letting people know that you are a person of substance. For Jupiter is now going to enlarge and expand your earnings and possessions. Wealth is going to accumulate now. Assets you own will increase in value. The means and methods for attaining your financial dreams and goals will be given. You are entering a period of great and increasing prosperity.

Love and romance improve after the 22nd. There is much greater synchronicity between you and the beloved. And while singles should not schedule a marriage just yet, there are many more love opportunities.

August

Best Days Overall: 1st, 2nd, 11th, 12th, 20th, 21st, 22nd, 29th, 30th

Most Stressful Days Overall: 6th, 7th, 13th, 14th, 15th, 27th, 28th

Best Days for Love: 6th, 7th, 8th, 9th, 11th, 12th, 18th, 19th, 20th, 21st, 27th, 28th, 29th, 30th

Best Days for Money: 3rd, 4th, 8th, 9th, 13th, 14th, 18th, 19th, 23rd, 24th, 29th, 30th

Health is improving day by day, but continue to rest and relax more until the 22nd. After then your health and vitality soar – and it has been months and months since you've felt this good. Those who have had health problems in recent months hear good news.

Most of the planets are now in the West, including Venus, your Ruler. Independence and self-will must give way to consensus and co-operation. Adapt to situations and try not to make waves with others.

Most of the planets are below the Horizon this month, and two powerful planets are still retrograde in your 10th House of Career. Let career issues slide and focus on home, family and psychological growth. Find your emotional 'comfort zone' and learn to function from there.

Home and family issues are emphasized in other ways as well. Your 4th House of Home and Family is a major House of Power during this period. Mars in your 4th House shows that this is a good period for heavy work around the house – major repairs and renovations – lifting and moving furniture, etc. Venus in your 4th House until the 6th makes this a good time for family gatherings and for entertaining from the home. It's also good for decorating and buying objects of beauty for the home. The Sun in your 4th House makes you shine in the home and increases your status within the family.

Love, too, is much improved this month. Pluto, your Love Planet, not only receives beautiful aspects but also starts moving forward during this period. Pluto's forward motion increases social confidence and strengthens social judgement. A current relationship starts moving forward again. Love opportunities come through family members and family connections until the 22nd. There could be conflicts with the beloved after the 6th, but these are short-term spats and not long-term trends. Compromise is the key.

Finances are getting stronger day by day. Saturn joins Jupiter in your Money House on the 11th. Earnings are soaring. Even brief conflicts after the 22nd cannot dim or slow earnings. You just have to work harder. There is so much wealth happening for you that financial management is a must – you need to know where to stash all this loot!

September

Best Days Overall: 7th, 8th, 17th, 18th, 25th, 26th

Most Stressful Days Overall: 2nd, 3rd, 10th, 11th, 23rd, 24th, 30th

Best Days for Love: 1st, 2nd, 3rd, 4th, 5th, 10th, 11th, 14th, 15th, 19th, 20th, 23rd, 24th, 30th

Best Days for Money: 1st, 10th, 11th, 19th, 20th, 27th, 28th, 29th, 30th

Most of the planets are in the West, including Venus, your Ruler. Social affairs are becoming ever more important. Popularity increases. You are going out of your way to please others and your current beloved. This is no time for undue self-assertion or self-will. Good comes to you through others and their good graces. Though Taureans are not known for their adaptability, this is a good period for you to develop more of this quality.

Most of the planets are still below the Horizon and your Career Planet is still retrograde. You can safely de-emphasize the career – coast for a bit – and focus on emotional and family issues. Though you coast career-wise, positive things are happening there – probably behind the scenes. This is still an excellent period for doing heavy work around the house.

Your important areas of interest this month are finance, parties, children, love affairs and creativity, health and work, love and romance, and your career.

Two powerful planets go retrograde in your Money House this month. This shows that while major financial developments are happening, there is a pause or a breather taking place. You are like the runner who needs to take a break and catch his or her breath. Review and perfect your financial goals and projects – especially the big ones.

Mercury, your Money Planet, moves swiftly through three different Signs and Houses of your Horoscope. Thus earnings are happening (everyday earnings) and you exhibit great financial confidence and judgement. Until the 7th, money comes from creativity, parties, speculations or while you are having fun. After the 7th, it comes from work and from opportunities created by co-workers. After the 28th, it comes though partnerships, your spouse or partner, social connections and friends. There is increased spending on children, lovers, and health and fitness items. Buy needed objects of beauty – jewellery, paintings, wall hangings and the like – until the 28th, when your aesthetic judgement will be most strong.

Your health is strong this month.

Pluto's forward motion and power in your House of Love is improving your love life tremendously. But love is stormy. Affections can change dramatically and swiftly. Financial disagreements can come between you and the beloved. The demands of your career are also not helping matters. The love is there but it is being tested by many factors.

October

Best Days Overall: 4th, 5th, 6th, 14th, 15th, 23rd, 24th

Most Stressful Days Overall: 1st, 7th, 8th, 20th, 21st, 27th, 28th

Best Days for Love: 1st, 2nd, 3rd, 9th, 10th, 11th, 12th, 13th, 20th, 21st, 27th, 28th, 29th, 30th

Best Days for Money: 1st, 7th, 8th, 9th, 10th, 11th, 16th, 17th, 18th, 19th, 25th, 26th, 27th, 28th

TAURUS

Saturn's retrograde back into your own Sign is the major headline this month. This, coupled with the presence of many planets in Scorpio after the 23rd, puts some temporary stress on your health. Rest and relax more and remember the discussion in the Health section, above. Keep in mind that the worst of the stress is over – it will not be nearly as severe as it was earlier in the year.

Most of the planets are in the West, and your 7th House of Love is a House of Power. Your way might not be the best way during this period. Hone and develop your social skills and let your good come to you through others. Adapt to situations during this period rather than trying to change them.

This is an important career month, Taurus. On the 23rd the balance of planetary power shifts decisively to the upper half of your Horoscope. Two planets long retrograde in your House of Career will start moving forward this month. Career delay now falls away and you enter your promised land. Inner developments that you were not aware of are now made manifest and your career is ready to spring forward.

The main challenge this month – after the 23rd – is balancing your career with your love and social life. Both areas are important but each pulls you in a different direction. This tension is short-term and will pass by the end of next month.

Though financial prospects and income have never been better, two important financial planets are retrograde this month – Mercury and Jupiter. Thus, deals and payments due you can be stalled. Misunderstandings in financial affairs are more likely than usual, and you must take steps to clarify things. Important purchases and investments made now are likely to be unrealistic, and your financial judgement is not up to its usually high standards. Avoid these things where possible until next month. You can do food shopping and the purchase of small items, but let big-ticket purchases wait.

Love is active this month but can be volatile. Part of the problem stems from your devotion to your career – which your lover takes as a slight. Perhaps a career development upsets plans you had with the beloved. Affections change rapidly. Communication between you and the beloved needs more work, as Mercury is retrograde in your House of Love. All of this is short term – but useful in testing love.

November

Best Days Overall: 1st, 2nd, 10th, 11th, 19th, 20th, 28th, 29th

Most Stressful Days Overall: 3rd, 4th, 17th, 18th, 23rd, 24th

Best Days for Love: 8th, 9th, 17th, 18th, 19th, 20th, 23rd, 24th, 26th, 27th, 28th, 29th

Best Days for Money: 3rd, 4th, 6th, 7th, 12th, 13th, 15th, 16th, 21st, 22nd, 23rd, 24th, 30th

The search for personal pleasure and physical beauty is taking you to some strange and exotic spaces – both physically and psychologically. There is experimentation with libido and perhaps travels or dealings with exotic, little known, foreign lands. It would come as no surprise if you were to explore the arcane regions of philosophy and theology during this period. An interesting and educational month lies ahead.

Most of the planets are still in the West and many planets are in your 7th House of Love and Social Activities – so this is a strong social period, a yearly social peak. Avoid power struggles and self-assertion and develop more adaptability now. Social grace will bring you good, where brute force and self-assertion never could.

The planetary power is now firmly above the Horizon – a trend that will get stronger in the coming months. Continue to de-emphasize home and family issues and focus on worldly ambitions. The family could kick up a brief fuss, but it will be short term. Your career is still stormy – hectic and active – until the 23rd, but great progress is going on there. Conflicts in career matters are temporary.

Your love life is active all month. Like last month, you need to balance the needs of love with your career urges. Difficult to satisfy both your boss and your beloved as they pull you in opposite directions. Each feels slighted when you give undue attention to the other. You are attending more weddings this month. Perhaps family members are getting married. There is more entertaining from home. Someone from your past comes into the romantic picture. Love comes through family connections.

Health is delicate until the 22nd. Rest and relax more. Most of the stress passes after the 22nd, but you still need to be careful and to focus on essentials.

Mercury, your Financial Planet, is retrograde until the 8th. Avoid major purchases, investments or financial commitments until after this day. Your financial power and judgement are much stronger after the 8th than before.

December

Best Days Overall: 8th, 9th, 16th, 17th, 25th, 26th, 27th

Most Stressful Days Overall: 1st, 2nd, 14th, 15th, 20th, 21st, 22nd, 28th, 29th

Best Days for Love: 6th, 7th, 10th, 11th, 14th, 15th, 18th, 19th, 20th, 21st, 22nd, 23rd, 24th, 28th, 29th

Best Days for Money: 1st, 6th, 7th, 10th, 11th, 14th, 15th, 18th, 25th, 26th, 28th

By the 8th the planets become evenly distributed between the Eastern and Western sectors. Venus, your Ruler, spends the month poised between the two sectors – on the cusp. The message is clear: neither independence nor social grace is the answer for you this month. Now you will go one way and now another. There are times you will have to adapt to situations, and times when you can go your own way. Each case will demand a specific decision on your part.

The planets are firmly above the Horizon and the power there gets stronger day by day. Handle home and family issues with dispatch and get right back – as soon as possible – to your career and outer ambitions. Family issues are still important but can safely be de-emphasized.

The Solar Eclipse of the 25th deals kindly with you. It could be disruptive for family members, or for the home, as the Sun is your Family Planet. If there are flaws in your present residence or in relations with family members they will come to the surface now so you can correct them. Some of you may move house. The Eclipse is especially powerful for those of you who are students. It signals a change in your schooling – which could be essentially good. This can be graduation, the acceptance to a university, an important educational decision, a change of focus for your studies, etc. Those of you involved in religion should see a shake-up or upheaval in your church, temple or mosque.

Venus, your Ruler, moves into your 10th House of Career on the 8th, making the coming period a yearly career peak. Venus conjunct Neptune on the 12th brings spiritual illumination, intuitive guidance about your career path, a significant dream, or a meeting with a psychic or clairvoyant. You are given glimpses into the future at these times. Venus conjunct Uranus on the 24th brings career joy and a pleasant job change – perhaps a promotion.

Health is excellent all month.

Love seems happy and harmonious most of the month, and with Mercury now forward in the House of Love communication with the beloved is much improved. Mars' move into your House of Love on the 23rd could cause power struggles in your relationship. Jealousy and over-intensity can be a serious problem. Singles become more aggressive in love.

Finances improve this month as your Money Planet moves into expansive Sagittarius. Earnings increase, but so does spending. Don't overdo the holiday shopping. Money comes through your spouse or partner or through social connections.

Gemini

Ⅱ

THE TWINS
Birthdays from
21st May
to 20th June

Personality Profile

GEMINI AT A GLANCE

Element – Air

Ruling Planet – Mercury
  Career Planet – Neptune
  Love Planet – Jupiter
  Money Planet – Moon
  Planet of Health and Work – Pluto
  Planet of Home and Family Life – Mercury

Colours – blue, yellow, yellow-orange

Colour that promotes love, romance and social harmony – sky blue

Colours that promote earning power – grey, silver

GEMINI

Gems – agate, aquamarine

Metal – quicksilver

Scents – lavender, lilac, lily of the valley, storax

Quality – mutable (= flexibility)

Quality most needed for balance – thought that is deep rather than superficial

Strongest virtues – great communication skills, quickness and agility of thought, ability to learn quickly

Deepest need – communication

Characteristics to avoid – gossiping, hurting others with harsh speech, superficiality, using words to mislead or misinform

Signs of greatest overall compatibility – Libra, Aquarius

Signs of greatest overall incompatibility – Virgo, Sagittarius, Pisces

Sign most helpful to career – Pisces

Sign most helpful for emotional support – Virgo

Sign most helpful financially – Cancer

Sign best for marriage and/or partnerships – Sagittarius

Sign most helpful for creative projects – Libra

Best Sign to have fun with – Libra

Signs most helpful in spiritual matters – Taurus, Aquarius

Best day of the week – Wednesday

Understanding the Gemini Personality

Gemini is to society what the nervous system is to the body. It does not introduce any new information but is a vital transmitter of impulses from the senses to the brain and vice versa. The nervous system does not judge or weigh these impulses – it only conveys information. And does so perfectly.

This analogy should give you an indication of a Gemini's role in society. Geminis are the communicators and conveyors of information. To Geminis the truth or falsehood of information is irrelevant, they only transmit what they see, hear or read about. Thus they are capable of spreading the most outrageous rumours as well as conveying truth and light. Geminis sometimes tend to be unscrupulous in their communications and can do great good or great evil with their power. This is why the Sign of Gemini is called the Sign of the Twins: Geminis have a dual nature.

Their ability to convey a message – to communicate with such ease – makes Geminis ideal teachers, writers and media and marketing people. This is helped by the fact that Mercury, the Ruling Planet of Gemini, also rules these activities.

Geminis have the gift of the gab. And what a gift this is! They can make conversation about anything, anywhere, at any time. There is almost nothing that is more fun to Geminis than a good conversation – especially if they can learn something new as well. They love to learn and they love to teach. To deprive a Gemini of conversation, or of books and magazines, is cruel and unusual punishment.

Geminis are almost always excellent students and take well to education. Their minds are generally stocked with all kinds of information, trivia, anecdotes, stories, news items, rarities, facts and statistics. Thus they can support any intellectual position that they care to take. They are awesome debaters and, if involved in politics, make good orators.

Geminis are so verbally smooth that even if they do not

know what they are talking about, they can make you think that they do. They will always dazzle you with their brilliance.

Finance

Geminis tend to be more concerned with the wealth of learning and ideas than with actual material wealth. As mentioned they excel in professions that involve writing, teaching, sales and journalism – and not all of these professions pay very well. But to sacrifice intellectual needs merely for money is unthinkable to a Gemini. Geminis strive to combine the two.

Cancer is on Gemini's Solar 2nd House (of Money) cusp, which indicates that Geminis can earn extra income (in a harmonious and natural way) from investments in residential property, restaurants and hotels. Given their verbal skills, Geminis love to bargain and negotiate in any situation, but especially when it has to do with money.

The Moon rules Gemini's 2nd Solar House. The Moon is not only the fastest-moving planet in the Zodiac but actually moves through every Sign and House every 28 days. No other heavenly body matches the Moon for swiftness or the ability to change quickly. An analysis of the Moon – and lunar phenomena in general – describes Gemini's financial attitudes very well. Geminis are financially versatile and flexible. They can earn money in many different ways. Their financial attitudes and needs seem to change daily. Their feelings about money change also: sometimes they are very enthusiastic about it, at other times they could not care less.

For a Gemini, financial goals and money are often seen only as means of supporting a family; these things have little meaning otherwise.

The Moon, as Gemini's Money Planet, has another important message for Gemini financially: in order for Geminis to realize their financial potential they need to develop more of an understanding of the emotional side of life. They need to combine their awesome powers of logic with an understanding of human psychology. Feelings have their own logic; Geminis need to learn this and apply it to financial matters.

Career and Public Image

Geminis know that they have been given the gift of communication for a reason, that it is a power that can achieve great good or cause unthinkable distress. They long to put this power at the service of the highest and most transcendental truths. This is their primary goal, to communicate the eternal verities and prove them logically. They look up to people who can transcend the intellect – to poets, artists, musicians and mystics. They may be awed by stories of religious saints and martyrs. A Gemini's highest achievement is to teach the truth, whether it is scientific, inspirational or historical. Those who can transcend the intellect are a Gemini's natural superiors – and a Gemini realizes this.

The Sign of Pisces is in Gemini's Solar 10th House of Career. Neptune, the Planet of Spirituality and Altruism, is Gemini's Career Planet. If Geminis are to realize their highest career potential they need to develop their transcendental – their spiritual and altruistic – side. They need to understand the larger Cosmic picture, the vast flow of human evolution – where it came from and where it is heading. Only then can a Gemini's intellectual powers take their true position and he or she can become the 'messenger of the gods'. Geminis need to cultivate a facility for 'inspiration', which is something that does not originate *in* the intellect but which comes *through* the intellect. This will further enrich and empower a Gemini's mind.

Love and Relationships

Geminis bring their natural garrulousness and brilliance into their love life and social life as well. A good talk or a verbal joust is an interesting prelude to romance. Their only problem in love is that their intellect is too cool and passionless to incite ardour in others. Emotions sometimes disturb them, and their partners tend to complain about this. If you are in love with a Gemini you must understand why this is so. Geminis avoid deep passions because these would interfere with their ability to think and communicate. If they are cool towards you, understand that this is their nature.

Nevertheless, Geminis must understand that it is one thing to talk about love and another actually to love – to feel it and radiate it. Talking about love glibly will get them nowhere. They need to feel it and act on it. Love is not of the intellect but of the heart. If you want to know how a Gemini feels about love you should not listen to what he or she says but rather observe what he or she does. Geminis can be quite generous to those they love.

Geminis like their partners to be refined, well educated and well travelled. If their partners are more wealthy than they, that is all the better. If you are in love with a Gemini you had better be a good listener as well.

The ideal relationship for the Gemini is a relationship of the mind. They enjoy the physical and emotional aspects, of course, but if the intellectual communion is not there they will suffer.

Home and Domestic Life

At home the Gemini can be uncharacteristically neat and meticulous. They tend to want their children and partner to live up to their idealistic standards. When these standards are not met they moan and criticize. However, Geminis are good family people and like to serve their families in practical and useful ways.

The Gemini home is comfortable and pleasant. They like to invite people over and they make great hosts. Geminis are also good at repairs and improvements around the house – all fuelled by their need to stay active and occupied with something they like to do. Geminis have many hobbies and interests that keep them busy when they are home alone.

Geminis understand and get along well with their children, mainly because they are very youthful people themselves. As great communicators, Geminis know how to explain things to children; in this way they gain their children's love and respect. Geminis also encourage children to be creative and talkative, just like they are.

Horoscope for 2000

Major Trends

1999 was a year of great social and intellectual expansion. Many of you expanded spiritually as well. University students or those involved in academia had a very good year. Philosophical concepts and understanding grew by leaps and bounds. Many of these trends are continuing in the year 2000. But there are new trends as well.

Both Saturn and Jupiter are moving into your own Sign this year and this is very significant. Saturn makes a brief visit, and gives a preview of things to come in 2001. Jupiter will enter your Sign permanently on 1st July.

Jupiter's entry into your Sign is a very happy transit. It brings increased earnings, foreign travel, optimism and enthusiasm, the expansion of horizons, overall good luck, the good life and serious love. Sensual desires and fantasies will be fulfilled.

Saturn, on the other hand, will tend to temper these tendencies. It will urge you to more stoicism and less self-indulgence. It will force you to balance the excesses of the good life with the correct diet and exercise programmes. Where Jupiter will expand your self-esteem beyond the stratosphere, Saturn will give this a good reality check. You will find that you are neither as lowly as you thought nor as exalted.

Pluto is still in your 7th House of Marriage, causing major transformations in your social life. Bad marriages are going down the pan. Power struggles in the marriage are going to be resolved in your favour – especially after 1st July.

The 9th House of Foreign Travel and Religion is still very strong and will continue to be important this year.

Paths to greatest fulfilment this year are the pursuit of intellectual interests, domestic travel, finance and earnings, friendships, group activities, spirituality, charity and volunteer activities, and personal pleasure.

Health

Your health should have been good in recent years. Most of the long-term planets have been kind to you. Pluto in Sagittarius has been stressing you out, but it is outgunned by all the positive help. The fact that your 6th House of Health is not a House of Power this year is another signal of good health. You take health for granted and don't pay much attention to it.

There are some issues you need to be aware of, however. When Jupiter moves into your own Sign on 1st July it is going to produce all kinds of happy events. Sensual fulfilment comes easily to you – perhaps too easily – and there is a tendency to over-indulge. Over-indulgence could cause health problems. If you listen to your body you can judge when you've had too much gourmet food, or too much good wine, etc. It will tell you when it has had enough.

When Jupiter moves into a person's Sign, weight gain can be a problem. Again this comes from over-indulgence.

Happily, Saturn's visit to your Sign from 11th August to 16th October will modify some of these tendencies. This is when you'll probably decide to diet and exercise more.

Saturn's move into your own Sign will make you aware of your physical limits, force you to manage your energy better, force you to work smarter and not harder and to focus on essentials. It has its ways of doing this – it is, after all, a genius.

From 11th August to 16th October we see a see saw battle going on: There will be alternate bouts of excessive bingeing and then bouts of excessive dieting; bouts of over-eating complemented with bouts of fasting; bouts of self-indulgence alternating with bouts of stoicism and self-denial. Getting the balance right seems difficult.

Pluto is your Health Planet and rules this domain from your 7th House of Love and Marriage. Thus there is a strong psychological connection between love and health. When there is harmony in love, health tends to be good and vice versa. Many of you are more concerned with the overall health of society, or with the health of partners, than with your own physical health. Since your love life seems good this year, health should be good as well. Health problems seem easily cleared when you resolve the love or relationship issues behind them. This connection will be especially dramatic after 1st July.

Home and Domestic Life

Your 4th House of Home and Family is not a House of Power this year, Gemini. You seem satisfied with the present arrangement and have no compelling urge to pay too much attention to these things. The status quo will probably prevail this year.

Jupiter's move into your own Sign from 1st July onwards often produces a renovation or enlargement of the personal sphere. This is not necessarily a move, but a renovation or expansion of a particular room (perhaps your favourite) – or the place where you spend most of your time. Career people may move to new and larger offices, while 'home-bodies' will renovate their bedrooms or studies. These things are sure to happen as Saturn's move into your Sign makes you feel cramped in these spaces as they exist and you will want to make changes.

One of your parents seems to have made major changes recently and is leading an exciting and 'liberated' lifestyle – unconventional, experimental, yet exciting. Another personality change is due around 5th February. A move or the acquisition of new property is likely after 1st July. This is a fortuitous move.

Siblings too are undergoing some long-term change. They might have moved house last year; this year the change is focused on the personality, image and physical appearance.

Relations with children seem to follow the status quo. Adult children's domestic situations are effected by the Eclipses of July and December. Thus they may move house or renovate the home due to a career change.

Love and Social Life

Both the 7th and 11th Houses are Houses of Power this year, so your love and social life is prominent and important. You are giving it a great deal of attention.

Married people are experiencing a prolonged power struggle in the marriage. Something will have to give. This year it seems fortunate for you, as your partner or spouse is 'giving in' and going way out of his or her way to please you. This could change next year, though.

As we mentioned, Pluto in your House of Marriage is going to annihilate bad relationships and totally renew the good ones. The bad ones will continue to get worse until they dissolve; the good ones will actually get better and better under Pluto's influence.

For many of you the marital status will change. Singles will marry and many married people will divorce. Jupiter's entry into your own Sign on 1st July is a classic marriage indicator – though it often produces 'live-in' relationships as well.

Singles need not run after love this year, as love is pursuing them. Early in the year love opportunities come through groups, organizations and friends. People you thought were just friends have more amorous things on their mind. After 15th February love comes through charities, ministries or volunteer activities. Love is idealistic and pure. Your standards are ultra-high and few mortals can live up to them. This is a period for formulating your ideal of love. Love is being arranged for you from the spirit world so there is no need for you to look for it in all the wrong places. Spiritually gifted people – pastors, ministers, gurus, psychics – are playing a matchmaking role during this period. Psychics and astrologers have important love guidance for you.

After 1st July, love starts becoming tangible and real. It will have its ups and downs – and will get tested (perhaps severely so) when Saturn moves into Gemini from 11th August to 16th October. This testing is important because before you can manifest your ideals of love, certain old attitudes and fears – both in you and in your lover – must be uprooted. Saturn will take care of this. Just hang in there.

There is an important Saturn—Jupiter conjunction happening this year. This only happens once in 20 years, and is thus very significant for your love life. A whole new social or marital cycle is beginning for most of you. A new love ideal is manifesting.

Your love and social life is unusual now – a year you will remember – as Jupiter behaves very unusually this year. It moves through three Signs and Houses in one year. Normally it moves through one or two. I read this as great social confidence and progress. Much dating and going out. Dating various types of people. Attaining much love and social experience in a short time.

Though you have many needs and urges in love this year (and many opportunities) I feel that the one who serves you best – serves your practical needs – will win your heart over time. He or she may not be as glamorous or as intellectually stimulating as some of the competition, but the urge to serve will carry the day.

Your love and social life will be unusually active from 1st to 24th January, 19th October to 13th November, and 22nd November to 21st December.

Children of marriageable age are likely to marry or have a significant relationship this year. Your parents' marriage (or the marriage of just one parent) goes through some upheavals and crisis – important flaws are being corrected. Siblings have an unstable love life – though neither the heights of rapture nor the depths of loneliness will be long lived. Both states are subject to sudden change.

Career and Finance

Though neither your Money House nor Career House is powerful this year, there is going to be much activity here in spite of your lack of interest. It is going to be a banner financial year.

The 1st July is an important date for you – both in love and in finance. There is a Solar Eclipse in your Money House, signifying dramatic long-term changes in the financial life – disruptive at first but leading to positive change. And, Jupiter, the Planet of Wealth and Abundance, moves into your own Sign on that day. Mark this on your calendar.

Jupiter is going to expand your self-esteem and feelings of self-worth. When this happens, earnings tend to increase as a side-effect. There are more honours and recognition this year. Self-confidence will be stronger – though Saturn will test it from 11th August to 16th October. There are pay rises and promotions in store. A new wardrobe and big-ticket personal accessories come. You dress for success. You lead a more opulent lifestyle. You travel more.

Your Career Planet and the South Node of the Moon travel together for many months. This shows a zeal and passion for career issues, and an instinctive – almost compulsive – drive to success, as if you can't help yourself. The Solar Eclipse of 5th February affects your Career Planet, bringing a job or career change. This will be positive, but disruptive.

Paths to financial success this year are investments in oil, natural gas, rubber, shipping, shipbuilders, retirement homes, foreign investments and technology. (Keep in mind that your full horoscope based on your exact date and time of birth could modify this.)

Paths to speculative increase are joint ventures, partnerships, foreign investments, publishing, import-export companies, re-cycling companies, tin and nuclear energy.

Job-seekers and employers have no problems for the first half of the year. After that, more discernment and caution are needed.

Self-improvement

Pluto has been hard at work transforming not only your love life and relationships but your body, image and personality as well. Much of this work has been going on in secret in the deep levels of the mind. Probably even your family and closest friends are not aware of it. This year, the work you've been doing starts to show. Come 1st July you will be birthing the 'new you'. You will dress differently, talk differently and have a totally new concept of yourself – totally superior to what you had in the past. You are becoming the 'you' that you've always dreamed of being and leading the lifestyle you've always dreamed of. This 'birthing of yourself' will of course change your relationships – this is inevitable. This fear of losing friendships or love has probably been the greatest barrier to this process. But the 'new you' comes equipped with friends; you must remember this.

There is much ferment going on in your mental life as well. As mentioned earlier, philosophical and religious concepts are being revamped and re-tooled. Educational opportunities are coming your way this year and you should take advantage of them. Foreign travel is not just a lark but serves to widen the mind and educate you as well.

Two powerful planets moving through your 12th House of Spirituality are going to both expand and solidify your connection to the Higher Power within. Jupiter will bring knowledge and happiness; Saturn will bring stability and the testing of your spiritual progress. Much psychological debris is being cleared out this year.

Month-by-month Forecasts

January

Best Days Overall: 8th, 9th, 17th, 18th, 25th, 26th

Most Stressful Days Overall: 3rd, 4th, 10th, 11th, 23rd, 24th, 30th, 31st

Best Days for Love: 3rd, 4th, 13th, 14th, 19th, 20th, 21st, 22nd, 30th, 31st

Best Days for Money: 3rd, 4th, 5th, 6th, 7th, 13th, 14th, 15th, 16th, 19th, 20th, 21st, 22nd, 25th, 26th, 30th, 31st

For half the month, *all* the planets will be in the top half of your chart, while 90 per cent of them will be there for the other half. You can safely ignore (or minimize) home and domestic concerns and focus on your 'outer' activities in the world. Mars crossing your Midheaven from the 4th onwards shows much activity in the career and that you are working very hard.

Between 90 and 100 per cent of the planets are moving forward this month so there is much (and quick) progress, achievement and change happening. Life is far from dull these days.

The Lunar Eclipse of the 21st is kind to you, but it would not be a bad idea to have your car, phones and computers checked out. Long-term financial changes – for the better – are happening as well, but the changes could be disruptive.

Love, personal transformation, making money for other people, debt, foreign travel and foreign affairs, religion and philosophy are the most important interests this month. This is where you will be spending most of your time, attention and energy. This is a great month in which to pursue educational opportunities or travel, or to regenerate the body and image.

Love is both romantic and passionate this month. Love is 'honeymoonish' and playful. Spiritual compatibility is the most important of all the compatibilities right now – and this trend will intensify in the coming months. It will not be enough if your beloved is a 'major babe' or has a lot of money – there must be a compatibility of spiritual ideals, interests and direction for any serious relationship to work. Relationships that lack this will be minor love affairs, those that have it have marriage potential.

Singles find love at the workplace, with co-workers, or at organizations and group activities.

Earnings per se are not particularly important during this period – though, as mentioned, the Lunar Eclipse of the 21st is going to shake things up. Money will come in a variety of ways and through a variety of opportunities. The new Moon of the 5th will clarify earnings and debt issues. This is a good month to focus on getting rid of debt.

February

Best Days Overall: 4th, 5th, 13th, 14th, 22nd, 23rd

Most Stressful Days Overall: 7th, 8th, 19th, 20th, 26th, 27th, 28th

Best Days for Love: 2nd, 3rd, 9th, 10th, 11th, 12th, 19th, 22nd, 26th, 27th, 28th, 29th

Best Days for Money: 4th, 5th, 9th, 10th, 13th, 14th, 15th, 16th, 19th, 24th, 25th, 29th

With 90 to 100 per cent of the planets above the Horizon of your chart, this indicates that the Cosmos is supporting your 'outer' life and career this month. It's OK to let home, domestic and emotional issues alone for a while. Outer success will lead to domestic harmony in due course.

With 90 to 100 per cent of the planets moving forward this month you will see great progress and achievement in your life and in the world around you. Major changes are going on in the world and in people around you, and they benefit you.

Mercury, your Ruler, goes retrograde from the 21st onwards. This is a period for re-evaluating personal goals. And though this retrograde usually makes you feel that you are going backwards in life, this feeling will be more muted during this period. For the overwhelming thrust of the planetary power is forward – you will be carried forward in spite of yourself and your doubts.

By the 20th, the planetary power will be evenly distributed between the Eastern and Western sectors. Thus a greater feeling of independence is happening now. You still can't ignore other people, or have things completely your way, but you can be more self-assertive than before. There is a need now to balance your own interests with those of others.

Your most important areas of interest this month are foreign travel, higher education, religion and philosophy, career and the parents, spirituality and charitable activities.

Your health and vitality are super until the 20th, but afterwards rest and relax more.

The Moon, your Financial Planet, will wax from the 5th to the 19th: this should be your strongest financial period. You are more involved with building career and professional status than you are with mere money right now. The demands of career are very great.

An important shift in love attitudes is happening during this period as Jupiter, your Love Planet, moves from your 11th House to your 12th. It will be there for many more months. Thus spiritual compatibility is becoming ever more important in love – perhaps more important than physical, intellectual or sexual compatibility. Singles are formulating their ideals of love – and they are high indeed. Love is found through spiritual activities, charities, volunteer work or in the pursuit of causes you hold dear.

March

Best Days Overall: 3rd, 4th, 12th, 20th, 21st, 30th, 31st

Most Stressful Days Overall: 5th, 6th, 18th, 19th, 25th, 26th

Best Days for Love: 1st, 3rd, 4th, 9th, 10th, 12th, 13th, 18th, 19th, 22nd, 23rd, 25th, 26th, 27th, 28th

Best Days for Money: 1st, 5th, 6th, 9th, 10th, 14th, 15th, 18th, 19th, 25th, 26th, 27th, 28th

Even though Mercury (your Ruling Planet) is retrograde, this is still going to be a month of forward progress and achievement. Mercury's retrograde operates in a context of overwhelming forward motion. Thus, you should use the retrograde – until the 14th – to review and clarify personal goals. Now that the planetary power is decisively shifted to the Eastern sector of your chart – and your ability to have things your way is increasing day by day – this period of review and clarification becomes ever more important.

Between 90 and 100 per cent of the planets are still above the Horizon of the chart and Mercury, also your Home and Family Planet, is retrograde. Let go of domestic issues for a while and focus on the outer world. This is a banner career month.

Your most important areas of interest this month are foreign travel, higher education, religion and philosophy, career, groups and group activities, friends and organizations, spirituality and charity.

Career matters are active and happy this month. This is not to say that there won't be some day-to-day problems or glitches, but the trend is good. The new Moon of the 6th is going to bring you all the information you need to resolve problems and take the next steps. Communication and networking skills are important for career success these days. Neptune, your Career Planet, has been travelling with the South Node of the Moon for the past month or so, perhaps making you overly obsessive about your career. Perhaps you've felt swallowed up by it – personally eclipsed – as if you were not a person but a job title or CV or performance record. Happily, being temporarily obsessed with your career is not a tragedy now, as home and family issues can be safely let go of for a while. Venus, moving through your House of Career from the 13th onwards, indicates the favour of bosses, fun at the job, the pursuit of career objectives through entertaining clients or through enjoyable activities, and a willingness to take a risk. Mercury's forward motion in your House of Career (after the 14th) suggests a new confidence in career issues and the support of family members for your career aspirations.

Health is basically good, but rest and relax more until the 20th.

Finances seem unimportant during this period, though earnings should be stronger from the 6th to the 20th. I expect the status quo to be maintained in financial matters.

Love is behind the scenes during this period. A relationship with a friend should also be kept low key. Your ability to love universally and unconditionally is expanding day by day.

April

Best Days Overall: 8th, 9th, 16th, 17th, 18th, 26th, 27th

Most Stressful Days Overall: 1st, 2nd, 14th, 15th, 21st, 22nd, 29th, 30th

Best Days for Love: 1st, 2nd, 6th, 7th, 12th, 13th, 14th, 15th, 21st, 22nd, 24th, 25th

Best Days for Money: 4th, 5th, 6th, 7th, 10th, 11th, 12th, 13th, 14th, 15th, 24th, 25th

Between 80 and 90 per cent of the planets are in the East; Mercury, your Ruler, is now moving forward; 90 per cent of the total planetary power is moving forward. The message is clear: Push forward towards your goals. Never mind what other people think or what others expect of you – you have to be concerned about your own happiness now. You have to build your life according to *your* tastes and desires – and you have the power to do it. You can expect to see much progress and achievement here.

Like last month, between 90 per cent and 100 per cent of the planets are above the Horizon of your chart. The Cosmos is urging you to focus on your career and worldly ambitions now. Home, family and psychological issues can safely be put on hold for a while. Their turn will come in due course.

Mercury, also your Family Planet, is in your 10th House of Career until the 13th. Thus, the family is still very supportive of your career aspirations. Emotional harmony comes from success in the world. Doing right leads to feeling right. Family members are themselves unusually ambitious, and you can further your own career by helping them in theirs. Career opportunities come from family members, family connections or in family-type businesses.

GEMINI

Your most important areas of interest this month are foreign travel, religion, philosophy and higher education, career, friends, groups and organizations, and spirituality and charity.

Pluto's retrograde suggests caution for job-seekers. Job offers are not what they seem and need more research. Pluto will not block employment opportunities – it has fabulous aspects most of the month – but you need to nail down the details in these things.

There is unusual power in your 12th House of Spirituality from the 19th onwards, and since many people are not aware of what this produces, it can make you feel strange. Your dreamlife will become hyperactive. There will be a greater interest in the invisible realms of life. There will be strong idealistic urges – urges to help and to heal others. Many of you will feel bored with the world, and crave more seclusion. The spiritual purpose behind your life – your current loves, sexual attractions, financial condition, etc. – will be explored.

Love is active, but still very much behind the scenes. A friend is becoming much more than that. Don't rush off and tell the world about your new love – let it be a mystery and let its purpose unfold.

Finances are unusually strong and come pretty easily. The North Node of the Moon makes a major shift into your Money House on the 10th, signalling that the attainment of financial goals and financial freedom brings fulfilment. The Moon waxes from the 4th to the 18th – and this will tend to be your strongest earning period. Use excess cash to pay off debts after the 18th.

May

Best Days Overall: 5th, 6th, 14th, 15th, 24th, 25th

Most Stressful Days Overall: 12th, 13th, 18th, 19th, 20th, 26th, 27th

Best Days for Love: 3rd, 4th, 12th, 13th, 18th, 19th, 20th, 21st, 22nd, 23rd, 31st

Best Days for Money: 3rd, 4th, 7th, 8th, 12th, 13th, 21st, 22nd, 23rd, 24th, 31st

This is a great month in a great year, and you still haven't peaked. The best is yet to come.

Retrograde activity increases this month but doesn't really obstruct your good or your overall happiness. You will feel the effect of the retrogrades (30 per cent of the planets) in work and career issues, not in your personal or love life.

The planets are very much in the Eastern sector of your chart now. By the 20th, your own Sign of Gemini and your 1st House will be an important House of Power. Mars will move into Gemini on the 3rd. Thus you are in a period of self-assertion and self-will. You can and will have things your way. You are in no mood for compromise or people-pleasing. Mind your tongue and your temper now as you have little patience for fools or obstructors.

With all this power available to you, it might be a good idea to spend the early part of the month in meditation and contemplation. There is a need to review the past year and set goals for the future. Honest introspection brings clarity, and clarity will produce better and more realistic goals.

This month the planetary power will be evenly distributed between the upper and lower halves. Thus there is a need now to balance inner and outer goals – home with career, psychological progress with career progress.

Your important areas of interest this month are religion, higher education, foreign travel and personal philosophy, spirituality and charity, and the body, image and personal pleasure and fulfilment.

Health is super this month. Mars in your own Sign brings aggressive energy. Your athletic performance is enhanced. You get things done very fast. Thoughts translate into actions very quickly. You are more impulsive than usual.

Libido is very powerful now and sex appeal radiates from every pore.

Important love developments are happening this month as Jupiter and Saturn make a once-in-20-year conjunction in your 12th House. Important, long-term social relationships are being formed. Singles are likely to meet the man or woman of their dreams. Geminis are connecting up to their spiritual groups and spiritual soulmates.

Finances are strong all month. You are spending more on yourself and your image – buying clothing and accessories – probably very expensive ones. You adopt the image of wealth during this period and this should help you manifest actual wealth much more easily.

June

Best Days Overall: 2nd, 10th, 11th, 20th, 21st, 29th, 30th

Most Stressful Days Overall: 8th, 9th, 15th, 16th, 22nd, 23rd

Best Days for Love: 2nd, 8th, 9th, 10th, 11th, 15th, 16th, 17th, 18th, 19th, 22nd, 23rd, 27th, 28th

Best Days for Money: 2nd, 3rd, 4th, 8th, 9th, 10th, 11th, 17th, 18th, 19th, 22nd, 23rd, 27th, 28th

The planets are mostly in the East, which would normally boost self-confidence and independence, but Mercury, your Ruler, goes retrograde on the 23rd. Retrograde activity in general is stronger during this period than last month. Thus, you should continue to build your life according to your personal specifications, but be more patient with things. Progress will be slower than usual. Perhaps what slows things down is confusion about or a need for re-evaluation of your true goals. Clarity about these things is essential, yet more difficult to attain right now.

Most of the planets will be below the Horizon this month – but this is not a powerful dominance, only a slight majority. Thus, while career and outer success are still important, you need to balance these things with family and emotional harmony. You're doing a juggling act during this period.

Three powerful planets are in your own Sign early in the month. The Sun is there until the 21st, adding star power, self-esteem and self-confidence to your nature. Venus adds charm, grace and beauty to your image. This is a good time (until the 18th) to buy clothing, jewellery and personal accessories, as your sense of style is very sharp. Mars in your Sign (until the 16th) brings aggressive energy, a strong libido and physical courage to your image. Of itself Mars could make you argumentative and overly aggressive – but Venus' presence is tempering things. You prefer to get your way through grace and charm, but are ready to fight if necessary. Mars pushes you to get things done in a hurry, but the many retrograde planets are slowing you down – patience is a virtue now.

Health is super all month.

Mars in your own Sign, and the general lack of the Water element until the 21st, can make you insensitive to other people's feelings. Be careful not to set up time-bomb situations by being overly aggressive or pushy. Resentments might not be expressed early in the month, but will probably be stored up for later.

Your Money House becomes very powerful after the 16th. There's much financial activity going on and many financial projects. Earnings are going to increase through sales, marketing, networking, intuition, creativity and perhaps some speculation. Earnings come easily.

Love is happy during this period. A power struggle in a current relationship can cause a breakup, but there is someone waiting in the wings. This power struggle could also manifest as a renewal of the current relationship.

July

Best Days Overall: 7th, 8th, 17th, 18th, 26th, 27th

Most Stressful Days Overall: 5th, 6th, 12th, 13th, 20th, 21st

Best Days for Love: 1st, 2nd, 6th, 7th, 10th, 11th, 12th, 13th, 14th, 15th, 22nd, 23rd, 25th, 26th, 30th, 31st

Best Days for Money: 1st, 2nd, 6th, 7th, 10th, 11th, 14th, 15th, 21st, 22nd, 25th, 26th, 29th, 30th, 31st

An epic and eventful month, both for you and the world. Major developments are taking place personally, socially and financially.

First of all, Jupiter makes an important move into your own Sign on the 1st. This coincides with a powerful Solar Eclipse in your Money House. Don't let short-term financial disruptions throw you for a loop; these changes are bringing financial opportunity to you along with a new sense of personal freedom. Many of these disruptions will come from positive events – large financial windfalls, marriage to someone wealthy, a significant business partnership, or the start of a new business. Good things can be as disruptive and time-consuming as stressful things.

Jupiter's move into your own Sign brings love and marriage opportunities into your life. Love is just the way you like it. Jupiter also brings increased self-esteem, self-confidence and public recognition. You are catching the lucky breaks now. Dame Fortune is smiling on you all the time.

Finances are very powerful as well – perhaps the major interest of the month. There is a new financial confidence in you. You are willing to take what the world calls risks – but for you they are sure things – and it looks like they work out. Money comes from sales, marketing, communication and high-tech enterprises. Your financial intuition is powerful, though it needs to be tested around the 1st.

Health will be excellent, though you should be careful of too much of the good life. If you over-indulge, Saturn will take care of it next month. Weight gain this month can be alarming to many of you.

Geminis of childbearing age are more fertile right now.

The Lunar Eclipse of the 16th is also kind to you. It creates long-term changes in your partner's finances and investments. Those of you seeking investors or outside capital might be turned down by one source and then accepted by another. Those of you in debt will be able to pay some of it off over the next six months – as the ways, means and methods will be revealed. Those of you who need working capital will be able to borrow.

The Solar Eclipse of the 30th is also kind to you. It causes long-term changes in your neighbourhood or with neighbours. Relations with a sibling become temporarily disruptive. Students change schools or experience upheavals in the school they attend.

All in all, a frenetic but happy month.

August

Best Days Overall: 4th, 5th, 13th, 14th, 15th, 23rd, 24th, 31st

Most Stressful Days Overall: 1st, 2nd, 8th, 9th, 16th, 17th, 29th, 30th

Best Days for Love: 3rd, 4th, 8th, 9th, 11th, 12th, 13th, 14th, 20th, 21st, 23rd, 24th, 29th, 30th

Best Days for Money: 3rd, 4th, 8th, 9th, 13th, 14th, 18th, 19th, 23rd, 24th, 25th, 26th, 29th, 30th

Saturn and Jupiter in your own Sign this month are creating contradictory and confusing attractions, and urges, in you. Jupiter in your Sign urges you towards the good life, to travel and sexual excess. It urges you to speculate, take a chance and be optimistic. Saturn is urging you in an opposite way. It wants physical and sensual stoicism, weight-loss regimes, and only as much of the good life as you can afford. Saturn abhors risks and gambles. Saturn urges you to look at the downside – to a sort of pessimism. So, you will probably shuttle between these two urges for a quite a while until you find a balance.

Jupiter and Saturn in your own Sign complicate the love life. It could show a testing of love – a caution regarding it – fears of commitment come up. Some of you may have difficulty expressing the love that you feel and can come off as a 'cold fish' – unfeeling. Of course this is not the case, but others could perceive you this way. On the other hand, this combination could bring someone older and more established into your life. Marriage is still quite possible, though you have to let love grow and develop. Your spouse, partner or lover is into money-making and seems generous with you.

The balance of planetary power will shift this month from the East to the West. Thus, you will have less of a need to be self-reliant, and more able to depend on others – especially your partner. You are entering a strong social phase of your life.

Finances are stable this month. The Moon (your Money Planet) will wax from the 1st to the 15th and from the 29th to the 31st. This should be the strongest earnings period. Spending needs to be controlled during this period. But too much hoarding and saving is also not good. Find the balance.

Most of the planets are below the Horizon and your Career Planet is still retrograde. Continue to focus on home, family and psychological issues. Your 4th House of Home and Family becomes a major House of Power after the 22nd, reinforcing the above. The new Moon of the 29th is also helping in family issues – bringing you all the knowledge you need to take wise decisions. This knowledge will come to you effortlessly and easily – no special effort on your part is needed.

Health is good, but rest and relax more after the 22nd.

September

Best Days Overall: 1st, 10th, 11th, 19th, 20th, 27th, 28th

Most Stressful Days Overall: 5th, 6th, 12th, 13th, 25th, 26th

Best Days for Love: 1st, 5th, 6th, 10th, 11th, 19th, 20th, 27th, 28th, 30th

Best Days for Money: 1st, 7th, 8th, 10th, 11th, 17th, 18th, 19th, 20th, 21st, 22nd, 27th, 28th, 30th

The planets are now mostly in the West; by the 17th, 80 per cent of them will be there. Two powerful planets go retrograde in your 1st House. The message is clear: avoid self-assertion and self-will; put other people first. Your good will come through others. Your way is not necessarily the best way during this period.

Most of the planets are below the Horizon, indicating a need to focus on inner harmony and inner goals, rather than outer, worldly goals. Home and family issues are a major focus this month. Mars moving into your 4th House on the 17th makes this an excellent period for doing heavy work around the house – major repairs, construction, demolition and furniture moving and lifting.

Mars in your 4th House can make the emotions volatile and create conflicts with family members. Mind your temper in this area.

Your important areas of interest are the body, image and appearance, the home and family, children, love affairs, creativity and amusement, and health and work.

Health is good, but rest and relax more until the 22nd. Like last month we see the alternation between bingeing and dieting – putting on weight and losing weight. Excess libido can stress the health. Balance and moderation in all things is called for.

Love is still happy and present in your life, but Jupiter's retrograde at the end of the month complicates things. The demands of work and conflicts about work need to be resolved with the beloved. Family issues also complicate your love life. But you are still getting your way in love during this period. Love becomes less stormy after the 22nd. Romance the beloved more, and do your best to make things more 'honeymoonish'.

Neptune, your Career Planet, is still retrograde, so evaluate career opportunities more closely. They are not what they seem.

Finances are stable during this period, though you should do better after the 22nd than before. You will have to work harder for earnings before the 22nd, but the Moon's waxing mode from the 1st to the 13th will give you the necessary energy.

After the 22nd you enter into one of the happiest, most carefree periods of your year. Speculations are favourable and you are in a party mood. Singles have opportunities for love affairs or serious committed love. There is good news from children.

October

Best Days Overall: 7th, 8th, 16th, 17th, 25th, 26th

Most Stressful Days Overall: 2nd, 3rd, 9th, 10th, 11th, 23rd, 24th, 29th, 30th

Best Days for Love: 1st, 2nd, 3rd, 7th, 8th, 9th, 10th, 11th, 16th, 17th, 20th, 21st, 25th, 26th, 29th, 30th

Best Days for Money: 7th, 8th, 16th, 17th, 18th, 19th, 25th, 26th, 27th, 28th

Saturn's move out of your own Sign on the 18th increases the urges to the good life. There is a tendency now to overdo things – to over-indulge in food, spirits and personal pleasures.

Be careful. On the other hand, there is more optimism and less worry and fear these days. Most of the month you are in a party mood.

You are still in one of the happiest, most successful periods of your life.

After the 23rd, the party will continue but at a slower pace. Work and work issues call to you, and so you will be alternating between work and play.

With most of the planets in the West and the retrograde of Mercury, your Ruler, on the 18th, this is a social month. A month to coast and not to force things. A month to allow good to happen in its own way and time. Your overall aspects are so good you can't even prevent good from happening.

On the 19th the planetary power shifts to the upper half of your Horoscope, making career and outer ambitions ever more important to you. The forward motion of Neptune, your Career Planet, on the 15th is another positive career signal. Long-delayed plans are moving forward again. Inner developments and subjective plans now start to bear objective, outward fruit. As the months go by, your career is going to be an ever greater focus for you.

Still, you can't simply ignore home and family issues, though you can de-emphasize them. Mars is in your 4th House of Home and Family all month, suggesting major repairs, renovations and perhaps some heavy lifting going on in the home. Relations with family members – and the general mood – can be volatile. But with so much other good happening in your life these short-term blowups are swallowed in a sea of harmony.

Students and academicians hear good news during this period as Uranus, the Lord of Gemini's 9th House, starts moving forward again. There is great success in all academic studies – whether they be at secondary school or university level. Sales and marketing projects go particularly well until the 18th – try to wrap them up before then.

112

GEMINI

Love is active and happy, but Jupiter's retrograde still shows a need for caution and for letting love grow and develop. There is great social popularity now, but your judgement regarding others might not be up to its usual standard.

November

Best Days Overall: 3rd, 4th, 13th, 21st, 22nd

Most Stressful Days Overall: 6th, 7th, 19th, 20th, 26th, 27th

Best Days for Love: 3rd, 4th, 8th, 9th, 12th, 13th, 19th, 20th, 21st, 22nd, 26th, 27th, 28th, 29th, 30th

Best Days for Money: 3rd, 4th, 6th, 7th, 12th, 13th, 15th, 16th, 21st, 22nd, 26th, 27th, 30th

Health is basically good this month, but rest and relax more after the 22nd. Enhancing the nervous system through relaxation, the avoidance of unnecessary thought and speech, and the massage of appropriate reflexes will enhance your health this month. Jupiter in your own Sign this month continues to bring the good life to you – your lover cannot do enough for you, sensual desires and fantasies are fulfilled and there is much good food and wine. Health regimes go well all month.

Many planets are in the West; Mercury, your Ruler, is retrograde until the 8th, and your 7th House of Love and Romance is a House of Power – thus, an active social month. Avoid power struggles and self-will. Allow good to come to you in its own way and time. Popularity soars during this period. Adapt to situations rather than trying to control or change them.

The planetary power has a slight bias towards the upper half of your Horoscope this month, but will get stronger there as the months go by. Handle home and family issues with alacrity, but give more focus to your career and your outer ambitions. Happy things are happening in your career. Your Career Planet (Neptune) is moving forward and receives especially beautiful aspects after the 22nd. Lovers, partners, neighbours and siblings – as well as your own personal efforts – are boosting your professional status and prestige. Promotions and pay rises are on their way to you.

Your important areas of interest this month are health and work, love and romance, and higher education, foreign travel, religion and philosophy.

Students, writers and lecturers have an outstanding month. There is good news about university and about academic work in general. Your normal mental sharpness – your ability to learn and communicate – is even stronger than usual.

Though most of you seem involved in a serious relationship, there are other contenders vying for your charms. This complicates your love life and throws some confusion into it – but this is a good confusion. You are loved. There is much going out and party-going these days.

Finances are stable and don't seem a concern during this period. The Moon's waxing period from the 1st to the 11th and from the 25th onwards should be your strongest earnings periods.

December

Best Days Overall: 1st, 2nd, 10th, 11th, 18th, 19th, 28th, 29th

Most Stressful Days Overall: 3rd, 4th, 16th, 17th, 23rd, 24th, 30th, 31st

Best Days for Love: 1st, 10th, 11th, 18th, 19th, 23rd, 24th, 28th, 29th

Best Days for Money: 1st, 6th, 7th, 10th, 11th, 12th, 13th, 14th, 15th, 18th, 25th, 26th, 28th

Love and social activities are active and happy. Both you and your beloved are going out of your way to please each other. Though the motives are right, there could be different opinions as to what 'pleasing' is – or as to what the other's interest really is. The important thing is that the love is there.

Most of the planets in the West and much power in your House of Love indicate that this is a social month – and not a period for going your own way. Good comes from others and you must put their interests ahead of your own – temporarily.

The upper half of your Horoscope is the strongest half, and is getting stronger day by day. Thus you can safely reduce attention to home and family issues and focus on your outer ambitions. Happy career events come about around the 4th and the 24th.

This time of year generally means more socializing with the family and from the home. But Mercury's position in your House of Social Activities indicates that this year these things go better than usual.

Your important areas of interest during this period are health and work, love and social activities, incurring or paying off debt, helping others prosper, and the deeper things of life: religion, philosophy, higher education and foreign travel, as well as the body, the image and personal pleasures.

Phone bills should be less this month as the power in the Air element is reduced.

The Solar Eclipse of the 25th is stressful to you, so please take a reduced schedule. It isn't only the Sun that is being eclipsed then, but also Mercury, your Ruler. Thus there will be a redefinition of your personality, an important change in your image, and the cleansing of bodily impurities. Those of you who are basically healthy should only experience a mild cleansing and physical detoxification. But those of you who have health problems will face a healing crisis. Though the Eclipse is not showing physical death, it does show a need to deal with the fears of death – and these kinds of emotional patterns will come up for cleansing.

Your partner is making important changes in his or her financial life – probably because of a short-term crisis. Siblings face a crisis and perhaps there is a short-term disruption in your relationship with them. Students (of secondary school age and younger) change schools or teachers.

Finances are stable during this period.

Cancer

♋

THE CRAB
Birthdays from
21st June
to 20th July

Personality Profile

CANCER AT A GLANCE

Element – Water

Ruling Planet – Moon
   Career Planet – Mars
   Love Planet – Saturn
   Money Planet – Sun
   Planet of Fun and Games – Pluto
   Planet of Good Fortune – Neptune
   Planet of Health and Work – Jupiter
   Planet of Home and Family Life – Venus
   Planet of Spirituality – Mercury

Colours – blue, puce, silver

Colours that promote love, romance and social harmony – black, indigo

Colours that promote earning power – gold, orange

Gems – moonstone, pearl

Metal – silver

Scents – jasmine, sandalwood

Quality – cardinal (= activity)

Quality most needed for balance – mood control

Strongest virtues – emotional sensitivity, tenacity, the urge to nurture

Deepest need – a harmonious home and family life

Characteristics to avoid – over-sensitivity, negative moods

Signs of greatest overall compatibility – Scorpio, Pisces

Signs of greatest overall incompatibility – Aries, Libra, Capricorn

Sign most helpful to career – Aries

Sign most helpful for emotional support – Libra

Sign most helpful financially – Leo

Sign best for marriage and/or partnerships – Capricorn

Sign most helpful for creative projects – Scorpio

Best Sign to have fun with – Scorpio

Signs most helpful in spiritual matters – Gemini, Pisces

Best day of the week – Monday

CANCER

Understanding the Cancer Personality

In the Sign of Cancer the heavens are developing the feeling side of things. This is what a true Cancerian is all about – feelings. Where Aries will tend to err on the side of action, Taurus on the side of inaction and Gemini on the side of thought, Cancer will tend to err on the side of feeling.

Cancerians tend to mistrust logic. Perhaps rightfully so. For them it is not enough for an argument or a project to be logical – it must *feel* right as well. If it does not feel right a Cancerian will reject it or chafe against it. The phrase 'follow your heart' could have been coined by a Cancerian, because it describes exactly the Cancerian attitude to life.

The power to feel is a more direct – more immediate – method of knowing than thinking is. Thinking is indirect. Thinking about a thing never touches the thing itself. Feeling is a faculty that touches directly the thing or issue in question. We actually experience it. Emotional feeling is almost like another sense which humans possess – a psychic sense. Since the realities that we come in contact with during our lifetime are often painful and even destructive, it is not surprising that the Cancerian chooses to erect barriers – a shell – to protect his or her vulnerable, sensitive nature. To a Cancerian this is only common sense.

If Cancerians are in the presence of people they do not know, or find themselves in a hostile environment, up goes the shell and they feel protected. Other people often complain about this, but one must question these other people's motives. Why does this shell disturb them? Is it perhaps because they would like to sting, and feel frustrated that they cannot? If your intentions are honourable and you are patient, have no fear. The shell will open up and you will be accepted as part of the Cancerian's circle of family and friends.

Thought-processes are generally analytic and dissociating. In order to think clearly we must make distinctions, comparisons and the like. But feeling is unifying and integrative.

To think clearly about something you have to distance your-self from it. To feel something you must get close to it. Once a Cancerian has accepted you as a friend he or she will hang on. You have to be really bad to lose the friendship of a Cancerian. If you are related to Cancerians they will never let you go no matter what you do. They will always try to maintain some kind of connection even in the most extreme circumstances.

Finance

The Cancer-born has a deep sense of what other people feel about things and why they feel as they do. This faculty is a great asset in the workplace and in the business world. Of course it is also indispensable in raising a family and building a home, but it also has its uses in business. Cancerians often attain great wealth in a family type of business. Even if the business is not a family operation, they will treat it as one. If the Cancerian works for somebody else, then the boss is the parent figure and the co-workers are brothers and sisters. If a Cancerian is the boss, then all the workers are his or her chil-dren. Cancerians like the feeling of being providers for others. They enjoy knowing that others derive their sustenance because of what they do. It is another form of nurturing.

With Leo on their Solar 2nd House (of Money) cusp, Cancerians are often lucky speculators, especially with resi-dential property or hotels and restaurants. Resort hotels and nightclubs are also profitable for the Cancerian. Waterside properties allure them. Though they are basically conven-tional people, they sometimes like to earn their livelihood in glamorous ways.

The Sun, Cancer's Money Planet, represents an important financial message: in financial matters Cancerians need to be less moody, more stable and fixed. They cannot allow their moods – which are here today and gone tomorrow – to get in the way of their business lives. They need to develop their self-esteem and feelings of self-worth if they are to realize their greatest financial potential.

Career and Public Image

Aries rules the 10th Solar House (of Career) cusp of Cancer, which indicates that Cancerians long to start their own business, to be more active publicly and politically and to be more independent. Family responsibilities and a fear of hurting other people's feelings – or getting hurt themselves – often inhibit them from attaining these goals. However, this is what they want and long to do.

Cancerians like their bosses and leaders to act freely and to be a bit self-willed. They can deal with that in a superior. Cancerians expect their leaders to be fierce on their behalf.

When the Cancerian is in the position of boss or superior he or she behaves very much like a 'warlord'. Of course the wars they wage are not egocentric but in defence of those under their care. If they lack some of this fighting instinct – independence and pioneering spirit – Cancerians will have extreme difficulty in attaining their highest career goals. They will be hampered in their attempts to lead others.

Since they are so parental, Cancerians like to work with children and make great educators and teachers.

Love and Relationships

Like Taurus, Cancer likes committed relationships. Cancerians function best when the relationship is clearly defined and everyone knows his or her role. When they marry it is usually for life. They are extremely loyal to their beloved. But there is a deep little secret that most Cancerians will never admit to: commitment or partnership is really a chore and a duty to them. They enter into it because they know of no other way to create the family that they desire. Union is just a way – a means to an end – rather than an end in itself. The family is the ultimate end for them.

If you are in love with a Cancerian you must tread lightly on his or her feelings. It will take you a good deal of time to realize how deep and sensitive Cancerians can be. The smallest negativity upsets them. Your tone of voice, your irritation, a look in your eye or an expression on your face can cause great distress for the Cancerian. Your slightest gesture is registered by them and reacted to. This can be hard to get used to, but stick by your love – Cancerians make great partners once you learn how to deal with them. Your Cancerian lover will react not so much to what you say but to the way you are actually feeling at the moment.

Home and Domestic Life

This is where Cancerians really excel. The home environment and the family are their personal works of art. They strive to make things of beauty that will outlast them. Very often they succeed.

Cancerians feel very close to their family, their relatives and especially their mothers. These bonds last throughout their lives and mature as they grow older. They are very fond of those members of their family who become successful, and they are also quite attached to family heirlooms and mementos. Cancerians also love children and like to provide them with all the things they need and want. With their nurturing, feeling nature, Cancerians make very good parents – especially the Cancerian woman, who is the mother *par excellence* of the Zodiac.

As a parent the Cancerian's attitude is 'my children right or wrong.' Unconditional devotion is the order of the day. No matter what a family member does, the Cancerian will eventually forgive him or her, because 'you are, after all, family'. The preservation of the institution – the tradition – of the family is one of the Cancerian's main reasons for living. They have many lessons to teach others about this.

Being so family-orientated, the Cancerian's home is always clean, orderly and comfortable. They like old-fashioned furnishings but they also like to have all the modern comforts. Cancerians love to have family and friends over, to organize parties and to entertain at home – they make great hosts.

Horoscope for 2000

Major Trends

1999 was a banner career year. Emphasis was on 'outer', career goals and the attainment of public or professional prestige. This trend continues a bit in 2000, but by February you will be where you want to be in terms of your career and will be exploring new friendships, joining groups and being active in professional organizations.

The Eclipses this year are affecting the body, image and personality, the love life and marriage, and finances. Long-term change is going on in these areas. More on these later.

Your Houses of Power (areas of greatest interest) in the coming year are health and work, transformation and other people's money, debt and the repayment of debt, sex, death and rebirth, career, friendships, organizations and group activities, and – later in the year – charity, ministry and spirituality.

Your paths to greatest fulfilment this year are finance, the body and image, personal pleasure, career, friendships and spirituality.

Health

Virtually all of the long-term planets are leaving you alone this year, Cancer – and some are actually making happy aspects to you. Thus health is good. Yet, Pluto in the 6th House of Health suggests that this area is important – and has been important for some years now.

Pluto in the House of Health shows that you are making an in-depth study of this field – learning its deepest laws and secrets. It shows that your attitudes to health are being transformed – that old learning on this subject is being uprooted and neutralized.

Pluto shows that surgery is seen or recommended as a quick fix to a health problem. This could be suggested later on in the year – during the summer. But get a second opinion.

Pluto in the 6th House indicates a heightened interest in diet and detoxification regimes. You are not taking these things for granted now. It also shows ways to enhance your health. Pluto rules the sexual organs generically. Thus there is a need for adequate and balanced (neither too much nor too little) sexual expression. It also rules the organs of elimination. These organs (sex and elimination) need special attention these days, and you can strengthen them in drugless, natural ways through systems such as reflexology, chiropractic, kinesiology, acupuncture and acupressure. The herbs and plants of Pluto – such as bananas, cherries, coconut – are good to add to your diet. Cherry and coconut are nice to wear as scents as well. Bloodstone is a good gem.

Pluto is the Lord of your 5th House of Fun, Joy, Creativity and Children. Thus, the cultivation of joy and creativity will enhance your health. Taking up a creative hobby and generally having more fun in life will be good for your health.

You seem more concerned with the health of children than with your own.

If health problems do arise, check out your relationship with children and work to clear that up before running to a health professional. Check to see whether you are allowing enough fun in your life. Once these issues are cleared, chances are the health condition will disappear of its own accord. If the services of a healer are still needed, his or her job will be that much easier.

Home and Domestic Life

Home is always important to you, Cancer, but this year less so. Your 4th House of Home and Family is not a House of Power, and this can be taken as a good sign. Things at home and with the family are basically as you want them to be – you are content with things and thus have little need to pay too much attention here.

With no long-term planets occupying your 4th House, the Cosmos is allowing latitude in this area. You have the power to shape things as you will. You need not react to situations.

Married people are facing pressure from their spouse to move house or enlarge the residence – even though you personally feel no especial need to do so.

If you are planning to buy or sell a home, or make investments in property, the period between 23rd September and 23rd October seems like a good time.

If you are redecorating or otherwise beautifying the home, 31st August to 24th September is a good time. This is also a good period for family gatherings and entertaining from the home.

If you are doing important renovations – tearing down walls, ripping out wires or plumbing – 4th November to 23rd December is a good time. This is also a good time to set up a home office or home-based business.

A parent is prospering, and if he or she hasn't moved this past year, he or she may do so in the year ahead.

Siblings are doing major renovations this year, and grown children are likely to move house – perhaps many times. Grown children seem very unsettled.

Grown grandchildren are either leaving for university or moving house. Perhaps there are changes of flatmates.

Love and Social Life

Though the 7th House of Love and Marriage is not a House of Power, three Eclipses this year guarantee much action and change. For singles this can indicate a marriage. You are forced to make a decision one way or another about a current relationship. It either gets more serious or dissolves. The Eclipse will not let you sit on the fence.

For married people, the Eclipses indicate crisis in the relationship. Hidden flaws that you never knew existed come up and must be dealt with. Good relationships will get even stronger, but weak ones are endangered.

The movements of Saturn, your Love Planet, are also adding complication to the brew. Saturn, a long-term planet, changes Signs this year – although briefly. Thus, your needs and attitudes in love are undergoing change. You feel the need for different things in a relationship.

While Saturn was in Taurus (1999 and most of 2000) you wanted the basics in a relationship: physical intimacy, financial support, touching, a sense of security. But as Saturn starts to move into Gemini (it will become established in this Sign next year) you want intellectual communion, communication, talking, the exchange of ideas and a shared spirituality. This combined with the Eclipses is producing the various crises.

Singles will find love at professional organizations or groups to which they belong. Perhaps a romance is struck up via e-mail, or over the Internet. Astrology plays a role in love this year.

When Jupiter conjoins your Love Planet in the summer, a significant love opportunity will come to you. But you must allow time for its development.

For married people, the conjunction of Jupiter with the Love Planet (Saturn) denotes an opportunity to enhance and deepen the present relationship and the coming of new and significant friends into the picture.

The South Node of the Moon moves into your House of Marriage on 10th April. This denotes heightened sexual activity in the marriage. Instincts and passions are aroused for good or ill. Sex can become compulsive rather than romantic or erotic. It can become addictive as well. If all this takes place within the relationship, all well and good – the problems arise if it takes place *outside* the relationship.

Singles may have to go through a few addictive relationships before finding Mr or Ms Wonderful. A hot physical chemistry does not a marriage make.

Your love and social life will be most active from 1st to 20th January, 24th January to 18th February, May and June, 13th November to 8th December, and 21st to 31st December.

Career and Finance

Last year should have been a banner career year. There should have been pay rises, promotions, favours from on high, honours and recognition and a great expansion of your public image and professional status. Those of you who are self-employed or in their own businesses could have moved offices to larger and more prestigious quarters. This trend continues in the year 2000.

With the 2nd House not a House of Power this year, the status quo regarding earnings can be expected. Three solar Eclipses this year – two of which occur in your Money House – will ensure that you fine-tune your spending and investments and make needed changes. But otherwise, money per se is not that important. You are much more concerned with status and prestige than with mere money. The North Node of the Moon moving into your Money House on 10th April counsels you to pay more attention to money and not to be so enamoured with titles and illusionary images.

Bottom-line virtues will bring the fullness of joy. Accept prestige by all means, but demand the rewards of it as well.

The Sun is your Money Planet and its positions and aspects are very important in your financial life. Since these are short-term things they will be covered more fully in the month-by-month forecasts.

Like the Moon, the Sun waxes and wanes – but it takes longer to do so. The Sun waxes (in the Northern hemisphere) from 21st December to 22nd June. This period will be stronger for earnings (given equivalent aspects) than after 22nd June. For those in the Southern hemisphere, the Sun waxes from 22nd June to 21st December – and those of you who live there will have stronger earnings during this period.

In general, make investments or start new financial projects when the Sun is waxing. Pay off bills, clear debts and finish up old financial projects when the Sun is waning – in the Northern hemisphere this is from 22nd June to 21st December, in the Southern hemisphere from 21st December to 22nd June.

The Sun moves through all the Signs and Houses of your Horoscope during a given a year. Thus money and earnings can come from a variety of places, projects or investments.

An important new business or earnings opportunity is coming late in May. This is a long-term thing which could keep you busy for the next 20 years.

A nice financial windfall occurs from 23rd September to 23rd October.

Job-seekers are having good success this year – especially until 11th August. Likewise, those who are hiring employees. May and June could be a period of laying off employees, or of consolidating the workforce or otherwise making the workforce more efficient. Job-seekers need to do more research during this period.

Those of you seeking investors or access to outside capital will have better success after 11th August than before. But you will feel a definite improvement beginning 1st July.

Those of you working to get out of debt need some patience. Steady, methodical, systematic payments will be powerful over the long term. Until 1st July you will sense little progress, but afterwards you get powerful assistance in this area.

A parent prospers greatly this year.

Your partner or spouse prospers but is working unusually hard for it.

Grown children go through a rough financial period from 11th August to 16th October.

Self-improvement

Pluto in your 6th House for years to come shows that the Cosmos is rehabilitating your health and health attitudes (as has been written earlier) and work and work attitudes. Deep changes are going on, over the long term, about your work ethic and what it means to be a good employee or employer. Challenges at the workplace will reveal where your concepts could be flawed.

Power in your 8th House – also for years to come – is revealing the secrets of how to make money with other people's capital and how to help others to prosper. More importantly it will show how to capitalize on things that other people consider to be junk or worthless. For you these can be gold mines. Secrets of financial transformation are being revealed in the years ahead.

Saturn in your 11th House most of the year continues to educate you about friendship and what it means to be a friend to someone. There are responsibilities in this and Saturn will reveal them to you. Saturn will also bring some disappointments here so that you can learn the art of forgiveness. It will show you the wisdom of focusing on the quality of your friendships rather than their quantity.

Saturn will make a brief foray into your 12th House of Spirituality. Thus you will start to improve this – most vital –

area of life. You will start to confront the major (and perhaps hidden) fears that obstruct your connection to the Higher Power within you. Always intuitive, you will start testing and confirming your intuitions – many feelings and thoughts disguise themselves as intuition but are really not. You will learn discernment and how to differentiate. But spirituality will really become important next year when Saturn becomes fully established in your 12th House.

Month-by-month Forecasts

January

Best Days Overall: 1st, 2nd, 10th, 11th, 19th, 20th, 28th, 29th

Most Stressful Days Overall: 5th, 6th, 7th, 13th, 14th, 25th, 26th

Best Days for Love: 3rd, 4th, 5th, 6th, 7th, 13th, 14th, 15th, 16th, 22nd, 23rd, 24th

Best Days for Money: 3rd, 4th, 5th, 6th, 7th, 13th, 14th, 15th, 16th, 21st, 22nd, 25th, 26th, 30th, 31st

Though home and family issues are always important to you, with 70 to 80 per cent of the planets above the Horizon you can safely minimize your attention here and get on with 'outer', career success. Doing right will lead to feeling right. Career harmony will lead to emotional harmony.

The Lunar Eclipse of the 21st is basically kind to you, though it will lead to one of your periodic image changes and to a redefinition of the personality. It will also lead to a financial 'house cleaning' as flaws in an investment or in your overall strategy are revealed. The end result will be positive.

Between 90 and 100 per cent of the planets are moving forward this month, indicating that there is great progress, change and achievement during this period.

Your most important areas of interest this month are health and work, the career, love, romance and social activities, and the libido, transformation, reinventing yourself, paying off debt, attracting investors and the deeper things of life.

The Moon waxes from the 5th to the 21st – a lucky break, as this is a period when your vitality is not at its best. This waxing Moon is giving you energy at a vulnerable time. Still, it would not be a bad idea to rest and relax more until the 20th.

Love is happy and active all month. As the month progresses it will get better and better. Two important developments are happening in love during this period – one, the new Moon of the 5th occurs in your House of Love and Romance, clarifying present relationships and bringing you all the knowledge you need to take important love decisions. The second is Saturn beginning to move forward on the 12th. This signals the end of a period of testing in a relationship. It can either go forward or you can move forward towards someone more in line with your interests. Your social confidence and judgement are going to be a lot stronger over the coming months.

Prosper this month by helping others to prosper. Follow your intuition, especially from the 20th to the 22nd. Channel spare cash into paying off debt. Your line of credit increases this month.

February

Best Days Overall: 7th, 8th, 15th, 16th, 24th, 25th

Most Stressful Days Overall: 2nd, 3rd, 9th, 10th, 22nd, 23rd, 29th

Best Days for Love: 2nd, 3rd, 11th, 12th, 19th, 20th, 22nd, 29th

Best Days for Money: 4th, 5th, 9th, 10th, 13th, 14th, 17th, 18th, 19th, 24th, 25th, 29th

Though family demands can be very intense from the 21st to the 23rd, with 80 to 90 per cent of the planets above the Horizon, these demands will soon fade and you can focus on furthering your career.

The planetary power is still mostly in the Western, social sector of your chart this month – though the percentage is dropping – so you are still in a social period, exercising social skills, getting your way through diplomacy and negotiation, and adapting to circumstances rather than creating them.

The Solar Eclipse of the 5th is basically kind to you, but is shaking up the world around you. It is bringing long-term changes in your financial life – and especially in the financial life of your spouse or partner. Flaws in present financial arrangements, plans, investments or strategies will surface so that you (and your spouse) can correct them. Those of you involved in insurance or estate claims will see a major development occur during this period. An important decision is made regarding debt. Some of you will take on a new loan and others will decide (and receive the wherewithal) to pay off an existing one. The status of debt – one way or another – is changing. This Eclipse in the 8th House often signals a need to deal with subconscious fears of death. These fears have probably been holding you back from cherished dreams and desires – and are probably unrealistic. It is good that you confront them and remove their power over you. A spiritually-orientated therapist can be of great help here.

Jupiter, your Planet of Health and Work, makes an important move from Aries into Taurus this month (the 15th). Many of you will be changing jobs in the coming months, as you will have new work attitudes and new needs you want fulfilled in your work. A job is more than your life's work now (though this is still important) – it needs to bring you friendships and a sense of teamwork. You need to feel that you are part of a team working towards a common goal. You will still be working hard, but you want a job where the pace is more orderly and structured. Working in a helter-skelter, frenetic way is losing its appeal.

Jupiter's move into Taurus is also having important effects on your love life. Your social life is going to expand. Singles are being prepared – in invisible and very subtle ways – to meet their Divine Intended One. It might not happen this month but will happen in the months to come.

Health will be excellent all month. Rest more when the Moon wanes from the 1st to the 5th and from the 19th to the 28th.

March

Best Days Overall: 5th, 6th, 14th, 15th, 22nd, 23rd, 24th

Most Stressful Days Overall: 1st, 7th, 8th, 20th, 21st, 27th, 28th, 29th

Best Days for Love: 1st, 3rd, 4th, 9th, 10th, 12th, 13th, 18th, 19th, 22nd, 23rd, 27th, 28th, 29th

Best Days for Money: 1st, 5th, 6th, 9th, 10th, 14th, 15th, 16th, 17th, 18th, 19th, 25th, 26th, 27th, 28th

This is a happy month in a happy year. Enjoy. Most of the planets are still in the Western, social sector of your chart – though the percentage is diminishing day by day. Still, this is a month for using your social graces, adapting to situations and allowing your good to happen, rather than making it happen. Power struggles and undue self-assertion should be avoided.

Between 80 and 90 per cent of the planets are still above the Horizon of the chart, showing your continued focus on the outer world and the attainment of career objectives. You can safely de-emphasize domestic issues and focus on the outer world.

With 90 per cent of the planets moving forward during this period, there's an indication of much forward momentum and progress in the world and in your life. The great current of life, and not so much your personal effort, is going to carry you to your goals.

Mercury's retrograde until the 14th suggests caution in communications. Important mass mailshots, advertising campaigns and the like are better off delayed. It would be a good idea to have your car and phone equipment checked out. Dreams, psychic readings and spiritual communications need to be confirmed and understood better before any action based on them is taken. Their message might be something radically different than you think.

Your important areas of interest during this period are debt and the payment of debt, helping others to prosper, the income of your partner, libido, religion, philosophy, higher education and foreign travel, career, and friends, groups, group activities and organizations.

Health is excellent this month but rest and relax more after the 20th. Strengthening the neck, throat and spine will enhance health even further.

Finances are happy and stronger this month. You spend more but you also earn more. When the Money Planet crosses your Midheaven after the 20th earnings will come from the career, elders, perhaps a parent, and from bosses. Cancerian investors are more speculative and risk-taking during this period – and probably succeed with this strategy. Job-seekers find work easily – through friends and social contacts.

Your love life and social magnetism are getting stronger day by day. Singles are not likely to be single very long. The workplace still seems the most fertile ground for romance.

April

Best Days Overall: 1st, 2nd, 10th, 11th, 19th, 20th, 29th, 30th

Most Stressful Days Overall: 4th, 5th, 16th, 17th, 18th, 24th, 25th

Best Days for Love: 1st, 2nd, 6th, 7th, 12th, 13th, 14th, 15th, 21st, 22nd, 24th, 25th

Best Days for Money: 4th, 5th, 6th, 7th, 12th, 13th, 14th, 15th, 24th, 25th

By the 13th the planetary powers make a decisive shift from the Western to the Eastern sector of your chart. Thus, the pendulum is swinging from a period of people-pleasing to a period of self-pleasing. More and more you will be able to have things your way – to create conditions as you like them to be. More self-assertion – in a constructive way – is healthy now. Have no fear, this self-assertion (provided you are not nasty about it) will not harm your social life – which is being highly stimulated now. On the contrary, those who really love you will admire your newfound independence.

The planetary power lies 80 to 90 per cent above the Horizon. Many planets in your 10th House of Career show that this is a yearly career peak. Push forward boldly in career matters. The new Moon of the 4th is also helping your career by supplying you with all the information you need to take your next steps. Mars, your Career Planet, receives intense stimulation on the 5th–6th and the 16th and 17th – both your career and social life receive unexpected boosts.

Having 90 per cent of the planets moving forward this month indicates that you are still in a period of great change, progress and achievement.

From the 13th to the 19th there are almost no planets in your home element of Water. Further, there is a strong dominance of the Fire element. Thus people around you are rushing about enthusiastically, unaware of people's feelings or of the costs and consequences of their actions. There is a general euphoria, but lack of sensitivity. Be patient with others during this period. If they hurt your feelings it is unintentional and will pass.

The North Node of the Moon shifts into your own Sign of Cancer on the 10th. This further reinforces your need to create personal happiness and to assert yourself. It also shows that getting your body and image in shape is a source of great fulfilment and should not be neglected. Your health is basically good this month, but rest and relax more until the 19th.

Finances are strong until the 19th and money is earned rather easily. Money comes from the good public and professional reputation that you've built up. Elders, bosses and parents are helping you in attaining your financial goals. Perhaps there is a pay rise at work – or you bring in a new client that increases your pay. After the 19th earnings become more volatile. Highs are unusually high and the lows unusually low. Hang in there and enjoy the roller-coaster ride.

May

Best Days Overall: 7th, 8th, 16th, 17th, 26th, 27th

Most Stressful Days Overall: 1st, 2nd, 14th, 15th, 21st, 22nd, 28th, 29th

Best Days for Love: 3rd, 4th, 12th, 13th, 21st, 22nd, 23rd, 31st

Best Days for Money: 3rd, 4th, 9th, 10th, 12th, 13th, 21st, 22nd, 23rd, 24th, 31st

The lack of the Water element this month makes others insensitive and out of touch with their (and others') feelings. To you they could seem cruel, but bear with it as it is not cruelty but lack of awareness. Their slights are not malicious and will pass when the astrological weather changes.

CANCER

Many planets in the Air element during this period make people more talkative and gossipy. Mind your phone bills now. Don't lend your phone card out to people.

The planetary power is still firmly in the East and you have unusual independence, self-reliance and the ability to have things your way. Important social developments are happening, but sticking to your own position and creating your life as you want it will not interfere with them – in fact will enhance your social life.

Most of the planetary power is above the Horizon of your chart – as it has been for the past few months. Continue to de-emphasize family and domestic issues and focus on your career. A successful career can enhance family life in other ways. Sometimes (not always) it is better to miss a soccer match with the kids and land that important deal instead. With the deal successfully completed you can buy needed things for the children. Everything is a choice; sometimes one way is right, sometimes another.

Your important areas of interest are personal transformation, dealing with addictions, getting rid of the unnecessary in your life, the deeper things of life, debts and their repayment, libido, friends, groups and group activities, organizations, spirituality and charity.

Health is basically good all month, but energy and self-confidence will be higher when the Moon waxes from the 4th to the 18th. Try to schedule your most demanding projects then. Wind down on the physical level from the 18th onwards. The conjunction of your Health Planet with Saturn suggests that health can be enhanced even further by taking special care of the spine and teeth. Social harmony will also enhance health in subtle ways.

Finances are strong, but stormy and volatile early in the month. There is dramatic improvement after the 20th. Volatility will enhance your income.

Singles meet significant others this month and the Love Planet makes a once-in-20-year conjunction with Jupiter.

This is the kind of conjunction where the boss marries the secretary or the prince weds the pauper. Love affairs happen at the workplace or at organizations. Important love meetings could happen via e-mail or while you're surfing the Internet. These love connections seem very long-term.

June

Best Days Overall: 4th, 12th, 13th, 14th, 22nd, 23rd

Most Stressful Days Overall: 10th, 11th, 17th, 18th, 19th, 25th, 26th

Best Days for Love: 2nd, 8th, 9th, 10th, 11th, 17th, 18th, 19th, 22nd, 23rd, 27th, 28th

Best Days for Money: 2nd, 3rd, 6th, 7th, 8th, 9th, 10th, 11th, 17th, 18th, 19th, 22nd, 23rd, 27th, 28th

The planets are mostly in the East and many of them are in your own Sign of Cancer. Your personal independence, self-reliance and confidence are very strong now. There is great power to assert the self and its will and to create conditions as you desire them. If there is a danger now it is of over-doing it – of being too self-willed, aggressive and unaware of other people's positions. This is especially possible when Mars moves into your own Sign on the 16th. It is one thing to be independent and another to be arrogant or domineering. Embrace the former and avoid the latter.

Until the 16th there is still a lack of your native Water element – but this is temporary. People's unawareness of feelings and seeming cruelty will pass by the 16th. Bear with this. By the 21st the opposite problem could arise. People – including yourself – become hypersensitive – often taking offence at innocent voice tones, gestures or other body language. This will be especially noticeable with children.

Though retrograde activity increases this month, your life moves forward. The delays in the world and the general slowing down of the pace works in your favour. This is one of your happiest months in a happy year.

The month begins with many planets in your 12th House of Spirituality. This produces a feeling of world-weariness and a desire for seclusion. The soul craves a deeper communion with the Higher Power within. Religious people will feel this as a desire to 'get right with God'. On a more mundane level it is a time to review the past year, recognize your failures and successes and set goals for the coming year which begins on your birthday. Since you have a lot of personal creative power now, it would be a good idea to get clear as to where you want to direct it. Clarity is 90 per cent of the battle in life.

Health will be super all month. Mars in your own Sign gives you great physical energy and courage. Exercise and athletic regimes go well. Brisk physical exercise enhances the health. Libido is stronger than usual. Venus moving into your Sign brings great personal beauty, grace, glamour and charm to your body and image. Your personal sense of style and taste shines. Love is in the air. The Sun in your own Sign (on the 21st) not only brings wealth and earnings opportunities, but a star quality to your image. This is another positive health indicator as well. The Sun will urge you to dress for success – to dress and accessorize expensively – to flaunt your wealth and your charms. Mercury, your Spiritual Planet, in your own Sign all month gives you an air of mystery and other-worldliness. Your personal beauty is not merely natural, but has a supernatural quality to it.

July

Best Days Overall: 1st, 2nd, 10th, 11th, 20th, 21st, 29th

Most Stressful Days Overall: 7th, 8th, 15th, 16th, 22nd, 23rd

Best Days for Love: 1st, 2nd, 6th, 7th, 10th, 11th, 14th, 15th, 16th, 22nd, 23rd, 25th, 26th, 30th, 31st

Best Days for Money: 1st, 2nd, 3rd, 4th, 6th, 7th, 10th, 11th, 14th, 15th, 21st, 22nd, 25th, 26th, 30th, 31st

This month there are three Eclipses taking place – an unusual number. Normally there are never more than two in a given month – often fewer than that. So this is an eventful month for the world as a whole. Watch the news.

All the Eclipses affect you dramatically, but two out of three seem stressful for you. Take a reduced schedule.

The Solar Eclipse of the 1st takes place in your own Sign. It shows one of your periodic redefinitions of your personality and image. For those who are lackadaisical in dietary or health matters the Eclipse will bring out physical impurities for their ultimate cleansing. These are not sicknesses per se – though many people confuse them with that – but physical cleansings. Co-operate with the process. This is actually a sign of health and not of disease. Many of you will change the way you dress and accessorize – or find that you are being misrepresented or slandered and need to define yourself clearly so that others don't do it for you. Take a reduced schedule for this Eclipse.

The Lunar Eclipse of the 16th is also stressful for you, so take a reduced schedule – two days before and a day after. This Eclipse again produces image and personality changes, a redefinition of these things. Since it occurs in your 7th House of Love and Marriage it could bring about disruption leading to long-term change in a current relationship or marriage. Good marriages will survive the disruption and become even stronger than before – but different. Faulty marriages, relationships or friendships can go by the wayside during this period. Singles can decide to marry and married people can decide to divorce. The Eclipse is changing the marital status for many of you.

The Solar Eclipse of the 31st is a bit kinder to you but still causes long-term financial changes – either with the way you earn your living or with your investments. Many people change brokers or financial advisors during this kind of Eclipse. Many change their investments or investment strategies. Flaws in current investments will be revealed so that you can take corrective action. Finances will swallow up much time, attention and energy over the next few months.

Your health and vitality are basically strong, so even physical cleansings caused by the Eclipse should have the best outcomes.

Jupiter's move into your 12th House on the 1st announces a new era of spirituality for you. Your spiritual growth will be important – and explosive – for the rest of the year.

August

Best Days Overall: 6th, 7th, 16th, 17th, 25th, 26th

Most Stressful Days Overall: 4th, 5th, 11th, 12th, 18th, 19th, 31st

Best Days for Love: 2nd, 3rd, 11th, 12th, 13th, 20th, 21st, 22nd, 23rd, 29th, 30th

Best Days for Money: 3rd, 4th, 8th, 9th, 13th, 14th, 18th, 19th, 23rd, 24th, 27th, 28th, 29th, 30th

Saturn joining Jupiter in the Sign of Gemini this month makes this one of the most important spiritual periods of your life. It has a profound effect on your love life as well.

Saturn (your Love Planet) in the 12th House of Spirituality is going to elevate your love life and a current relationship. Those of you already married or involved in a happy relationship will see it become more idealistic, more altruistic, and learn of the past-life connections between you and your lover. You are also going to widen your love to include all people in all countries and climes. Though you are committed physically to one person, this doesn't stop you from radiating love vibrations to all people. This is as it should be.

For singles, this brings about a spiritual relationship. Spiritual compatibility – a compatibility of ideals and spiritual goals – will become more important than any other compatibility – whether it be of physical appearance, sexual tastes or financial habits. Unless there has been some important spiritual connection it is doubtful whether any relationship will last in the coming years.

Saturn near Jupiter in your 12th House is going to change the way you express love as well. Love will be expressed through service – through practical deeds – and not merely through sentiment and romantic niceties. This trend has been going on for a while.

Those of you on a spiritual path are likely to meet important mentors, gurus and teachers. You will learn in the coming years that true spirituality is not a mass of vague feelings, but an exact, scientific – testable – process.

Your intuitions and dreamlife will be more active than usual and you will need to test them out in the real world.

Health is wonderful all month.

Finances are powerful as well. You have more control over your financial destiny than you've had all year. There is a stronger risk-taking, speculative urge in you and this seems to pay off. Cancerian investors have a flair for gold, utilities, athletic suppliers, military contractors and telecommunications companies. Your career prestige is also an important factor in earnings. Bosses, elders and parents are supporting your financial goals. There are some financial disagreements with your spouse or partner, but you will probably win out. You are confident and sure, where your partner seems confused.

September

Best Days Overall: 7th, 8th, 17th, 18th, 25th, 26th, 30th

CANCER

Most Stressful Days Overall: 1st, 7th, 8th, 14th, 15th, 16th, 27th, 28th

Best Days for Love: 1st, 7th, 8th, 10th, 11th, 19th, 20th, 27th, 28th, 30th

Best Days for Money: 1st, 7th, 8th, 10th, 11th, 17th, 18th, 19th, 20th, 23rd, 24th, 27th, 28th, 30th

Most of the planets are still below the Horizon of your chart. Mars, your Career Planet, moves ever closer to the lowest point (nadir) of your chart, day by day. Your 4th House of Home and Family is a major House of Power during this period. The message is clear: Career issues are less important, home and family issues are most important. The affairs of your eldest child seem especially pressing. The new Moon of the 27th occurs in your 4th House and will clarify – rather effortlessly – any family issues that confront you. This month you foster your career by shoring up and strengthening your home base.

With Venus in your 4th House for most of the month this is an excellent period for family get-togethers, entertaining from home, decorating the home and buying objects of beauty for the home.

This month – after the 22nd – there is an important shift of planetary power from the Eastern to the Western sector. This represents a psychological shift in yourself. This is an important month. Gradually you will start to exercise the social gifts and graces more and more. You will depend less on yourself and your own independent powers and more on the co-operation of other people. Life will start to present you with situations over which you have little control and you will be forced to adapt to them.

Your important areas of interest will be neighbours, siblings, short-hop travel, communication and intellectual interests, home and family, children, creativity, amusement, love affairs, and the deeper things of life, personal transformation, debt and its repayment, helping others prosper, and the libido.

Finances will be strong all month but become absolutely super-charged after the 22nd. Your Money Planet receives beautiful aspects from all of the long-term planets. Money comes easily and effortlessly – from family members or family connections, property or industries that cater to the home. You almost can't avoid getting rich during this period. You are also spending more on the home right now.

Health is strong, but rest and relax more after the 22nd.

The retrograde of your Love Planet on the 12th shows that love needs time to develop. Your social confidence is not as strong as usual. A current relationship seems on hold.

October

Best Days Overall: 1st, 9th, 10th, 11th, 18th, 19th, 27th, 28th

Most Stressful Days Overall: 4th, 5th, 6th, 12th, 13th, 25th, 26th

Best Days for Love: 1st, 4th, 5th, 6th, 7th, 9th, 10th, 11th, 15th, 16th, 20th, 21st, 24th, 25th, 29th, 30th

Best Days for Money: 7th, 8th, 16th, 17th, 20th, 21st, 25th, 26th, 27th, 28th

Saturn's retrograde changes your attitudes about love and the direction of a current relationship. Some of you are going back to loves that you thought you had outgrown or were over with. Others feel that a current relationship is going backwards instead of forwards. Many of you are finding love opportunities in groups, organizations or through introductions made by friends. All of this is short term, and designed to give you breathing space to re-evaluate your love situation. Neither a marriage nor a divorce should be scheduled now.

CANCER

The combined retrograde of Mercury (from the 18th to the 31st) and Jupiter (all month) impacts on your spiritual life. Meditators find it more difficult to meditate and spiritual studies seem to go backwards instead of forwards. Dream messages and psychic readings need more careful interpretation, as their true meanings could be far from what you think.

Most of the planets are still in the West, indicating a greater emphasis on the social life and the needs of others. You are more popular this month and are developing your social skills. Continue to adapt to situations rather than trying to change them.

Most of the planets below the Horizon of your Horoscope (like last month) show a continuing need to focus on home and family issues and to de-emphasize the career.

Health is excellent, but rest and relax more until the 23rd. After this time your vitality returns with a vengeance.

When the Sun enters Scorpio on the 23rd you enter one of the best overall periods of your year. Health is good, optimism and self-confidence are strong and you are in a party mood. This is a period for exploring the 'rapture' side of life – enjoying life and helping others to do the same. Creativity is at a yearly high, and there will be many parties, entertainments and amusements. Singles will have love affairs or opportunities for love affairs. Speculations are favourable, and children bring you great happiness. Your ability to enter the 'child-like' state and thus understand and get on with children is stronger now as well.

Finances are very powerful and happy until the 23rd. Afterwards they become more volatile. Too much speculating can be a problem. Over-spending on the children or on entertainment can be another. Earnings can come to you suddenly – out of the blue – but also be spent just as suddenly. Spend proportionally after the 23rd. It's wonderful to make grand gestures and make other people happy, but do so within your budget.

November

Best Days Overall: 6th, 7th, 15th, 23rd, 24th

Most Stressful Days Overall: 1st, 2nd, 8th, 9th, 21st, 22nd, 28th, 29th

Best Days for Love: 1st, 2nd, 8th, 9th, 11th, 19th, 20th, 28th, 29th

Best Days for Money: 3rd, 4th, 6th, 7th, 12th, 13th, 15th, 16th, 17th, 18th, 21st, 22nd, 26th, 27th, 30th

Looks like major construction or repairs going on in the home. A parent could be visiting or staying with you. Home and family issues are very prominent now as most of the planets are below the Horizon of your Horoscope. Emotions can be volatile and this is a good opportunity to resolve old wounds.

Still and all this is a happy month. The Sun in Scorpio until the 22nd boosts finances, gives speculative good fortune, and brings easy money. There are more parties and entertainments during this period. Relations with children seem happy – though you can over-spend on them. Singles find ample love opportunities.

Those of you involved with mass mailshots or telemarketing should postpone these things until after the 8th, when Mercury goes forward again. It would not be a bad idea to have your phones, cars and computers checked out during this period. Malfunctions in these areas are more likely to happen when Mercury is retrograde.

Venus in your 7th House and many planets in the West boost your love life. Other people's concerns come before your own. Good comes through other people and not by self-assertion or self-will. Adapting to situations brings more success than trying to create new conditions.

Venus 'out of bounds' all month suggests that you are going way out of your normal orbit in love situations, in order to meet friends, and to expand your social sphere. Love can be addictive during this period. Singles find romantic opportunities outside the normal social sphere and in unusual ways. This is an exciting love period. The retrograde of your Love Planet counsels caution and allowing more time for love to develop. Your urges are to rush a marriage or commitment, but you're better off waiting.

Job-seekers have plenty of opportunity after the 22nd, but job offers must be researched more carefully. Don't make a move until you understand all the ins and outs of the situation. There could be hidden time-bombs in your contract that will detonate later on.

Health is excellent all period. Mars is the lone planet stressing you out, suggesting the avoidance of haste and impatience in all things.

December

Best Days Overall: 3rd, 4th, 12th, 13th, 20th, 21st, 22nd, 30th, 31st

Most Stressful Days Overall: 6th, 7th, 18th, 19th, 25th, 26th, 27th

Best Days for Love: 8th, 9th, 10th, 11th, 16th, 17th, 18th, 19th, 25th, 26th, 27th, 28th, 29th

Best Days for Money: 1st, 6th, 7th, 10th, 11th, 14th, 15th, 18th, 25th, 26th, 28th

Most of the planets are in the West and your 7th House is an important House of Power this month. This is a yearly social peak. There is, temporarily, less independence and self-reliance and a greater need to cultivate the good graces of others. Your way is probably not the best way during this period. Adapt to situations rather than trying to force change. Avoid power struggles as much as possible.

The planetary power makes an important shift to the upper half of your Horoscope later in the month. Thus, as the months go by, career and outer achievement will become ever more important to you. Your ambitions are strengthened.

The Solar Eclipse of the 25th is a powerful one, Cancer, affecting many areas of your life. Do take a reduced schedule two days before and one day after. This is a time of year when many of you will be travelling. Try to schedule your travels around this period. Activities that don't have to be done – and only you can decide this – are better off rescheduled.

The Solar Eclipse affects your love life and/or marriage. Whatever your marital state, the flaws in these areas will be revealed – in dramatic and perhaps disruptive ways – so you can make the necessary changes. Understand that the Eclipse doesn't create anything new but brings out what was always there and which you have been ignoring or sweeping under the carpet. The time for action one way or another has come. Good relationships and marriages will only improve because of the Eclipse. Irreparably flawed marriages and relationships will dissolve. Singles who are miserable in their single state will become acutely aware of this misery and take steps – in the coming months – to change this condition. Singles who are happily single will not be affected.

The Sun is also your Financial Planet. Thus the Solar Eclipse is going to bring needed changes in your financial life. Investments could change as flaws in these things will be revealed. Many of you will change your investment strategy, or financial advisors, brokers and banks. A business partnership comes under review. This is all to the good. This Eclipse also affects Mercury, the Lord of both your 12th and 3rd Houses. Thus students will face some educational crisis, or change schools or teachers. Relations with neighbours and siblings could change for the long term. Those on a spiritual path (the 12th House) will change gurus or meditative practices. The Eclipse will stimulate your dreamlife, but don't give too much credence to these images, as much of them are just 'psychic flotsam and jetsam' stirred up by the Eclipse.

Leo

♌

THE LION

Birthdays from
21st July
to 21st August

Personality Profile

LEO AT A GLANCE

Element – Fire

Ruling Planet – Sun
   Career Planet – Venus
   Love Planet – Uranus
   Money Planet – Mercury
   Planet of Health and Work – Saturn
   Planet of Home and Family Life – Pluto

Colours – gold, orange, red

Colours that promote love, romance and social harmony – black, indigo, ultramarine blue

Colours that promote earning power – yellow, yellow-orange

LEO

Gems – amber, chrysolite, yellow diamond

Metal – gold

Scents – bergamot, frankincense, musk, neroli

Quality – fixed (= stability)

Quality most needed for balance – humility

Strongest virtues – leadership ability, self-esteem and confidence, generosity, creativity, love of joy

Deepest needs – fun, elation, the need to shine

Characteristics to avoid – arrogance, vanity, bossiness

Signs of greatest overall compatibility – Aries, Sagittarius

Signs of greatest overall incompatibility – Taurus, Scorpio, Aquarius

Sign most helpful to career – Taurus

Sign most helpful for emotional support – Scorpio

Sign most helpful financially – Virgo

Sign best for marriage and/or partnerships – Aquarius

Sign most helpful for creative projects – Sagittarius

Best Sign to have fun with – Sagittarius

Signs most helpful in spiritual matters – Aries, Cancer

Best day of the week – Sunday

Understanding the Leo Personality

When you think of Leo, think of royalty – then you'll get the idea of what the Leo character is all about and why Leos are the way they are. It is true that, for various reasons, some Leo-born do not always express this quality – but even if not they should like to do so.

A monarch rules not by example (as does Aries) nor by consensus (as do Capricorn and Aquarius) but by personal will. Will is law. Personal taste becomes the style that is imitated by all subjects. A monarch is somehow larger than life. This is how a Leo desires to be.

When you dispute the personal will of a Leo it is serious business. He or she takes it as a personal affront, an insult. Leos will let you know that their will carries authority and that to disobey is demeaning and disrespectful.

A Leo is king (or queen) of his or her personal domain. Subordinates, friends and family are the loyal and trusted subjects. Leos rule with benevolent grace and in the best interests of others. They have a powerful presence; indeed, they are powerful people. They seem to attract attention in any social gathering. They stand out because they are stars in their domain. Leos feel that, like the Sun, they are made to shine and rule. Leos feel that they were born to special privilege and royal prerogatives – and most of them attain this status, at least to some degree.

The Sun is the Ruler of this Sign, and when you think of sunshine it is very difficult to feel unhealthy or depressed. Somehow the light of the Sun is the very antithesis of illness and apathy. Leos love life. They also love to have fun; they love drama, music, the theatre and amusements of all sorts. These are the things that give joy to life. If – even in their best interests – you try to deprive Leos of their pleasures, good food, drink and entertainment, you run the serious risk of depriving them of the will to live. To them life without joy is no life at all.

LEO

Leos epitomize humanity's will to power. But power in and of itself – regardless of what some people say – is neither good nor evil. Only when power is abused does it becomes evil. Without power even good things cannot come to pass. Leos realize this and are uniquely qualified to wield power. Of all the Signs, they do it most naturally. Capricorn, the other power Sign of the Zodiac, is a better manager and administrator than Leo – much better. But Leo outshines Capricorn in personal grace and presence. Leo loves power, where Capricorn assumes power out of a sense of duty.

Finance

Leos are great leaders but not necessarily good managers. They are better at handling the overall picture than the nitty-gritty details of business. If they have good managers working for them they can become exceptional executives. They have vision and a lot of creativity.

Leos love wealth for the pleasures it can bring. They love an opulent lifestyle, pomp and glamour. Even when they are not wealthy they live as if they are. This is why many fall into debt, from which it is sometimes difficult to emerge.

Leos, like Pisceans, are generous to a fault. Very often they want to acquire wealth solely so that they can help others economically. Wealth to Leo buys services and managerial ability. It creates jobs for others and improves the general well-being of those around them. Therefore – to a Leo – wealth is good. Wealth is to be enjoyed to the fullest. Money is not to be left to gather dust in a mouldy bank vault but to be enjoyed, spread around, used. So Leos can be quite reckless in their spending.

With the Sign of Virgo on Leo's 2nd House (of Money) cusp, Leo needs to develop some of Virgo's traits of analysis, discrimination and purity when it comes to money matters. They must learn to be more careful with the details of finance (or to hire people to do this for them). They have to be more cost-conscious in their spending habits. Generally, they need to manage their money better. Leos tend to chafe under financial constraints, yet these constraints can help Leos to reach their highest financial potential.

Leos like it when their friends and family know that they can depend on them for financial support. They do not mind – even enjoy – lending money, but they are careful that they are not taken advantage of. From their 'regal throne' Leos like to bestow gifts upon their family and friends and then enjoy the good feelings these gifts bring to everybody. Leos love financial speculations and – when the celestial influences are right – are often lucky.

Career and Public Image

Leos like to be perceived as wealthy, for in today's world wealth often equals power. When they attain wealth they love having a large house with lots of land and animals.

At their jobs Leos excel in positions of authority and power. They are good at making decisions – on a grand level – but they prefer to leave the details to others. Leos are well respected by their colleagues and subordinates, mainly because they have a knack for understanding and relating to those around them. Leos usually strive for the top positions even if they have to start at the bottom and work hard to get there. As might be expected of such a charismatic Sign, Leos are always trying to improve their work situation. They do so in order to have a better chance of advancing to the top.

On the other hand, Leos do not like to be bossed around or told what to do. Perhaps this is why they aspire so for the top – where they can be the decision-makers and need not take orders from others.

Leos never doubt their success and focus all their attention and efforts on achieving it. Another great Leo characteristic is that – just like good monarchs – they do not attempt to abuse the power or success they achieve. If they do so this is not wilful or intentional. Usually they like to share their wealth and try to make everyone around them join in their success.

Leos are – and like to be perceived as – hard-working, well-established individuals. It is definitely true that they are capable of hard work and often manage great things. But do not forget that, deep down inside, Leos really are fun-lovers.

Love and Relationships

Generally, Leos are not the marrying kind. To them relationships are good while they are pleasurable. When the relationship ceases to be pleasurable a true Leo will want out. They always want to have the freedom to leave. That is why Leos excel at love affairs rather than commitment. Once married, however, Leo is faithful – even if some Leos have a tendency to marry more than once in their lifetime. If you are in love with a Leo, just show him or her a good time. Travel, go to casinos and clubs, the theatre and discos. Wine and dine your Leo love – it is expensive but worth it and you will have fun.

Leos generally have an active love life and are demonstrative in their affections. They love to be with other optimistic and fun-loving types like themselves, but wind up settling with someone more serious, intellectual and unconventional. The partner of a Leo tends to be more political and socially conscious than he or she is, and more libertarian. When you marry a Leo, mastering the freedom-loving tendencies of your partner will definitely become a life-long challenge – and be careful that Leo does not master you.

Aquarius sits on Leo's 7th House (of Love) cusp. Thus if Leos want to realize their highest love and social potential they need to develop a more egalitarian, Aquarian perspective on others. This is not easy for Leo, for 'the king' finds his equals only among other 'kings'. But perhaps this is the solution to Leo's social challenge – to be 'a king among kings'. It is all right to be royal, but recognize the nobility in others.

Home and Domestic Life

Although Leos are great entertainers and love having people over, sometimes this is all show. Only very few close friends will get to see the real side of a Leo's day-to-day life. To a Leo the home is a place of comfort, recreation and transformation; a secret, private retreat – a castle. Leos like to spend money, show off a bit, entertain and have fun. They enjoy the latest furnishings, clothes and gadgets – all things fit for kings.

Leos are fiercely loyal to their family and of course expect the same from them. They love their children almost to a fault; they have to be careful not to spoil them too much. They also must try to avoid attempting to make individual family members over in their own image. Leos should keep in mind that others also have the need to be their own people. That is why Leos have to be extra careful about being over-bossy or over-domineering in the home.

Horoscope for 2000

Major Trends

1999 was a stressful year, Leo, as major long-term planets were pummelling and mauling you, pulling you off your natural centre, forcing you into necessary but uncomfortable changes. The fact that you got through it with your health and sanity intact is a testament to the strength and power of your soul. Those of you who persisted, who measured your energies, focused on the essentials and refused to be discouraged, had great career success. Those of you who squandered your energy could have experienced health problems.

Happily the year 2000 is a lot easier than 1999. Saturn is getting ready to move out of Taurus – where it has been setting up obstructions and perhaps frustrating you – and moving into Gemini, a much more harmonious placement. Saturn will still be in Taurus for most of the year, so you can't relax your vigilance, but the worst of the transit is over.

The stresses of 1999 forced many of you to re-evaluate your world view, your personal philosophy of life and many of your religious beliefs. All of you grew spiritually and philosophically in 1999. This growth helped you get through the year a bit more easily. This inner, spiritual growth continues in the year 2000.

Jupiter will cross your Midheaven point this year and move through your 10th House of Career. Thus, if you have learned to manage your energy efficiently there is more career progress in store. There are pay rises and promotions and increased public recognition. The year 2000 is a banner career year.

Your areas of greatest interest this year are children, creativity, love affairs, romance, and career.

Your paths of greatest fulfilment this year are the body, self-image, personal appearance, spiritual growth, charities, career and friendships.

Health

Though your health should be better this year than last, your vitality is still not what it should be nor what you are used to. You've got to find ways to take it easy – to give time to yourself – to maximize your energy.

Any therapy that is drugless and boosts overall energy and strengthens the overall system is good. Thus it might be a good idea to have regular body massages or Alexander Technique sessions. Foot and hand reflexology is an excellent general preventative and energy-booster. Increase your vitamin intake – especially of the B vitamins. Wear the colours, metal, gems and scents of your Sign. Citrus fruits are healthful eating for many of you, as these are ruled by Leo.

You have enough energy to handle the tasks and responsibilities that are truly yours, but not enough for things that are not yours – that are imposed on you. You must be sharply discerning these days. Focus on the essentials and let the lesser things go – or delegate lesser things to others.

The art of relaxation is a great art to learn. Few people ever truly relax – even when they are in leisure activities. Observe them, they are tensed up – the shoulders and neck are tensed, even when they are going to sleep. Twenty minutes of pure relaxation is equivalent to many hours of sleep – and is a real energy-booster. Try to cultivate a relaxed state even in your work. Take breaks and stretch and move your head from side to side.

Work rhythmically. Alternate activities. Do brain work for a while and then do something physical. Then go back to your brain work.

Try to schedule activities (where you have some choice in the matter) on your best days. Things will tend to go more smoothly if you do this. Lighten up on your schedule on your stressful days. (See the month-by-month forecasts.)

Once you've done all in your power in a given area, relax, let go and be happy. The results are not in your power any more and so you may as well be happy.

Your Health Planet will be in the Sign of Taurus for most of the year. Thus you should pay special attention to your neck and throat. Keep them massaged and loose. Massage the reflexology or acupressure points for these areas – or have a professional do it.

From 11th August to 26th October Saturn will be in Gemini. Try to avoid excessive or needless speech. There's no need to be rude to others, just avoid gossip or idle talk. This is a great waster of energy. The lungs and nervous system need special attention then.

LEO

The period between 19th April and 20th May will be particularly stressful for you, so be sure to rest and relax more at this time. Other stressful periods are 20th January to 19th February and 23rd October to 22nd November.

Few Signs are blessed with as much vitality as yours. If you don't waste it, you'll get through the year with flying colours.

Home and Domestic Life

Your 4th House of Home and Family is not a House of Power for most of the year, Leo, thus you have much free will in this area. The Cosmos doesn't push you one way or the other.

Pluto, your Family Planet, is in the expansive Sign of Sagittarius for many years to come. This can be seen as a positive thing. It indicates general emotional happiness, family support, domestic harmony and pleasant changes in the family and domestic pattern. Children and their welfare – always important to you – are now even more so. There is great creativity in the home and from the home. And, early on in the year, perhaps a fortunate property speculation – the fortunate purchase or sale of a home.

But later in the year – in the summer – Pluto receives some intense stimulation from Jupiter and Saturn. Saturn opposing Pluto could make you feel cramped in the home – in many cases this will come as a result of new additions to the family, in other cases as a result of visits from friends. Jupiter's opposition to Pluto – from 1st July onwards – could force you into a move or renovation that you don't feel ready for. Perhaps peer pressure is a factor. All your friends are installing such and such a device, or making such and such a renovation, and you feel compelled to do likewise. Many of you will be installing new high-tech gadgets in the home – and perhaps you are premature with it. Do the necessary research on these things and make sure that the technology is up to scratch. Be careful with property speculations after 1st July. Strategies that worked earlier in the year might not work after then.

A parent could be having a marital crisis and may move house as a result. The Eclipses of 16th July and 25th December could bring moves (and perhaps major repairs in the home) for siblings. Many of you will become grandparents this year as adult children seem very fertile. And in general, Leos of childbearing age are more fertile this year.

Those of you who are pregnant and are due to give birth in the summer or afterwards need to take more care with the pregnancy – go for more antenatal checkups, and rest and relax more than usual. Multiple births are a strong possibility.

Love and Social Life

Your 7th House of Love and Marriage is a major House of Power this year – just as it has been for many years. It will be powerful for many more years to come.

Two powerful planets – Uranus and Neptune – are camped out in your House of Marriage. On the one hand they bring idealism about love – a desire for the highest and the best, a knowledge of what true love is. On the other hand they bring an experimental attitude to love – a desire to upgrade the love life and marriage constantly. All of this makes for an exciting love life, but a very unstable one.

Current and new marriages are not written in stone. Affections can change at the drop of a hat. Many of you are filled with grand visions of what is available to you, and so the partner must not only compete against what is really out there, but also against your grand visions.

Singles can marry (and remarry), married people can divorce and remarry. Love happens suddenly – out of the blue. There are many love-at-first-sight experiences. The minute you think you've found Mr or Ms Right, someone else comes along who seems 'more' right. It's very difficult for Leos to commit right now – even if they want to.

This high idealism in love has both an upside and a down-side. The upside is that, because you demand more, expect

160

more, you will attract better love opportunities. The down-side is that often these ideals are so high that no human person can ever fulfil them. And so there is disappointment. The disappointments will continue until a basic lesson is learned: Perfect love can only come from a perfect power. Humans are by nature imperfect so we cannot expect more from them than they are capable of. But if you look to the Power that loves you perfectly, you will always have perfect love. You will become more tolerant of your human lover and things will go better between you. Neptune will teach you to love the Higher Power in your lover, not his or her physical embodiment. This doesn't mean that you despise the physical, but that you know that the physical is only an effect of the spiritual.

There are other issues in love going on this year. Uranus in the 7th House brings a love of change, excitement, and unconventional types of relationships. Neptune brings a desire for the Divine Selection – the mate who was destined for you long before you were born. These are, on the surface, contradictory urges. One can lead to promiscuity and playing the field, the other wants one committed, life-long marriage. But the Cosmos is very clever. As you play the field, experiment and learn from trial and error you will be processed and prepared to meet your Divine Selection. Until there is a certain amount of experience (both positive and negative) you won't be able to recognize the Divine Selection when he or she appears.

In the meantime, enjoy the gaining of experience.

Your 11th House of Friendship and Group Activities becomes powerful after 1st July. Thus new and happy friendships are coming into the picture this year. These are people who are on your wavelength, with whom you have intellectual affinity. Group activities, organizations and introductions made by friends also bring romantic opportunities. The reverse is true as well: Romantic liaisons bring a whole new set of friendships.

Career and Finance

Your 2nd House of Finance is not a House of Power this year, Leo, which means money per se is not that important to you. Perhaps it comes so easily to you that you give it little respect. It is not a challenge and doesn't require undue attention. You seem satisfied with your earnings.

Career, on the other hand, is very important this year. Status, prestige and public recognition are much more important than mere money. You will trade money for glory at the drop of a hat.

Saturn in your 10th House for the past year and a half has been making you serious about career issues. You are working hard, focusing on real and true achievement. You are doing a good day's work (and perhaps more) for a good day's pay. Bosses and authority figures have been harsh and demanding – like drill sergeants at boot camp. Never mind. Keep producing consistently. The payoff is near. On 15th February Jupiter moves into your 10th House and stays there until 1st July. This shows pay rises and promotions at work. Your previous unsung efforts are now recognized. Perhaps there is a new regime at work – bosses are now softer with you, treating you with more respect and becoming more eager to bestow favours. And, though you will still be working hard, the whole atmosphere at work is easier and happier.

Jupiter is the Lord of your 5th House of Children, Happiness and Speculations. So, in your Horoscope Jupiter is not only expanding your career horizons, but bringing you happiness and creative satisfaction as well. Many of you will pursue career objectives 'out of the dungeon' – at the golf course, the tennis club, at parties or elegant restaurants. Those of you who have expense accounts will see their limits increased. Those of you who never had an expense account will now have one.

Many of you will decide to make children your career and leave the corporate world altogether. Still others will be motivated in your career efforts by new mouths to feed.

LEO

Jupiter's transit is especially significant for those of you in the entertainment or artistic fields. These fields are disproportionately filled with Leos (sometimes Leo rising as well). The period from 15th February to 1st July signals a major stretch of success and public popularity.

Paths to financial increase and speculative success this year are property, agriculture and the pursuit of career objectives.

Self-improvement

The main area of self-improvement will be the health area, as mentioned. It is very important that you learn to maximize your energy and learn relaxation. The outer world – love and career – calls very strongly to you now, and is very alluring. It is tempting to lose yourself in these things, for most of the events taking place in these realms are happy. But if your energy levels get too low, you endanger yourself. Never allow yourself to become over-tired.

Two major planets enter your 11th House of Friendship this year. Jupiter moves in on 1st July, Saturn on 11th August. Many new friends are coming into the picture and the tendency will be to be indiscriminate about them. But Saturn will force you to discriminate – either through harsh lessons and disappointments, or through your own intelligence. Focus on quality, not quantity. Friendships need to be tested. Friendship implies responsibility and is not just a free ride. A true friend wants your own fondest hopes and wishes to come true – those who don't desire this for you are not true friends.

Saturn in the 11th House implies learning the art of forgiveness. Some friends – true friends – can disappoint, and you must learn to forgive. When you forgive you will see that the disappointment they caused came from their own problems and were not related to you.

Month-by-month Forecasts

January

Best Days Overall: 3rd, 4th, 13th, 14th, 21st, 22nd, 30th, 31st

Most Stressful Days Overall: 1st, 2nd, 8th, 9th, 15th, 16th, 28th, 29th

Best Days for Love: 3rd, 4th, 8th, 9th, 13th, 14th, 17th, 18th, 22nd, 25th, 26th

Best Days for Money: 3rd, 4th, 5th, 6th, 7th, 13th, 14th, 15th, 16th, 21st, 22nd, 23rd, 24th, 25th, 26th, 30th, 31st

The planets are making an important shift to the upper half of your Horoscope after the 19th, making career and 'outer' activities more and more important as the months progress. Emotional harmony is still important, but becoming less so. Start focusing on your outer life.

Between 80 and 90 per cent of the planets are in the Western, social sector of your chart this month – making this an important social month. Put other people first and your own good will come to you. This is not a great period for self-assertion or trying to have your own way. Seek consensus, negotiate, compromise and above all adapt to situations and you will get through the month with flying colours.

As 90 to 100 per cent of the planets are moving forward this month, there is great social progress and achievement happening. Good is coming from other people – allow it to happen, don't try to *make* it happen.

The most important areas of interest this month are parties, love affairs, sports and entertainment, health and work, love and romance, and your personal image.

The Lunar Eclipse of the 21st is a strong one on you, Leo, so be sure to take a reduced schedule two days before and a day after. The Eclipse occurs in your own Sign, showing a cleansing of the body, a redefinition of the personality and long-term changes in both your image and spiritual life. Those of you on a spiritual path will find that they change gurus or meditation techniques around this time. There could be disruptive upheavals in a charity or ministry that you're involved with. Hang on and let the dust settle – the changes are all to the good.

Love is happy and exciting all month. A marriage, or involvement with marriage, would not be a surprise. Love comes suddenly, out of the blue. You are unusually popular, eager to please the beloved and in great demand socially. You are on a charm offensive and you succeed.

Rest and relax more after the 20th. Remember what we've written about previously about the need to maximize energy.

Finances are strong all month. Financial judgement is strongest until the 19th – a good time to shop and make big-ticket purchases as you will not overpay. It's a good time to make long-term investments as well. Money comes from work and being productive until the 19th. After that it comes from social activities, the support of your spouse and partner, and through partnership activities. A happy (and unexpected) windfall comes around the 28th–29th.

February

Best Days Overall: 9th, 10th, 17th, 18th, 26th, 27th, 28th

Most Stressful Days Overall: 4th, 5th, 11th, 12th, 24th, 25th

Best Days for Love: 2nd, 3rd, 4th, 5th, 11th, 12th, 13th, 14th, 22nd, 23rd

Best Days for Money: 6th, 9th, 10th, 15th, 16th, 19th, 20th, 24th, 25th, 29th

An eventful but stressful month, Leo. Be sure to rest and relax more. Though the Cosmos never gives more than we can handle, it sometimes tests our limits. This is one of those months for you. Consider it a tempering process. When you emerge you will be purer, stronger, tougher than you ever thought you could be. We are all vehicles through which a Higher Power operates, and periodically these vehicles need to be road-tested. You will be laughing and telling stories about this period, years from now – as examples of what can be overcome. Your superhuman sense of humour will be a great help now.

The planetary power is still overwhelmingly in the Western sector of your chart. You must adapt to situations and let patience do its perfect work. You can't force things to happen now, you must allow them to happen. Your social and diplomatic skills are being tested and refined. Avoid self-assertion and power struggles like the plague.

The planetary power is slowly shifting from the bottom half of your chart to the top half. Thus the career and outer, worldly activities are becoming ever more important. Jupiter, moving into your Career House on the 15th, indicates an important – and very happy – career change. Perhaps you are promoted, or offered a dream job in another company. A boss who was harsh on you for the past year is replaced by someone more appreciative of your gifts. Elders and authority figures who were stern and unsupportive suddenly become more favourably disposed.

Favours come from those on high – but they are not free rides – strictly conditional.

The Solar Eclipse of the 5th is very powerful on you, so do take a reduced schedule – two days before and a day after. This Eclipse affects you both personally, in terms of the body and the image, and socially, in a current relationship. Many of you will redefine your personality. You will dress differently and revise your concept of yourself. You will start projecting a different image. A current relationship is unstable during this period; if the flaws can't be fixed it seems doomed. In many cases important decisions about the direction of a relationship must be taken – if you or your lover have been sitting on the fence, letting things ride and develop, now you must decide one way or another where things are going. Many a marriage will happen now too. Obstructions to your path of True Love are being blasted away during this period.

Mercury, your Money Planet, goes retrograde from the 21st onwards. Be more cautious with purchases, investments and important financial commitments. Best to delay major expenditures until Mercury goes forward again on the 14th March.

March

Best Days Overall: 7th, 8th, 16th, 17th, 25th, 26th

Most Stressful Days Overall: 3rd, 4th, 9th, 10th, 22nd, 23rd, 24th, 30th, 31st

Best Days for Love: 3rd, 4th, 12th, 13th, 20th, 21st, 22nd, 23rd, 30th, 31st

Best Days for Money: 1st, 5th, 6th, 9th, 10th, 14th, 15th, 18th, 19th, 22nd, 23rd, 24th, 27th, 28th

Though Mercury's retrograde until the 14th won't stop earnings, it will create all kinds of delays or minor irritations in that department. Continue to study all major purchases, contracts, financial commitments and investments very thoroughly. Execute your financial plans after the 14th. Your spouse or partner should do the same.

The retrograde of your Home and Family Planet, Pluto, shows that big-ticket purchases for the home or major renovations need to be studied more carefully. Besides, with 80 to 90 per cent of the planets above the Horizon, it is safe (and desirable) to let go of domestic concerns and focus more on the career and outer activities.

With 60 to 70 per cent of the planets still in the Western sector of your chart, this indicates that other people and their concerns are most important now. Good will come through the good graces of others and not by self-will, undue independence or personal power struggles. Continue exercising all the social graces.

As 90 per cent of the planetary power is forward, this is still a period of great forward momentum and achievement in your life – only, like the sunbather in search of a tan, you let it happen rather than make it happen.

Your important areas of interest this month are love, romance and social activities, debts and their repayment, the libido, the income of your partner or shareholders, personal transformation, religion, philosophy, higher education and foreign travel, and the career.

Health is still delicate. Rest and relax more, pace yourself and work rhythmically. Delegate wherever possible. Keep the spine and thighs in good shape.

Your love life is still active but less frenetic than last month. Singles can find love suddenly and out of the blue. This is a month where love can happen with a boss or with someone who works for you. The main challenge in love now is the conflict between the demands of your career and the demands of your lover – both want all your time and attention. Even an office romance won't solve the tension. This is what makes love so volatile this month.

The new Moon of the 6th will clarify debt issues and help your partner to take the right financial decisions. Your line of credit will increase this month and tax issues will end with a best-case scenario. Your personal financial focus should be the prosperity of others. As you help others to prosper you will prosper personally.

LEO

April

Best Days Overall: 4th, 5th, 12th, 13th, 21st, 22nd

Most Stressful Days Overall: 6th, 7th, 19th, 20th, 26th, 27th

Best Days for Love: 1st, 2nd, 8th, 9th, 12th, 13th, 16th, 17th, 21st, 22nd, 26th, 27th

Best Days for Money: 1st, 2nd, 6th, 7th, 10th, 11th, 14th, 15th, 21st, 22nd, 24th, 25th

This is one powerful career month. Seldom in your life have you ever been so busily engaged in the outer world. Seldom have the demands of your career been so overwhelming – threatening even to destroy your love and social life and interfere with people you love dearly.

Between 80 and 90 per cent of the planets are above the Horizon, and your 10th House of Career is a *major* House of Power. Four planetary gangbusters are moving through this House – most of them kindly and benefic. Thus, recent blockages and obstructions to your career success are now getting blasted away – overcome and overpowered. Rivals for a position you covet are outgunned. Competitors are outflanked. You sail to the heights with a strong wind at your back.

But this success is like a bombshell on your social life. It will prove very difficult to integrate the two areas and make them co-operate. One of these areas will have to go, and it looks like it is your social life. Old friends and people you dearly love are shaken up now. It is not that they don't wish you success, but that their status in your life is now changed. They feel some insecurity about that. Assure them of your love and undying devotion, but hammer away at your career.

With 90 per cent of the planets in forward motion there is great forward momentum and progress happening. With many planets in the Fire element – your native element – things are happening with bewildering rapidity. A week is like an aeon of time. So much can happen, so much can change.

The danger for you with all this fire is that you can leap into things with little thought and without regard to costs or consequences. Remember that life will give you everything you ask for, but you do have to pay the bill.

Earnings are soaring this month – especially after the 13th. Financial confidence is back. You earn more and spend more. Impulsive, reckless spending can be a problem. You enjoy making the 'grand gesture' financially – perhaps treating a whole group of people to dinner, a night out or some other extravagance. But earnings come easily and you don't seem to care. You might be better off buying big-ticket items after the 19th when there is more Earth in the Horoscope – it's less likely that you will overpay.

Career and social demands are stressing your health, so be sure to rest and relax more after the 19th. Don't burn the candle at both ends and remember the discussion in the Health section, above.

May

Best Days Overall: 1st, 2nd, 9th, 10th, 18th, 19th, 20th, 28th, 29th

Most Stressful Days Overall: 3rd, 4th, 16th, 17th, 24th, 25th, 31st

Best Days for Love: 3rd, 4th, 5th, 6th, 12th, 13th, 14th, 15th, 22nd, 23rd, 24th, 25th

Best Days for Money: 3rd, 4th, 12th, 13th, 14th, 21st, 22nd, 24th, 25th, 31st

Health is still very delicate until the 20th, so rest and relax more. There is dramatic improvement in your vitality after the 20th, but you still need to maximize your physical and mental energy all month. Proper care of the thighs and spine will enhance health. A sense of humour will also help.

Happily, the planets have shifted eastward, making you more independent and self-reliant. You are more in control of your destiny these days – less a plaything for others. With your Love and Social Planet going retrograde on the 25th, you can safely de-emphasize social issues and focus on personal fulfilment.

Like last month, the career is a major focus. Your 10th House is ultra-powerful and most of the planets are above the Horizon. You can safely let go of family and domestic concerns and focus on your ambitions.

Career is going great guns this month, and is still stressing your social and love life. Your single-minded ambition and the career demands put on you are making a loved one or spouse rethink the relationship. They feel that your career comes before them. Social issues should improve after the 20th when your career cools down a bit. After the 20th you feel more social and this helps matters as well.

Jupiter and Saturn's rare conjunction in your House of Career signals long-term (probably for the next 20 years) developments there. For many it shows a creative type of career or work for a creative type of organization – an entertainment type of company. For others it shows a choice to make between children and career. Even those who are staying at their jobs are being motivated by their children. A career gamble looks like it pays off.

Finances are stormy and volatile until the 14th. Money can come suddenly and be spent just as suddenly. Money comes from the career and from the professional reputation you've built up. After the 14th networking, sales and marketing become very important to your bank balance – and these activities will be successful. Trading brings profits, and professional investors will be doing more trading than usual.

June

Best Days Overall: 6th, 7th, 15th, 16th, 25th, 26th

Most Stressful Days Overall: 12th, 13th, 14th, 20th, 21st, 27th, 28th

Best Days for Love: 2nd, 10th, 11th, 20th, 21st, 22nd, 23rd, 29th, 30th

Best Days for Money: 4th, 5th, 8th, 9th, 12th, 13th, 14th, 17th, 18th, 19th, 22nd, 23rd, 27th, 28th

Health is much improved, but you still need to rest and relax more. Let your body determine your schedule.

The majority of planets are in the East and your social planets are retrograde. Let go of social issues and of trying to be popular and work on personal fulfilment – building a lifestyle and conditions that create happiness. Work on becoming the person you want to be and love will happen naturally.

Between 80 and 90 per cent of the planets are still above the Horizon. And, though career is less hectic than it was a few months ago, it is still prominent and important. Let go of psychological and domestic issues and focus on the outer world. Doing right will lead to feeling right.

Though most of the planets are still moving forward, retrograde activity increases this month. Progress is still happening in your life, but more slowly.

Your career involves a lot of work but it seems fun. There is joy in your work.

Much power in your 11th House until the 21st shows that this is a month for realizing your fondest hopes and wishes. There is more socializing with friends and groups during this period. There seems more satisfaction in friendship than in romantic love.

After the 21st the power shifts to the spiritual 12th House, activating your dreamlife and creating a yearning for 'getting right with God' and for introspection and seclusion.

LEO

World-weariness is a perfectly natural feeling these days. Those on a spiritual path will make important spiritual breakthroughs – in knowledge and understanding. And even secular-minded people will be more involved in charitable and ministerial projects.

Romantic love is calming down and there is better synchronicity between you and the beloved. But caution needs to be exercised in love. It would not be wise to schedule either a marriage or a divorce now, as your social judgement is not up to its usual standards. Singles need to let love grow and develop – love cannot be rushed this month.

Finances are stable, but Mercury's retrograde on the 23rd suggests a need for caution in spending and investing. Wrap up important purchases and financial commitments before the 23rd.

Mercury in the Sign of Cancer in your 12th House suggests earnings that come from intuition and in behind-the-scenes ways. This it not the time to flaunt your wealth. There is more charitable giving. Dream and psychic guidance regarding finances need confirmation after the 23rd – these indicators might not mean what you think.

July

Best Days Overall: 3rd, 4th, 12th, 13th, 22nd, 23rd, 31st

Most Stressful Days Overall: 10th, 11th, 17th, 18th, 24th, 25th

Best Days for Love: 1st, 2nd, 7th, 8th, 10th, 11th, 17th, 18th, 22nd, 23rd, 26th, 27th, 30th, 31st

Best Days for Money: 1st, 2nd, 5th, 6th, 7th, 10th, 11th, 14th, 15th, 20th, 21st, 25th, 26th, 29th, 30th

We have three Eclipses this month which will cause major change in the world and in your environment. Many planets now in the Eastern sector show that these changes will blast away many obstructions to your personal happiness and will clear the ground so you can create conditions as you want them. Have clear goals and a clear plan, and when the dust settles from the Eclipses act on your plan.

Two out of three of the Eclipses are kind to you. Only the Solar Eclipse of the 30th seems stressful – take a reduced schedule during this period (two days before and a day after). Since your health and self-confidence are improving day by day I expect that the physical cleansings brought on by this Eclipse will be ultimately helpful.

The Solar Eclipse of the 1st occurs in your 12th House of Spirituality, bringing long-term changes – and perhaps upheavals – in a spiritual, charitable or religious organization to which you belong. Those on a spiritual path will make important changes in their meditative techniques or practices. Many will change gurus, pastors and/or ministers during this period. Your dreamlife becomes more active during this period, but these dreams will be unreliable and shouldn't be taken too seriously. Much of it is psychic 'flotsam and jetsam' brought up by the Eclipse.

The Lunar Eclipse of the 16th occurs in your 6th House of Health and Work. Since it is basically kind to you it is probably indicating changes in health regimes, doctors or health plans. Job changes could also occur. Employers could have a shake-up in their staff.

The Solar Eclipse of the 30th brings on image and personality changes, a redefinition of the personality. (The Solar Eclipse of the 1st will also cause some of this, but this second Solar Eclipse is more dramatic.) Old wardrobes and modes of dress change, and new ones come into replace them.

Jupiter's move into Gemini on the 1st increases your social circle and brings new and prominent friends into the picture. You are more involved (and happily) in groups, organizations and group activities. New high-tech equipment – big-ticket items – are coming to you.

LEO

Finances should be strong this month as Mercury's forward motion on the 17th restores both confidence and judgement. Mercury's position in your 12th House of Spirituality shows that financial problems are not what they seem. This is just the way that the Higher Power gets your attention. Intuition is getting trained through financial issues this month.

August

Best Days Overall: 8th, 9th, 18th, 19th, 27th, 28th

Most Stressful Days Overall: 6th, 7th, 13th, 14th, 15th, 20th, 21st, 22nd

Best Days for Love: 4th, 5th, 11th, 12th, 13th, 14th, 15th, 20th, 21st, 23rd, 24th, 29th, 30th

Best Days for Money: 1st, 2nd, 3rd, 4th, 8th, 9th, 13th, 14th, 18th, 19th, 23rd, 24th, 29th, 30th

Many planets in the East and many planets in your own Sign give you an energy and independence that you haven't felt in a long time, Leo. Go forward boldly towards your goals now. You have the power to create conditions as you like them and have little need for compromise. Let the world adapt to you for a while.

Most of the planets are now below the Horizon, so you are entering a period of psychological progress and a focus on inner versus outer growth. Find your emotional comfort zone and work from there.

Health is truly fabulous this month. Health problems of the past just melt away. Both the Sun and Mars in your own Sign fill you with explosive, dynamic energy. You have drive and enthusiasm now. You assert yourself with great power and are not a person to be opposed or trifled with. Exercise and health regimes go very well. Things get done in a hurry. Libido, always powerful in you, is even more so now. Athletes perform at their peak these days.

Mars in your own Sign – opposed by Uranus – shows a need to mind your temper. Sudden flare-ups can be deadly to love. Both the Sun and Mars in opposition to Uranus, your Love Planet – show a battle of wills in love – you and your lover are pulling in opposite directions. You will probably win the tug of war, but it is not good for the relationship. Rush, haste and impatience are enemies to guard against.

This is one of the best financial periods in your year. Mercury (your Money Planet) is moving forward speedily, showing great financial confidence and astute judgement. Your Money House becomes very powerful after the 23rd. Mercury moves into its own Sign and House on that day – making it even more powerful on your behalf. The new Moon of the 29th occurs in your Money House as well, showing that all relevant financial information will come to you easily and effortlessly in the next month.

Until the 6th, money comes from financial intuition and dreams. Hunches are profitable. There is more charitable giving, which clears off bad karma and allows more wealth to come to you. On the 10th a sudden windfall could come out of the blue, perhaps through a speculation. You might have to work harder for it as there is great resistance. From the 6th to the 23rd your image and personality play a big role in financial success. Dressing for success is important. You are spending on yourself. Shopping for big-ticket items goes better after the 23rd, as you will then be more careful about spending. Deal with mundane accounting chores and bookkeeping after the 23rd.

September

Best Days Overall: 5th, 6th, 14th, 15th, 16th, 23rd, 24th

Most Stressful Days Overall: 2nd, 3rd, 10th, 11th, 17th, 18th, 30th

LEO

Best Days for Love: 1st, 10th, 11th, 19th, 20th, 27th, 28th, 30th

Best Days for Money: 1st, 10th, 11th, 19th, 20th, 25th, 26th, 27th, 28th, 29th, 30th

The planets are more or less evenly distributed between the Eastern and Western sectors this month – thus you need balance between your personal desires and those of other people. Life will confront you with various types of situations – some you will be able to change and recreate according to your liking, while others will require adaptability on your part. The Moon's position will probably determine the issue – when it is in your Eastern sector you will have more independence, when it is in your Western sector you will need to be more adaptable. Your interests and those of others take equal priority now.

The planets are mostly below the Horizon of your chart during this period. Your 4th House of Home and Family becomes a House of Power by the end of the month. Venus, your Career Planet, crosses the nadir (lowest point) of your Horoscope on the 24th. The message is clear: focus on inner harmony and emotional comfort; let career issues go for a while. You must handle your career, of course, but give most of your attention to the home, family and psychological issues. Your career needs a stable home base upon which to rest.

Your important areas of interest this month are finance, local travel, intellectual interests, neighbours, siblings and communication, home and family, love and romance, and friendships, groups and organizations.

Health is still much improved. You can enhance it further by giving special attention to your knees, skeleton, teeth and ankles. The retrograde of your Health Planet on the 12th suggests caution when it comes to new diets, medicines and health regimes. Research these things more carefully as they are not what they seem to be. Medical diagnoses should be taken with many grains of salt. Get a second opinion where possible.

Job-seekers, too, need to exercise more caution. You will eventually find work but need to be careful that it's the right kind of work – the work you've been hired to do.

Finances are stormy early in the month and you need to work harder for earnings than you are used to. Perhaps you are hit with unexpected expenses or repairs. But don't despair. Handle the needs of each day. By the 7th, your Money Planet moves into fabulous alignment with many planets and earnings will soar. Money will come from sales, marketing, communication, trading, buying and selling, and social networking.

Your love life is very energetic but needs caution. Neither a marriage nor a divorce should be scheduled now. Let love grow and develop. Singles need to beat admirers off with a stick – the prospects and options are numerous.

October

Best Days Overall: 2nd, 3rd, 12th, 13th, 20th, 21st, 29th, 30th

Most Stressful Days Overall: 1st, 7th, 8th, 14th, 15th, 27th, 28th

Best Days for Love: 1st, 7th, 8th, 9th, 10th, 11th, 16th, 17th, 20th, 21st, 25th, 26th, 29th, 30th

Best Days for Money: 1st, 7th, 8th, 9th, 10th, 11th, 16th, 17th, 18th, 19th, 23rd, 24th, 25th, 26th, 27th, 28th

With Saturn's retrograde back into the Sign of Taurus, and with many planets in the Sign of Scorpio, there's some temporary health stress on you, Leo. Rest and relax more. This stress condition is nowhere near as severe as it was early in the year, but more so than it has been in the past few months. Remember the discussion in the Health section, above.

LEO

Many planets below the Horizon of your chart, and many planets in your 4th House of Home and Family, indicate a need to focus on inner rather than outer success. The emotional comfort zone is the Holy Grail for you this month, and once found must never be relinquished.

Let go of career issues and focus on your home base.

Venus in your 4th House until the 19th makes this an excellent period to patch up family relationships, work from the home, entertain from home and otherwise beautify and decorate the home. Mercury's retrograde in your 4th House (from the 18th to the 31st) reinforces the need to wrap up these projects early on and be especially careful of how you communicate to family members. Miscommunication is likely to be the biggest cause of disharmony there – not lack of love or caring.

Mercury's retrograde affects finances as well. Financial judgement is not up to its usual standard and you must be extra careful when making large purchases or investments. Earnings seem more difficult during this period. Social demands don't seem to mesh well with your financial needs and goals. A lover might resent the time you spend on financial issues. Avoid overspending on social matters.

Love is getting much better as two powerful planets start moving forward in your House of love. Your social confidence is improving. The direction of a current relationship is clarified. But the storms are not over. Family, domestic and financial issues come between you and the lover. There is a battle of wills going on as well – your lover wants to do one thing, you want to do another. If you can weather the short-term stress things will get better next month. The long-term outlook on love is very positive.

The full Moon of the 13th gives you extra energy to achieve academic and religious goals. The new Moon of the 27th will clarify emotional and domestic concerns.

November

Best Days Overall: 8th, 9th, 17th, 18th, 26th, 27th

Most Stressful Days Overall: 3rd, 4th, 10th, 11th, 23rd, 24th

Best Days for Love: 3rd, 4th, 8th, 9th, 13th, 19th, 20th, 21st, 22nd, 28th, 29th

Best Days for Money: 3rd, 4th, 6th, 7th, 12th, 13th, 16th, 19th, 20th, 21st, 22nd, 23rd, 24th, 30th

Though this is an exciting career month, Leo, with many planets below the Horizon and your 4th House powerful, you must handle career issues but place your focus on the home and family. The attainment of emotional harmony will help your career in the long run.

Venus, your Career Planet, is 'out of bounds' all month. You are venturing into strange and unknown areas in career matters – perhaps breaking with established tradition in the pursuit of career objectives. A parent or elder is also embarking on a strange course during this period.

Venus travels very close to the South Node towards the end of the month, perhaps making you obsessive in the pursuit of career and work objectives – the danger is of losing your identity because of runaway ambition.

Most of the planets are now in the West, making this a more social month. The good graces of others become ever more important in attaining your goals as the months progress. Love is still stormy and conflicted early in the month, but becomes happy and harmonious again after the 22nd. Good relationships will easily weather the storms. The domestic situation can also be volatile early in the month. This too will pass when the Sun moves into jovial Sagittarius on the 22nd. Expect to make important psychological breakthroughs this month. That is the purpose behind all of this.

LEO

Health is stressful until the 22nd, so rest and relax more. Focus on essentials and let lesser things go. Health and vitality rebound strongly after the 22nd.

After the 22nd you enter into a party period. Optimism returns. There are amusements, entertainments, sporting events and parties. There is more dealing with children and children's issues, and your creativity will be at a yearly high.

Finances are improving after the 8th as your Financial Planet begins to move forward. Your financial judgement is penetrating and your confidence is sound. But there are financial disagreements and disputes with your spouse or partner which need to be resolved. Too much focus on money-making is not helping your love life. On the other hand, love cannot so dominate you that you ignore your financial well-being. Tread the middle ground.

December

Best Days Overall: 6th, 7th, 14th, 15th, 23rd, 24th

Most Stressful Days Overall: 1st, 2nd, 8th, 9th, 20th, 21st, 22nd, 28th, 29th

Best Days for Love: 1st, 2nd, 10th, 11th, 18th, 19th, 28th, 29th

Best Days for Money: 1st, 6th, 7th, 10th, 11th, 14th, 15th, 16th, 17th, 18th, 25th, 26th, 28th

The planets are mostly in the West, and your 7th House of Love is unusually strong after the 8th. Avoid power struggles, develop your social graces and don't try to change situations too much. Adapt, compromise and seek consensus. Good comes from the good graces of others and not so much through your personal efforts.

By the 8th the planetary power will be evenly distributed between the upper and lower halves of your Horoscope (there's only a slight bias to the upper half). This is a period for juggling and balancing career and family duties. Both are more or less equally important and you can't lean too far one way or the other.

Every Solar Eclipse is important to you, Leo, but the one on the 25th seems especially significant. Every Solar Eclipse produces a change of the image, a re-evaluation and redefinition of the personality, and physical cleansings. This one is not different. But this Eclipse occurs in your 6th House of Health and Work, signalling long-term changes in these areas. For many of you this shows a job change – ultimately good – but which can be disruptive initially. Many of you will change doctors, health plans and health regimes. Those of you who have been experiencing health problems will confront a healing crisis. The condition will seem to get worse before it dissolves. This Eclipse affects finances as well, Leo. Mercury, your Financial Planet, gets eclipsed. Thus you are making long-term changes in investments, brokers, bankers and/or financial planners. Your financial strategy will change. Job changes also relate to the changes in your financial goals. Take a reduced schedule two days before and for a day after this Eclipse. Try to schedule holiday travel around the Eclipse – arrive at your destination earlier than you might otherwise have planned, and leave a little later.

Aside from the Eclipse phenomena, finances will be strong most of the month – especially before the 23rd. You are earning more and spending more. You are buying toys – both as gifts for others and for yourself. Speculations are favourable. There is great financial optimism. You will be a smarter shopper after the 23rd than before.

Love is still very exciting these days, though unstable. Sudden love opportunities come around the 12th and the 24th. An office romance is a strong possibility.

Health is reasonable. As mentioned, take things easy around the time of the Eclipse.

Virgo

♍

THE VIRGIN

Birthdays from
22nd August
to 22nd September

Personality Profile

VIRGO AT A GLANCE

Element – Earth

Ruling Planet – Mercury
  Career Planet – Mercury
  Love Planet – Neptune
  Money Planet – Venus
  Planet of Home and Family Life – Jupiter
  Planet of Health and Work – Uranus
  Planet of Pleasure – Saturn
  Planet of Sexuality – Mars

Colours – earth tones, ochre, orange, yellow

Colour that promotes love, romance and social harmony – aqua blue

Colour that promotes earning power – jade green

Gems – agate, hyacinth

Metal – quicksilver

Scents – lavender, lilac, lily of the valley, storax

Quality – mutable (= flexibility)

Quality most needed for balance – a broader perspective

Strongest virtues – mental agility, analytical skills, ability to pay attention to detail, healing powers

Deepest needs – to be useful and productive

Characteristic to avoid – destructive criticism

Signs of greatest overall compatibility – Taurus, Capricorn

Signs of greatest overall incompatibility – Gemini, Sagittarius, Pisces

Sign most helpful to career – Gemini

Sign most helpful for emotional support – Sagittarius

Sign most helpful financially – Libra

Sign best for marriage and/or partnerships – Pisces

Sign most helpful for creative projects – Capricorn

Best Sign to have fun with – Capricorn

Signs most helpful in spiritual matters – Taurus, Leo

Best day of the week – Wednesday

Understanding the Virgo Personality

The virgin is a particularly fitting symbol for those born under the Sign of Virgo. If you meditate on the image of the virgin you will get a good understanding of the essence of the Virgo type. The virgin is, of course, a symbol of purity and innocence – not naïve, but pure. A virginal object has not been touched. A virgin field is land that is true to itself, the way it has always been. The same is true of virgin forest: it is pristine, unaltered.

Apply the idea of purity to the thought processes, emotional life, physical body, and activities and projects of the everyday world, and you can see how Virgos approach life. Virgos desire the pure expression of the ideal in their mind, body and affairs. If they find impurities they will attempt to clear them away.

Impurities are the beginning of disorder, unhappiness and uneasiness. The job of the Virgo is to eject all impurities and keep only that which the body and mind can use and assimilate.

The secrets of good health are here revealed: 90 per cent of the art of staying well is maintaining a pure mind, a pure body and pure emotions. When you introduce more impurities than your mind and body can deal with, you will have what is known as 'dis-ease'. It is no wonder that Virgos make great doctors, nurses, healers and dietitians. They have an innate understanding of good health and they realize that good health is more than just physical. In all aspects of life, if you want a project to be successful it must be kept as pure as possible. It must be protected against the adverse elements that will try to undermine it. This is the secret behind Virgo's awesome technical proficiency.

One could talk about Virgo's analytical powers – which are formidable. One could talk about their perfectionism and their almost superhuman attention to detail. But this would be to miss the point. All of these virtues are manifestations of a Virgo's desire for purity and perfection – a world without Virgos would have ruined itself long ago.

A vice is nothing more than a virtue turned inside out, misapplied or used in the wrong context. Virgos' apparent vices come from their inherent virtue. Their analytical powers, which should be used for healing, helping or perfecting a project in the world, sometimes get misapplied and turned against people. Their critical faculties, which should be used constructively to perfect a strategy or proposal, can sometimes be used destructively to harm or wound. Their urge to perfection can turn into worry and lack of confidence; their natural humility can become self-denial and self-abasement. When Virgos turn negative they are apt to turn their devastating criticism on themselves, sowing the seeds of self-destruction.

Finance

Virgos have all the attitudes that create wealth. They are hard-working, industrious, efficient, organized, thrifty, productive and eager to serve. A developed Virgo is every employer's dream. But until Virgos master some of the social graces of Libra they will not even come close to fulfilling their financial potential. Purity and perfectionism, if not handled correctly or gracefully, can be very trying to others. Friction in human relationships can be devastating not only to your pet projects but – indirectly – to your wallet as well.

Virgos are quite interested in their financial security. Being hard-working, they know the true value of money. They do not like to take risks with their money, preferring to save for their retirement or for a rainy day. Virgos usually make prudent, calculated investments that involve a minimum of risk. These investments and savings usually work out well, helping Virgos to achieve the financial security they seek. The rich or even not-so-rich Virgo also likes to help his or her friends in need.

Career and Public Image

Virgos reach their full potential when they can communicate their knowledge in such a way that others can understand it. In order to get their ideas across better, Virgos need to develop greater verbal skills and fewer judgemental ways of expressing themselves. Virgos look up to teachers and communicators; they like their bosses to be good communicators. Virgos will probably not respect a superior who is not their intellectual equal – no matter how much money or power that superior has. Virgos themselves like to be perceived by others as being educated and intellectual.

The natural humility of Virgos often inhibits them from fulfilling their great ambitions, from acquiring name and fame. Virgos should indulge in a little more self-promotion if they are going to reach their career goals. They need to push themselves with the same ardour that they would use to foster others.

At work Virgos like to stay active. They are willing to learn any type of job as long as it serves their ultimate goal of financial security. Virgos may change occupations several times during their professional lives, until they find the one they really enjoy. Virgos work well with other people, are not afraid to work hard and always fulfil their responsibilities.

Love and Relationships

If you are an analyst or a critic you must, out of necessity, narrow your scope. You have to focus on a part and not the whole; this can create a temporary narrow-mindedness. Virgos do not like this kind of person. They like their partners to be broad-minded, with depth and vision. Virgos seek to get this broad-minded quality from their partners, since they sometimes lack it themselves.

Virgos are perfectionists in love just as they are in other areas of life. They need partners who are tolerant, open-minded and easy-going. If you are in love with a Virgo do not waste time on impractical romantic gestures. Do practical and useful things for him or her – this is what will be appreciated and what will be done for you.

Virgos express their love through pragmatic and useful gestures, so do not be put off because your Virgo partner does not say 'I love you' day-in and day-out. Virgos are not that type. If they love you, they will demonstrate it in practical ways. They will always be there for you; they will show an interest in your health and finances; they will fix your sink or repair your video recorder. Virgos deem these actions to be superior to sending flowers, chocolates or St Valentine's cards.

In love affairs Virgos are not particularly passionate or spontaneous. If you are in love with a Virgo, do not take this personally. It does not mean that you are not alluring enough or that your Virgo partner does not love or like you. It is just the way Virgos are. What they lack in passion they make up for in dedication and loyalty.

Home and Domestic Life

It goes without saying that the home of a Virgo will be spotless, sanitized and orderly. Everything will be in its proper place – and don't you dare move anything about! For Virgos to find domestic bliss they need to ease up a bit in the home, to allow their partner and kids more freedom and to be more generous and open-minded. Family members are not to be analysed under a microscope, they are individuals with their own virtues to express.

With these small difficulties resolved, Virgos like to stay in and entertain at home. They make good hosts and they like to keep their friends and families happy and entertained at family and social gatherings. Virgos love children, but they are strict with them – at times – since they want to make sure their children are brought up with the correct sense of family and values.

Horoscope for 2000

Major Trends

Love and libido were very important in 1999, and this trend continues for a while in the year 2000. Many of you succeeded in getting out of debt last year – or if you didn't pay it off completely made serious progress with it. This trend also continues in the coming year.

Work, always important to you, is now (and for years to come) even more important. There are great changes going on in the workplace and in your attitude towards work. Serial job changes are occurring.

Those of you who are students faced rough going in 1999. You worked unusually hard at your studies. You had to earn good marks, and the experiences at university were less than benign. But when Jupiter moves into your 9th House on 15th February, this will start to change. Education becomes happier, studying goes better and good marks are easier to attain. This transit also shows more foreign travel and happy educational opportunities for those who are not students.

But the most important trend this year is the career. Both Jupiter and Saturn will cross the Midheaven of your chart in the summer. Jupiter crosses on 1st July, and Saturn on 11th August. (Saturn will make two moves over this point – this one, going forward, and a backward-moving one on 27th October). Pay rises, promotions, fortunate job offers and career changes are in the works. True, you will have to work hard, but there are also great rewards – both financially and in terms of status.

Your paths to greatest fulfilment this year are spirituality, charity, friends and group activities, (from 1st January to 15th February) paying off debt and reinventing yourself, (from 15th February to 1st July) foreign travel, higher education, religion and philosophy, and (from 1st July to 31st December), career.

Health

Health is always important to you, but this year (and for years to come) it seems ultra-important. This is an unusual focus for you, Virgo. Your 6th House is an important House of Power and there is much ferment and change going on here.

Like last year we see changes of attitude towards health and important breakthroughs in your understating of it. Uranus in your House of Health makes you very experimental in this area. You find new therapies, healing techniques, health technologies, diets, pills, potions and 'miracle' foods unusually alluring. You want to try them all. There is an almost complete break with orthodox and traditional medicine. This kind of experimentation has its upside and downside. On the positive end, it yields – through trial and error – great knowledge about health. You learn what things your body responds to. You learn how to clear up perennial problems. On the negative side, this can be very expensive, with many false leads and hopes. Follow your intuition in your experimentation. Change in order to upgrade and improve – don't change merely for the sake of change. If something is working for you, stay with it.

Neptune is now firmly established in your House of Health, indicating the importance of spiritual and metaphysical techniques and their importance on health. Neptune will show you that there is really only *one* disease – though it produces all the others. This disease is lack of energy. Lack of energy can occur for many reasons, but the primary and root reason is a lack of connection to our inner source of power – the Higher Power, or life-force – within. Neptune will teach you (after you've finished experimenting with every physical method under the sun) how to re-establish your connection with this power and let it re-charge your cells and bodily systems.

Neptune in your House of Health also has other messages. It is the most spiritual planet. It is the planet of the Divine Will. Thus it reveals how the Higher Power gets your attention. Health problems are not what they seem for you – they are only calls to get into closer unity with the Higher Power. Once this is done, the health problem will usually disappear. Neptune is also your Love Planet. Thus health problems probably have some love issue at their root. Explore the relationship issue, cleanse it, forgive yourself and the other and restore harmony, and the health problem will in all likelihood clear up by itself.

The Higher Power is training your intuition through health and love issues now.

It is good that you are focusing on health and are very involved in health regimes and exercise now – even though your health is excellent for the first half of the year. Come the summer when both Jupiter and Saturn start making inharmonious aspects to you, your regime will be tested. If it's a good one, you'll come through with flying colours. If it's a bad one, the facts of life will force you to change it.

The 11th August to 27th October is the most stressful health period during this coming year. Be sure to rest and relax more then.

Home and Domestic Life

Your 4th House of Home and Family is an important House of Power this year and for years to come. Add to this unusual movements of Jupiter (your Family Planet) and its once-in-20-years conjunction to Saturn, and you have a very interesting domestic year ahead.

Pluto in your 4th House all year suggests deep psychological growth and transformation. The deep mysteries of the subconscious mind are being revealed – the deep origins of most of your feelings and day-to-day habit patterns. Great emotional cleansing is happening.

Pluto in your 4th also suggests (and there is a strong connection to what is said above) deep and major renovations of the home. These are not cosmetic things, such as new paintwork or the rearranging of furniture – but a radical overhaul of the home. Wires and walls are being ripped out – perhaps old plumbing is being ripped out and replaced with new. Many of you moved house in the past year, but if not, it could still happen this year.

Pluto is Lord of your 3rd House of Neighbours and Siblings. This suggests that your domestic situation is changing because of developments in your neighbourhood – or that you have different neighbours who impact on your day-to-day lifestyle. Perhaps new construction work is going on in your neighbourhood that unduly impacts on your home, or perhaps the character and flavour of your neighbourhood is changing.

Jupiter in your 8th House until 15th February reinforces the psychological progress and the radical renovations written of earlier. Important changes have happened in your relations with family and family members in the past year – seems like an emotional separation – and this trend continues until 15th February. The family pattern has changed dramatically.

Jupiter's move into your 9th House on 15th February is a very positive emotional and domestic indicator. It shows expansion of the home, a happy move, new additions to the family and the fortunate sale or purchase of a home. Emotions, moods and feelings will tend to be upbeat and positive. There is greater emotional stability during this period (15th February to 1st July). You can enjoy the psychological progress you've made.

On 1st July, Jupiter will cross your Midheaven – a very powerful and important transit. This could show a move related to your career, or the career advancement of family members. It also indicates that your top priority is placed on home and domestic issues, the need to make your home a show place and a status symbol. Your family supports your career activities and vice versa. Many of you will decide to make the family and home your career, and will leave the corporate world. Many of you will decide to work from home. Inner, psychological progress becomes just as important as career progress.

Jupiter and Saturn will go conjunct in late May. This could show new children or grandchildren and the beginning of a new domestic cycle. Adult children could move house.

Love and Social Life

1998 was your most important love year. Jupiter moved through your House of Marriage, and your Love Planet (Neptune) changed Signs after many years in Capricorn. Not only did your relationships expand – many of you married or got involved in serious relationships – but your whole attitude to love changed. You found a new freedom in this area. This attitudinal change is still going on now.

Though many of you have found love, there is still much work to be done. The Lunar Eclipse of 21st January is going to force flaws in your relationship to the surface so that they can be corrected. Singles could still marry in the coming months as well, as the Eclipse shows a change in the marital status. Love becomes very disruptive to your normal habit patterns.

Neptune travels in conjunction with the South Node of the Moon during the early part of the year. For married people this shows intense, instinctual – almost addictive – sexuality. For singles, it shows addictive – almost obsessive – love relationships. The hunger for the object of love is so intense that one can think of little else. It dominates the whole mind and attention. Even you workaholic Virgos will have trouble focusing on work during this period. Singles can elope, marry out of instinct without taking into account costs or side issues such as lifestyle, cultural differences or domestic compatibility. Virgo will learn the power of a love addiction this year. It will overpower all your vaunted discernment and critical faculties – it will swallow you up.

High-speed love has its thrills. But high speeds also increase the likelihood of crashes. And these will be the test of love. True love will weather these inevitable crashes. Superficial love won't.

Your Love Planet in the 6th House of Health and Work shows that you find love at the workplace, perhaps with a fellow worker, boss or employee – it all depends on your status. Some of you will find it at the doctor's surgery, or while visiting someone in hospital – it could also be with someone involved in your health.

Love also flourishes from 19th February to 6th April.

The marriage of a sibling has been stressed out lately; this can change after 15th February. Either the current relationship improves or there is a new marriage. A parent could remarry after the summer. The marital status of children of marriageable age could change around 1st July, as the Solar Eclipse changes attitudes and feelings.

Virgos working towards a second marriage face an important opportunity from 15th February to 1st July. This will not be a smooth ride, though, and there could be many delays. There is much mistrust and fear to overcome.

Those working towards a third marriage will probably see the status quo maintained this year.

Career and Finance

Your 2nd House of Money is not a House of Power this year, Virgo, so earnings are not a big priority. Probably you are satisfied and have no need to give this undue attention. Though you will undoubtedly be earning more money this year, these extra earnings come almost as a side-effect to career advancement and increased education.

The career becomes important in the summer as both Jupiter and Saturn cross your Midheaven point. Jupiter crosses on 1st July and will be in your Career House for the rest of the year. This signals pay rises and promotions, fortunate job changes or job offers, travelling related to the career, and the favour of elders, authorities, parents and bosses.

Of course every elevation of status brings more work and responsibility – and this is shown by Saturn crossing the Midheaven twice – on 11th August and 27th October. Jupiter bestows the glory and honour, Saturn demands the results.

Saturn crossing the Midheaven often indicates dealings with the government. On the surface these could look fearsome, but Jupiter nearby assures that the best-case scenario will be the outcome.

It would be wise to take all the educational opportunities available until the summer, as these will pay off afterwards.

Jupiter will be in your 8th House of Other People's Money until 15th February. It was there for most of 1999 as well. As mentioned earlier, this increases your access to outside capital, enables you to attract investors to your projects and helps to you pay off debt. If there are tax issues with the government, best-case scenarios will be the result. If there are legal issues with insurers or involving property, there is fortunate news.

Your spouse or business partner prospers greatly and seems generous with you. Your spouse is more money-focused than you are.

Self-improvement

Health, psychology and religious and metaphysical beliefs are the main areas that will be improved in your life this year. All of these things relate to each other, and when one improves the others automatically flourish. Now, as a Virgo you will probably feel that health is the most important area to work on. But really it is your metaphysical and philosophical beliefs that are most important. When these are fine-tuned, corrected and aligned with reality there will be an automatic improvement in your physical and emotional health. Philosophy (your world view) is much more important than psychology, for the first causes the other and not vice versa.

Psychology deals with how you feel and the memories associated with it. But philosophy deals with your interpretation of events, which shapes how you feel.

Much new and happy metaphysical knowledge is coming to you this year – and there will be opportunities to study more. This area is worth your attention, and meditation.

Saturn, moving briefly into your 10th House of Career, shows ambition and hard work. Now for most people this would be a hard transit. For you it will be a snap. What Virgo is afraid of hard work? But you will probably have to deal with a hard and demanding boss – briefly this year, but for the long-term from next year. So, the challenge will be to deal with these demands in a way that preserves your health, sanity and well-being. Our advice – give the dictator more than he or she asks for.

Month-by-month Forecasts

January

Best Days Overall: 5th, 6th, 7th, 15th, 16th, 23rd, 24th

Most Stressful Days Overall: 3rd, 4th, 10th, 11th, 17th, 18th, 30th, 31st

Best Days for Love: 3rd, 4th, 8th, 10th, 11th, 13th, 17th, 14th, 22nd, 25th

Best Days for Money: 3rd, 4th, 13th, 14th, 21st, 22nd, 25th, 26th, 30th, 31st

Between 60 and 70 per cent of the planets are still below the Horizon of the chart during this period (though this percentage is getting ready to change in the coming months), so you still need to find your emotional comfort zone and to function from there. This is more important than outer, career success. Feeling right leads to doing right.

Between 80 and 90 per cent of the planets are in the Western, social sector of your chart, showing that this is a month for attaining social goals, for compromise and getting your way through negotiating and gaining the good graces of others. Self-assertion will delay your good luck.

With 90 to 100 per cent of the planets moving forward – including Mercury, your Ruler – this is a month of progress and forward momentum in your life. Just remember that your good is coming from others now.

The Lunar Eclipse of the 21st deals kindly with you. It occurs in your 12th House of Spirituality. Thus there are shake-ups and disruptions in charities, ministries or spiritual organizations that you are involved with. Spiritually-orientated Virgos are changing gurus or meditative techniques now. There could be disruptions with a friend or a professional organization. All of these disruptions are good as they will lead to a better pattern later on.

The new Moon of the 5th occurs in your 5th House of Love Affairs, creativity and children. You can expect that all these areas will clarify as the month progresses. The Moon will illuminate and bring the necessary knowledge to take any needed decision.

Love is active but stormy during this period. Mars moving into your House of Love and Marriage on the 4th shows a power struggle in a current relationship. This relationship is in trouble right now. For singles (those uninvolved) it shows great social aggressiveness. But these things should be resolved by the 20th when a new idealism – a new attitude towards love – starts taking hold. Only a Higher Power can resolve certain problems. And, a Higher Power has selected someone to be your mate and companion – trust its guidance.

Finances are strong all month. Be careful of debt around the 9th. Sales and marketing bring profits during this period. Investing in the home from the 1st to the 24th seems like a good idea – especially if you're decorating or buying objects of beauty. But be careful of overspending – your financial judgement can be over-optimistic. After the 24th sound, rational judgement returns. Your investment skill is strong. Money comes through creativity and through calculated, well-hedged risks.

February

Best Days Overall: 2nd, 3rd, 11th, 12th, 19th, 20th, 29th

Most Stressful Days Overall: 7th, 8th, 13th, 14th, 26th, 27th, 28th

Best Days for Love: 2nd, 3rd, 4th, 7th, 8th, 11th, 13th, 12th, 22nd, 23rd

Best Days for Money: 2nd, 3rd, 9th, 10th, 11th, 12th, 19th, 22nd, 23rd, 29th

All the planets (with the exception of the Moon, and that for only two weeks out of the month) are in the Western, social sector of your chart. Mercury, your Ruling Planet, goes retrograde from the 21st onwards. And while this will be a month of great change, progress and achievement – it will happen through others and not from your personal or wilful efforts. Adapt to situations, exercise your social skills, avoid self-assertion and the Great Current of Life will carry you, effortlessly, to your heart's desire.

Perhaps it is good that Mercury's retrograde weakens your self-confidence somewhat. If you were too confident you might spoil things.

The Solar Eclipse of the 5th is kind to you, though it might bring a job change. Employers might see shake-ups in their staff over the coming months. The Eclipse also affects those of you on a spiritual path. Gurus, meditation techniques and your status in a spiritual organization will change for the long term.

Finances will be happy this month, though you seem swallowed up by minutiae from the 21st to the 23rd. This period signals an important business partnership or some financial negotiation with your spouse or partner. Money comes from social contacts and partners as well as work. Financial success can come suddenly – out of the blue. Financial intuition needs confirmation from the 21st to the 23rd. Dreams and visions are not necessarily what they seem.

The power struggle in a current relationship still seems intense. You seem to be the one compromising – which is probably the right thing to do. Your social life is active and passionate. Singles are meeting significant others after the 20th.

On an overall level your health is good and will improve as the months progress, but rest and relax more after the 20th. Cater to other people by all means, but don't give more than your capacity or endanger your health.

Jupiter, your Family Planet, makes an important move from Aries into Taurus on the 15th. Thus a long-term shift of mood is happening. Moods are calmer and more stable – at least you are working towards that. Thoughts are turning to expanding the home or acquiring new properties. Family members are going off to university or travelling more.

March

Best Days Overall: 1st, 9th, 10th, 18th, 19th, 27th, 28th, 29th

Most Stressful Days Overall: 5th, 6th, 12th, 25th, 26th

Best Days for Love: 3rd, 4th, 5th, 6th, 12th, 13th, 20th, 22nd, 23rd, 30th

Best Days for Money: 1st, 3rd, 4th, 9th, 10th, 12th, 13th, 18th, 19th, 20th, 21st, 22nd, 23rd, 27th, 28th

With Mercury (your Ruling Planet) retrograde, and with 90 to 100 per cent of the planets in the West, avoid power struggles like the plague. Your social grace will carry you to heights that sheer force of will could never dream of. This is an important and happy social month. Let other people and their interests come first.

By the 13th, 60 to 70 per cent of the planets will be above the Horizon, showing an ever increasing interest in career and worldly activities. With Mercury (also your Career Planet) retrograde until the 14th, this is a good period for reviewing, re-evaluating and setting career goals. Executing these plans can come later.

Though Mercury is retrograde this is still a month of great personal progress and achievement, as 90 per cent of the planets are in forward motion. But progress will come from and through others.

Your important areas of interest this month are health and work, love and social activities, transformation, the libido, debts and their repayment, helping others to prosper, religion, philosophy, higher education, foreign travel and foreign affairs.

Health is superb on an overall level, but rest and relax more until the 20th. You will start feeling more zippy and self-confident when Mercury goes forward on the 14th, and really energetic when the Sun enters Aries on the 20th. Health and financial issues are unusually connected until the 13th. Many of you are more concerned with financial health than with physical health. Many of you are spending more on health products now – and perhaps investing in health industries. Job-seekers have excellent prospects until the 13th. After that the prospects are average.

Finances are strong this month as Venus gets electrified as it passes Uranus. Money comes out of the blue – when you least expect it. Money comes from work, perhaps from overtime opportunities, and from co-workers. After the 13th, money comes through your spouse or lover – or through social contacts. Social affairs play a big role in earnings after the 13th. Parties and social gatherings boost your bank balance.

Love is active and happy now. Like last month, there is a tendency to be obsessive about it – a feeling of being addicted to love or to the beloved. As time goes on this feeling will ease up, but for now it is intense. Love is both practical and idealistic during this period. You want romance and all the niceties, but also someone who can help you attain financial goals and feel secure. Spiritual compatibility is still very important.

April

Best Days Overall: 6th, 7th, 14th, 15th, 24th, 25th

Most Stressful Days Overall: 1st, 2nd, 8th, 9th, 21st, 22nd, 29th, 30th

Best Days for Love: 1st, 2nd, 8th, 12th, 13th, 16th, 21st, 22nd, 26th, 27th, 29th, 30th

Best Days for Money: 1st, 2nd, 6th, 7th, 12th, 13th, 14th, 15th, 16th, 17th, 18th, 21st, 22nd, 24th, 25th

A happy month in a happy year. With 90 to 100 per cent of the planets in the Western sector – including Mercury, your Ruler – your social popularity should be at an all time high. Much good comes this month, through others and their good graces. Your way is probably not the best way during this period. Let the Great Current of Life carry you effortlessly to your goals. People will think of you as lucky during this period, but you are merely reaping the rewards of past actions.

Though home and family issues are going to be active during this period, with most of the planets now above the Horizon you should focus more on your career and outer life. Handle the domestic things that come up, then go right back to your career activities.

With 90 per cent of the planets in forward motion – including Mercury, your Ruler – this is a month of great forward momentum and progress. If anything, things move too quickly for your taste.

From the 13th to the 19th there is a dominance of Fire in the Horoscope. People around you move in a euphoria. They act impulsively and quickly, without thought to costs or consequences. This is a bit uncomfortable for you as you are a more cautious type – costs and consequences are important to you. Your mentality is a bit out of favour during this period, but hold on and don't give in, you are vindicated after the 19th.

The North Node of the Moon shifts (on the 10th) from your 12th House of Spirituality to your 11th House of Friends and Groups. Thus there is much fulfilment in these areas in the coming year.

Now that the South Node of the Moon has moved away from Neptune love is calmer and happier – less addictive – less compulsive. You can love and still be your own person. Venus in your 7th House of Love brings romance for singles. For others it brings parties, social gatherings and an expansion of the social sphere. Mercury leaves your 7th House on the 13th, making love less romantic but more passionate and sexual.

Health is superb all month – but especially after the 19th. You have so much energy these days you could raise the dead.

Finances are strong all month, but especially after the 6th. This is a good period to pay off debt or refinance existing debts at more favourable rates. You will prosper as you help others prosper. Your own financial interests and those of others are not separate things as you have thought – they are one, inextricably intertwined. Your spouse or partner is more generous with you during this period. Those of you seeking outside capital meet with success. Tax issues end in best-case scenarios.

May

Best Days Overall: 3rd, 4th, 12th, 13th, 21st, 22nd, 31st

Most Stressful Days Overall: 5th, 6th, 18th, 19th, 20th, 26th, 27th

Best Days for Love: 3rd, 4th, 5th, 12th, 13th, 14th, 15th, 22nd, 23rd, 24th, 26th, 27th

Best Days for Money: 3rd, 4th, 12th, 13th, 14th, 15th, 21st, 22nd, 23rd, 31st

The increase in retrograde activity this month will not stop the progress and achievement in your life, but only slow it down somewhat. Major developments in education and career are happening now.

This is a major career month, a yearly career peak. Most of the planets are above the Horizon and your 10th House is a strong House of Power. And though important developments are happening with the home and family, your main focus should be your career.

This month the planetary power makes an important shift from the Western to the Eastern sector of your chart. This signals a shift in attitude. You are becoming ever more independent and self-reliant as the months go by. More and more you have the power to create conditions rather than just adapt to them. More and more you are being empowered to have things your way. Pleasing the self becomes more important than pleasing others. If you truly please yourself, you will find – magically – that others are also pleased.

The important areas of interest this month are health and work, religion, philosophy, higher education and foreign travel, and the career.

Jupiter and Saturn's conjunction in your 9th House is a very powerful and benefic financial signal for the next 20 or so years. A new business cycle is being born on the planet and you are right in synch with it. You are entering a long-term prosperity period. You will have your ups and downs over the next 20 years to be sure, but the trend will be towards prosperity.

Jupiter and Saturn also have other meanings in your chart. Jupiter is your Family Planet and Saturn is your Planet of Children. This conjunction signals greater fertility for Virgo and a general expansion of the family through births and marriage.

For singles this shows a love affair, which may or may not result in marriage but which will linger for many years. The torch will be carried inside regardless of your marital status.

A new religious and philosophical cycle is being born in many of you. A new world view and personal philosophy grips you and will probably hold you for years to come.

Rest and relax more after the 20th. Career demands are stressful (probably intensely competitive) but necessary. Pace yourself and focus on essentials.

June

Best Days Overall: 8th, 9th, 17th, 18th, 19th, 27th, 28th

Most Stressful Days Overall: 2nd, 15th, 16th, 22nd, 23rd, 29th, 30th

Best Days for Love: 2nd, 10th, 11th, 20th, 21st, 22nd, 23rd, 29th

Best Days for Money: 2nd, 8th, 9th, 10th, 11th, 17th, 18th, 19th, 22nd, 23rd, 27th, 28th

VIRGO

The planets are shifting eastward, giving you more independence and self-reliance. But Mercury's retrograde weakens this somewhat. It's a good idea to review your personal goals and objectives – fine-tune them – and then launch into action when Mercury moves forward next month. If you are already clear on your personal goals, launch your projects before the 23rd.

Most of the planets are still above the Horizon so it is still safe to let go of domestic and psychological issues and focus on the career.

The 10th House of Career is a House of Power until the 21st. Career demands are intense. You are working hard. Important career breakthroughs are happening this month and you have great courage and tenacity in pursuing them. You shine in career activities. Higher-ups are favourably disposed towards you but they demand 'deeds' as well as words.

After the 21st your 11th House of Friends and Groups becomes powerful. This is an excellent social period – though not necessarily a romantic one. You are dealing with people of like mind, with platonic relationships, rather than relationships of the heart. New breakthroughs come in astrology and science.

Love is on hold right now, though there is plentiful opportunity until the 21st. The zest and enthusiasm seem lacking as Neptune's retrograde makes you more cautious and doubtful of your judgement. Love needs to develop and grow. Don't try to overtest it – let the normal circumstances of life test it. Don't try to rush things either. Time is your best friend in love.

Finances are stable this month, though they seem stronger before the 21st than afterwards. Career and professional status seem more important than money these days. Money comes as a result of your good reputation and professional status. Elders, bosses, friends and higher-ups are financially supportive and provide you with earnings opportunities. Your Money Planet's move into the Sign of Cancer on the

18th suggests moodiness in finances. You earn according to your mood and spend that way too. In an overly optimistic mood you can overspend, in a down mood you can reject or bypass a significant opportunity. Try to sleep on things before taking any important financial decision. This is especially important for investors or traders. The upside is that when you are in a serene and stable frame of mind your financial intuition will be uncanny.

Health is excellent long term, but rest and relax more until the 21st.

July

Best Days Overall: 5th, 6th, 15th, 16th, 24th, 25th

Most Stressful Days Overall: 12th, 13th, 20th, 21st, 26th, 27th

Best Days for Love: 1st, 2nd, 7th, 8th, 10th, 11th, 17th, 20th, 21st, 22nd, 23rd, 26th, 27th, 30th, 31st

Best Days for Money: 1st, 2nd, 6th, 7th, 8th, 10th, 11th, 14th, 15th, 22nd, 23rd, 25th, 26th, 30th, 31st

Though there are three Eclipses this month and major changes are happening all around you, you sail right through. They deal kindly with you. In fact, the disruptions they cause create opportunities for you.

Jupiter makes a major move into your 10th House on the 1st – another major – and happy – development in your life. With most of the planets above the Horizon of your chart you are unusually ambitious. Jupiter is going to ensure that your ambitions succeed. Though the career is ultra-important you won't be able to ignore home and family issues as these two areas of your life are inter-related. Many of you are choosing family life as a career these days. Others are experiencing an expansion of the family circle through births and marriage. Still others are learning to integrate emotional comfort with a successful career. Both your career and family life should be happy during this period.

The Solar Eclipse of the 1st occurs in your 11th House and causes long-term changes with friends and with organizations to which you belong. Internal shake-ups in the organization affect your relationships there. A flawed friendship (which you never knew was flawed) can go by the wayside.

The Lunar Eclipse of the 16th occurs in your 5th House of Children, Creativity and Love Affairs. Since the 5th House also rules speculation, avoid this now. This Eclipse is kind to you so the disruptions are actually helping. A flawed love affair or fun-and-game type of relationship can be disrupted – perhaps end. A creative project hits a snag which will ultimately improve it. A child goes off to university or gets married or moves house, causing a change in your relationship with him or her.

The Solar Eclipse of the 30th occurs in your 12th House of Spirituality, causing your dreamlife to be hyperactive and unreliable. Spiritual messages during this period (two days before and about a day after) are not to be relied on without confirmation. There is a change in your meditation practice or in your charitable giving. Shake-ups in your church or ministry could cause you to move on.

Finances will be stable but the Eclipse of the 1st does affect them.

Health is strong all month. Romantic love needs patience.

August

Best Days Overall: 1st, 2nd, 11th, 12th, 20th, 21st, 22nd, 29th, 30th

Most Stressful Days Overall: 8th, 9th, 16th, 17th, 23rd, 24th

Best Days for Love: 4th, 5th, 11th, 12th, 13th,
14th, 16th, 17th, 20th, 21st, 23rd, 29th, 30th, 31st

Best Days for Money: 3rd, 4th, 5th, 11th, 12th,
13th, 14th, 20th, 21st, 23rd, 24th, 29th, 30th, 31st

A hectic but unusually successful month, Virgo – enjoy.

Until the 22nd the planets are still mostly above the Horizon of your chart. Your 10th House of Career is very powerful as well. Thus important career developments are happening and it is good to focus your energy here. And though your 10th House of Career will still be powerful after the 22nd, there is a shift of planetary power below the Horizon. This complicates things. You have strong career demands, but also a strong need to deal with family and psychological issues. Inner and outer growth must be balanced in the coming months. The conflict between the home and the career will be dramatic. Stay in the middle.

Last month probably brought pay rises, promotions and expanded career horizons. This trend continues this month and for many months to come. But Saturn's move into your 10th House on the 11th shows that these gifts do not come free – there is increased responsibility as well. Power and authority must be used justly and dispassionately. The misuse of authority will backfire. This is going to be the lesson in the coming years.

The planets are now firmly in the East with many planets in your own Sign after the 23rd. Thus you are much more independent, self-reliant and self-contained these days. You can have things your way if you like. You create your destiny for a while. Create wisely. Spend some time early in the month on reviewing the past year. Acknowledge and then forgive past mistakes and set goals for the future. Create from a place of clarity of mind.

Until the 22nd it will be normal to feel that you want more seclusion, or that you are somewhat weary of the world. With career demands so strong this feeling is normal.

With much power in your 12th House of Spirituality you are wondering about the purpose of all this activity and worldliness – is this what life is all about? The Higher Power within has the answer if you consult it.

After the 22nd these feelings will pass and you will be more involved in the body, the image and personal pleasure. Love issues start improving as well. You look and feel great. Others take notice. You can have your way in love.

Finances are strong this month. Your Money Planet in your own Sign after the 6th indicates spending on yourself and for personal pleasures. It shows a personal control over earnings and over your financial destiny. You are an astute shopper and investor during this period. Money comes from work and personal effort – from taking the bull by the horns.

September

Best Days Overall: 7th, 8th, 17th, 18th, 25th, 26th

Most Stressful Days Overall: 5th, 6th, 12th, 13th, 19th, 20th

Best Days for Love: 1st, 10th, 11th, 12th, 13th, 19th, 20th, 27th, 28th, 30th

Best Days for Money: 1st, 10th, 11th, 19th, 20th, 27th, 28th, 30th

Health is improved over last month. Many planets in your own Sign are neutralizing the stress of the long-term planets. Mars in your own Sign after the 17th bestows energy, courage, enthusiasm and drive. You excel in exercise and athletic regimes.

Mars in your own Sign and most of the planets in the East give you a new and powerful sense of independence. You know what you want and you go after it with great energy. You are in no mood for compromise – nor should you, as you can have things your way now. Things get done quickly and, in spite of the increased retrograde activity, your personal progress is swift.

Though there is still tremendous growth and ferment in your career during this period, it seems safe to take a breather and focus on home, family and psychological issues. Most of the planets are below the Horizon, and the planets in your House of Career are retrograde.

Finding the balance between a satisfying and successful career and a happy home is going to be a major challenge for the next few years. This month you are getting a preview of things to come.

Finances are supercharged most of the month. Money is earned effortlessly. You catch the lucky breaks. Elders and people in authority are eager to grant favours – especially financial ones. Your financial intuition is especially keen during this period and you will most likely follow it. Charitable giving increases after the 22nd – and this is a good thing that enriches you even further. There is great financial enthusiasm and interest this month. The New Moon of the 27th helps you even further by clarifying prospective purchases, investments or financial confusion.

Your love life is active and happy and there is abundant romantic opportunity almost everywhere you turn. Your personal magnetism and self-confidence are truly impressive. But Neptune's retrograde urges caution and warns against taking all this attention too seriously. Love needs time to grow and develop. Romantic opportunities are not what they seem. Take time and let the circumstances of life test love.

Mind your temper after the 17th and try not to be in too much of a rush.

October

Best Days Overall: 4th, 5th, 6th, 14th, 15th, 23rd, 24th

VIRGO

Mixed signals in this month's Horoscope show many contradictory urges and desires. Things are not clear-cut or neatly packaged now. Half of the planets in the West urge you to compromise and adapt. Half of the planets in the East urge you to be independent. Mars in your own Sign makes you feel that you can do anything and be anything. The retrograde of Mercury, your Ruler, introduces doubt and an urge to review. Mars in Virgo urges you to rush and get things done in a hurry. Power in the 10th House urges you towards ambitions in the world, while Jupiter in that House urges you to build a stable home and family base. But there is a beautiful method behind all this madness. This is a month for balancing and for conscious action. All sides of an issue need to be looked at. Once clarity is attained, Mars and the planets in the East will give you the firepower needed to attain your ends. Or, if other action is called for, many planets in the West will help you adapt to and compromise with existing situations.

Though career issues are still very important this month, Saturn's retrograde out of your 10th House along with most planets below the Horizon are making your career less important than last month. Career progress needs to be balanced with emotional harmony and good family relationships.

Finances are still very strong this month. Your financial intuition carries you to the heights until the 23rd. Your Money Planet receives beautiful aspects, and money should come easily now. Money comes from writing, teaching, communication, sales and marketing. Neighbours and siblings are supportive of your financial goals. Money is earned close to home. Investors have a knack for the telecommunications and transportation sectors. Speculative success comes from high-tech goods, science and computers. Financial increase comes from property, restaurants, hotels and industries that cater to the home.

Love is starting to improve as your Love Planet, Neptune, starts moving forward after many months of retrograde activity. Your social confidence and judgement are getting stronger. A blow-up after the 23rd reveals the path you should take in love.

Health is reasonable this month. Mars in your own Sign gives you energy, vitality and athletic prowess. It also gives you the urge for dieting and detoxification regimes. There is much work on improving your image this month.

November

Best Days Overall: 1st, 2nd, 10th, 11th, 19th, 20th, 28th, 29th

Most Stressful Days Overall: 6th, 7th, 13th, 26th, 27th

Best Days for Love: 3rd, 4th, 6th, 7th, 8th, 9th, 13th, 19th, 20th, 21st, 22nd, 28th, 29th

Best Days for Money: 3rd, 4th, 8th, 9th, 12th, 13th, 19th, 20th, 21st, 22nd, 28th, 29th, 30th

Your financial drives are so strong as to be almost obsessive during this period. The lure of easy money can lead you into strange and untrodden spaces and even stranger behaviour. Be careful. While it is good to be experimental and be open to the new, take care not to be victimized. If you lose your identity and judgement then all is lost. Be especially careful in speculations. No matter how sure you think you are, don't wager more than you can afford to lose. Mars in your Money House and your Financial Planet 'out of bounds' can bring you money through unknown ways – but there are dangers. Temper aggressiveness with good judgement and a sound plan.

Most of the planets are shifting westward after the 22nd. You are in a more social period, where good comes through and from other people and not so much by your own efforts. Though your personal confidence is stronger after the 8th, you are not in a position to go it alone during this period. Adapt to situations and avoid power struggles.

Most of the planets are still above the Horizon, and after the 22nd there is power in your 10th House. Focus on career issues and let home and domestic activities take a back seat for a while. You are in a yearly career peak and you should make the most of it. Though your Career Planet is retrograde, it won't stop career progress now but perhaps delay things and force you to work a little harder. Charities and volunteer activities will boost your career during this period. So will sales, marketing and advertising.

There could be a pay rise during this period, or extra income that comes in other ways – you land a new client and earn extra commissions, or the boss gives you an extra (and unusual) perk or reimbursement.

Love is improved over last month. Conflicts are winding down. Your social confidence is getting stronger. Love opportunities for singles are abundant. Married people are meeting new friends and expanding socially. There is much love talk and communicating with friends during this period. Mind your phone bill as it can easily escalate out of all proportion.

Rest and relax more after the 22nd.

December

Best Days Overall: 8th, 9th, 16th, 17th, 25th, 26th, 27th

Most Stressful Days Overall: 3rd, 4th, 10th, 11th, 23rd, 24th, 30th, 31st

Best Days for Love: 1st, 2nd, 3rd, 4th, 10th, 11th, 18th, 19th, 28th, 29th, 30th, 31st

Best Days for Money: 1st, 10th, 11th, 18th, 19th, 28th, 29th

Mercury, your Ruler, crosses over to the Western hemisphere of your chart on the 3rd. It joins six other planets in that sector, making the West much stronger than the East. Adapt to situations, compromise and seek consensus in all things. Independence and self-will are not virtues right now and will probably get you nowhere. This doesn't mean that you have to be a door mat for others or that you allow yourself to be abused – only that you exercise social grace in getting your way.

Between 70 and 80 per cent of the planets are below the Horizon of your chart – including Mercury, your Ruler – so focus on finding your emotional comfort zone and all else will follow from there.

Your important areas of interest this month are the home and family, children, parties, entertainment, speculations and love affairs, and health and work.

Rest and relax more until the 21st. Do all you can to maximize your energy. Pace yourself, work within a rhythm and focus only on essentials.

The Solar Eclipse of the 25th is mixed for you. Take a reduced schedule. Though the Eclipse itself is benign, it does affect Mercury, your Ruler. Thus there are image changes, redefinitions of the personality, and perhaps physical changes. Those of you who are mindful of your diet need not fear the physical cleansings – the Eclipse will probably manifest as a change in image and personality. Those of you who are not careful about diet might be shown why you need to be. The Eclipse occurs in your 5th House. Thus a love affair that has outlived its usefulness could dissolve. There are changes with children – probably very natural ones – such as a child graduating, going off to university, getting married, etc. Children and children's issues swallow up much of your time, attention and energy.

Finances seem excellent all month. Until the 8th they come easily, through creativity or speculations. Perhaps you have a brilliant idea – or meet someone significant – at a party, sporting event or nightclub. Money comes as you are having fun and enjoying life. After the 8th money comes through work and service. Your partner or spouse can present you with a happy financial surprise (or big-ticket item) on the 12th. Sudden money comes on the 24th as well – perhaps from your employer (a bonus) or through a co-worker.

Love seems status quo, though singles may meet someone special around the 12th and 24th.

Libra

♎

THE SCALES
Birthdays from
23rd September
to 22nd October

Personality Profile

LIBRA AT A GLANCE

Element – Air

Ruling Planet – Venus
   Career Planet – Moon
   Love Planet – Mars
   Money Planet – Pluto
   Planet of Communications – Jupiter
   Planet of Health and Work – Neptune
   Planet of Home and Family Life – Saturn
   Planet of Spirituality and Good Fortune –
   Mercury

Colours – blue, jade green

Colours that promote love, romance and social harmony – carmine, red, scarlet

Colours that promote earning power –
burgundy, red-violet, violet

Gems – carnelian, chrysolite, coral, emerald,
jade, opal, quartz, white marble

Metal – copper

Scents – almond, rose, vanilla, violet

Quality – cardinal (= activity)

Qualities most needed for balance – a sense of
self, self-reliance, independence

Strongest virtues – social grace, charm, tact,
diplomacy

Deepest needs – love, romance, social harmony

Characteristic to avoid – violating what is right
in order to be socially accepted

Signs of greatest overall compatibility – Gemini,
Aquarius

Signs of greatest overall incompatibility – Aries,
Cancer, Capricorn

Sign most helpful to career – Cancer

Sign most helpful for emotional support – Capricorn

Sign most helpful financially – Scorpio

Sign best for marriage and/or partnerships – Aries

Sign most helpful for creative projects – Aquarius

Best Sign to have fun with – Aquarius

Signs most helpful in spiritual matters – Gemini,
Virgo

Best day of the week – Friday

Understanding the Libra Personality

In the Sign of Libra the universal mind – the soul – expresses its genius for relationships, that is, its power to harmonize diverse elements in a unified, organic way. Libra is the soul's power to express beauty in all of its forms. And where is beauty if not within relationships? Beauty does not exist in isolation. Beauty arises out of comparison – out of the just relationship between different parts. Without a fair and harmonious relationship there is no beauty, whether it be in art, manners, ideas or the social or political forum.

There are two faculties humans have that exalt them above the animal kingdom: their rational faculty (expressed in the Signs of Gemini and Aquarius) and their aesthetic faculty, exemplified by Libra. Without an aesthetic sense we would be little more than intelligent barbarians. Libra is the civilizing instinct or urge of the soul.

Beauty is the essence of what Librans are all about. They are here to beautify the world. One could discuss Librans' social grace, their sense of balance and fair play, their ability to see and love another person's point of view – but this would be to miss their central asset: their desire for beauty.

No one – no matter how alone he or she seems to be – exists in isolation. The universe is one vast collaboration of beings. Librans, more than most, understand this and understand the spiritual laws that make relationships bearable and enjoyable.

A Libra is always the unconscious (and in some cases conscious) civilizer, harmonizer and artist. This is a Libra's deepest urge and greatest genius. Librans love instinctively to bring people together, and they are uniquely qualified to do so. They have a knack for seeing what unites people – the things that attract and bind rather than separate individuals.

Finance

In financial matters Librans can seem frivolous and illogical to others. This is because Librans appear to be more concerned with earning money for others than for themselves. But there is a logic to this financial attitude. Librans know that everything and everyone is connected and that it is impossible to help another to prosper without also prospering yourself. Since enhancing their partner's income and position tends to strengthen their relationship, Librans choose to do so. What could be more fun than building a relationship? You will rarely find a Libra enriching him- or herself at someone else's expense.

Scorpio is the Ruler of Libra's Solar 2nd House of Money, giving Libra unusual insight into financial matters – and the power to focus on these matters in a way that disguises a seeming indifference. In fact, many other Signs come to Librans for financial advice and guidance.

Given their social grace, Librans often spend great sums of money on entertaining and organizing social events. They also like to help others when they are in need. Librans would go out of their way to help a friend in dire straits, even if they have to borrow from others to do so. However, Librans are also very careful to pay back any debts they owe, and like to make sure they never have to be reminded to do so.

Career and Public Image

Publicly, Librans like to appear as nurturers. Their friends and acquaintances are their family and they wield political power in parental ways. They also like bosses who are paternal or maternal.

The Sign of Cancer is on Libra's 10th House (of Career) cusp; the Moon is Libra's Career Planet. The Moon is by far the speediest, most changeable planet in the Horoscope. It alone among all the planets travels through the entire

Zodiac – all 12 Signs and Houses – every month. This is an important key to the way in which Librans approach their careers, and also to what they need to do to maximize their career potential. The Moon is the Planet of Moods and Feelings – Librans need a career in which their emotions can have free expression. This is why so many Librans are involved in the creative arts. Libra's ambitions wax and wane with the Moon. They tend to wield power according to their mood.

The Moon 'rules' the masses – and that is why Libra's highest goal is to achieve a mass kind of acclaim and popularity. Librans who achieve fame cultivate the public as other people cultivate a lover or friend. Librans can be very flexible – and often fickle – in their career and ambitions. On the other hand, they can achieve their ends in a great variety of ways. They are not stuck in one attitude or with one way of doing things.

Love and Relationships

Librans express their true genius in love. In love you could not find a partner more romantic, more seductive or more fair. If there is one thing that is sure to destroy a relationship – sure to block your love from flowing – it is injustice or imbalance between lover and beloved. If one party is giving too much or taking too much, resentment is sure to surface at some time or other. Librans are careful about this. If anything, Librans might err on the side of giving more, but never giving less.

If you are in love with a Libra make sure you keep the aura of romance alive. Do all the little things – candle-lit dinners, travel to exotic locales, flowers and small gifts. Give things that are beautiful, not necessarily expensive. Send cards. Ring regularly even if you have nothing in particular to say. The niceties are very important to a Libra. Your relationship is a work of art: make it beautiful and your Libra lover will appreciate it. If you are creative about it, he or she will appreciate it even more; for this is how your Libra will behave towards you.

Librans like their partners to be aggressive and even a bit self-willed. They know that these are qualities they sometimes lack and so they like their partners to have them. In relationships, however, Librans can be very aggressive – but always in a subtle and charming way! Librans are determined in their efforts to charm the object of their desire – and this determination can be very pleasant if you are on the receiving end.

Home and Domestic Life

Since Librans are such social creatures, they do not particularly like mundane domestic duties. They like a well-organized home – clean and neat with everything needful present – but housework is a chore and a burden, one of the unpleasant tasks in life that must be done, the quicker the better. If a Libra has enough money – and sometimes even if not – he or she will prefer to pay someone else to take care of the daily household chores. However, Librans like gardening; they love to have flowers and plants in the home.

A Libra's home is modern, and furnished in excellent taste. You will find many paintings and sculptures there. Since Librans like to be with friends and family, they enjoy entertaining at home and they make great hosts.

Capricorn is on the cusp of Libra's 4th Solar House of Home and Family. Saturn, the Planet of Law, Order, Limits and Discipline, rules Libra's domestic affairs. If Librans want their home life to be supportive and happy they need to develop some of the virtues of Saturn – order, organization and discipline. Librans, being so creative and so intensely in need of harmony, can tend to be too lax in the home and too permissive with their children. Too much of this is not always good; children need freedom but they also need limits.

Horoscope for 2000

Major Trends

1999 was a happier year than 1998, and the year 2000 will be even happier. All the major, long-term planets are lining up in wonderful ways to you. Summer will be an important turning point.

1999 was an important social year for you. Many of you married or entered into significant love relationships. There were many parties and entertainment events. Much fun and creativity. And this trend continues in the year 2000. Those of you who have not yet married still have opportunity – especially if you were born late in the sign – after 15th October.

In the year 2000 the focus shifts from romance to physical, sensual pleasures. Libido is heightened and is more easily expressed than in 1999.

Students looking to enter university hear good news in the summer. And those who are already in university have an easier year with their studies.

When Jupiter enters your 9th House on 1st July there will be more foreign travel – and happy travel – though you might have to be on a budget.

The pursuit of intellectual interests and relations with neighbours and siblings were important in 1999 and are important this year. Bottom-line issues are involved; this will be discussed in more detail later.

Your paths to fulfilment this year are friends and group activities, astrology, career issues, romance, the healthful expression of libido, paying off debt, helping others to prosper, religion, metaphysics and foreign travel.

Health

Your 6th House of Health is not a House of Power this year, thus you have no need to pay undue attention to health issues now. Health is good, and as the saying goes, 'if it ain't broke, don't fix it.'

After 15th February when Jupiter leaves Aries, there will be no long-term planet stressing you out. In fact, most of them are making positive and harmonious aspects to you. Come the summer, even Jupiter (and for a brief period, Saturn) will make beautiful aspects to you. Thus you have seldom experienced this much energy and vitality. You have the energy of 10 people. You are being powered from on high.

If you have had health problems in the past you will hear good news this year. Chances are that your health problem was never what you thought it was – or what it was diagnosed as being – it was an energy problem. When the Cosmos turns the energy back on – boom – the health problem disappears.

Neptune, your Health Planet, is basically beautifully aspected, which is another positive health signal. But it travels with the South Node of the Moon in the early months of 2000. This could indicate dealing with addictions – whether it be food, substance abuse or behavioural/habit patterns. Addictive behaviour becomes so strong that you are forced to take actions to correct it – this is the purpose behind it. So this will be the main health challenge in the year 2000.

Steady readers of these reports know that Neptune rules the feet. Thus, health can be enhanced even further by having the feet massaged regularly and by wearing shoes that fit and are comfortable. Neptune is in the Sign of Aquarius, which rules the ankles – thus have your ankles massaged while you are doing your feet. Give them support if you are doing strenuous exercise.

The health of your spouse seems to maintain the status quo. The health of parents seems more delicate. The Solar

Eclipses of 1st July and 25th December, and the Lunar Eclipse of 16th July force physical impurities to the surface. The health of a sibling could be better.

Home and Domestic Life

Though your 4th House of Home and Family is not a House of Power this year, three Eclipses ensure that there will be plenty of change and excitement in this area.

The fact that your 4th House is not especially active is a good sign. It shows that you are basically satisfied with the home and with the current domestic pattern. You have freedom and leeway to create these things as you desire them to be. The tendency is towards the status quo. But the Eclipses show that though you might be consciously satisfied, a deep part of you – and the Cosmos itself – is not satisfied. There are flaws in the domestic arrangements, or in the home itself, that you might not be aware of. It is the job of the Lunar Nodes – the Heavenly Dragon – to force these to the surface so you can correct them. In fact you will have little choice but to correct them. Is there a weak pipe to the washing machine? Is the carpeting old and worn? Do you have rodents or termites lurking around somewhere? Is your roof about ready to give out? The Eclipses will reveal this to you in very dramatic ways. The weak pipe can burst, flooding the old and worn carpet, forcing you to replace both – something you wouldn't have done off your own bat.

Is there some hidden flaw or problem with a family member? With your relationship to him or her? The Eclipse will bring these out as well.

Often the Eclipse will indicate a move, as you decide that the flaws you find in the present home are not worth correcting.

The Eclipses you need to be especially mindful of are the Lunar Eclipse of 16th July and the Solar Eclipse of 25th December.

The Solar Eclipse of 1st July is especially interesting in that it indicates a possible move due to a career change, not because of any flaw in the home.

Jupiter and Saturn go conjunct this year, in late May. They travel together in May and June. This is very important domestically, as Saturn is your Home and Family Planet and this conjunction only happens once every 20 years. This shows a move into your dream home and the establishment of your heart's desire in the home. Begin now to visualize and design this home in your mind; jot down notes on paper and review them every night before you go to sleep; feel yourself living in your dream home as you do so – and then let the Cosmic Genii, Jupiter and Saturn, bring it to pass.

Love and Social Life

The year begins with benevolent Jupiter still in your 7th House of Marriage. Most of you have either married, entered significant relationships or added new and prominent friends to your social circle. But if not, the early part of the year – until 15th February – is still good for these things. If you were born late in the Sign of Libra – from 15th to 22nd October – Jupiter will still be in your 7th House for the first half of the year. Love is blooming now. Singles will marry or meet a significant other.

Love is in the neighbourhood these days. No need to run off to exotic climes or out-of-town resorts, it is right where you are. If a sibling invites you to a party or to meet someone, take the invitation seriously. Street parties or local social activities are also likely meeting places. Love can bloom through the post as well. There is much communication about love this year.

The first half of the year is almost a perfect love year as you have wonderful options. With your 5th House strong you have plenty of romantic opportunities that are not serious; they are fun-and-games type relationships. And, with your 7th House strong, you have an opportunity for more serious relationships. It all depends on what you want. The Cosmos will give you either.

Those of you looking towards a second marriage are likely to meet that special someone after 1st July. The Cosmos is offering you choices as well – either romantic flings or serious, committed love.

Two Eclipses – a Lunar one on 21st January and Solar one on 30th July – are impacting on those who are either married for the third time or looking towards a third marriage. If you are attached, the Eclipses will test the relationship, bringing out hidden flaws for correction – perhaps producing a crisis in the relationship. If you are unattached, the Eclipses could bring love to you – but with much disruption of your personal life and normal patterns. Yes, love is good but it can be very disruptive.

A sibling is likely to marry after the summer. Romantic opportunity is there, but there is a need to go slow and let love develop. Your parents' marriage is stormy and the Eclipses of 1st July, 16th July and 25th December will test it.

Career and Finance

This is not an especially important career or financial year for you, Libra, as neither your 10th House of Career nor your 2nd House of Money is a House of Power. The Cosmos is allowing much freedom for you to shape these areas as you will. But can freedom compensate for lack of interest? Other things are much more important to you and you are focusing your attentions there.

Two Eclipses affect your career this year. The first one – on 21st January – will be felt by those of you born later in the Sign of Libra. The second one – 1st July – will be felt by those of you born early in the Sign. Some of you will feel both these Eclipses. These are indicating career changes, shake-ups and perhaps disruptions in the company you work for. The end result will be good, but while the Eclipse is working itself out things are frenetic. You feel swallowed up by events. Some of you may suddenly discover that you hate your job and want to be elsewhere. Some of you may take an entirely new career path. Others might find that a shake-up in the corporate hierarchy brings changes to your status and position. The company you work for could merge or be taken over, causing massive shifts of jobs and responsibilities. Your boss could resign or be promoted, and you are now working for someone new. Hang in through the changes and see the good. The end result is good.

Financially I expect the status quo. Earnings are relatively stable this year. Debt issues, which have been a problem of late, become much easier when Jupiter moves into your 8th House on 15th February. This shows help. Debts are more easily made and more easily paid. Access to outside capital is easier. Money comes to you through the generosity of a spouse or partner. Insurance or property claims have fortunate outcomes. If you have good ideas, attracting investors is easier.

Jupiter in your 8th House from 15th February to 1st July shows prosperity for a spouse or partner. But Saturn in their Money House still shows a need for good financial management. Organizing the spouse's financial life is still a top priority.

Pluto (your Financial Planet) is still in Sagittarius in your 3rd House. It was there last year and will be there for many years to come. This indicates that earnings come through communication, teaching, writing, sales and/or marketing. The telecommunications and transportation industries seem like good investments – but your personal horoscope (based on your precise date and time of birth) could modify this.

Your paths to financial increase are residential property, companies that cater to the home, home-builders, restaurants and hotels.

Your paths to speculative success are oil, natural gas, footwear, shipping, water utilities, the fishing industry, boat-builders. High-tech companies also look interesting.

Self-improvement

The Eclipses that effect your 10th House of Career bring opportunities to become more stable and secure. There are few of us who are totally secure in our jobs or status. It is said that job insecurity is a fact of life. The Eclipses of 21st January and 1st July will bring these insecurities to the surface and force you to confront them. Confronting these things boldly will bring great psychological growth. The only thing to fear is fear itself. When push comes to shove there are always solutions.

Your 5th House of Creativity is very strong this year and for years to come. There are many ways that this power will be expressed. Some of you will lose yourself in amusements and parties, some in love affairs and some with child-rearing. All these things are good, but not enough. It would be a good idea to get involved in a creative hobby – something that you do for the sheer joy of the doing. Creativity will not only bring happiness and release pent-up emotions but also improve your health as well.

Your 9th House of Religion, Philosophy, Higher Education and Metaphysics becomes very important in the summer. Many of you will attract educational opportunities, and you should take them. Others will become more involved with religion and philosophy. Illumination on these subjects is coming to you. Many of you will meet an important teacher or mentor during this period. This is one of the great experiences of life – recognize it for what it is. A good mentor can save you years and years of wandering in the wilderness. And while he or she cannot do the work for you, this person can put you on a straight path and help you to avoid pitfalls and hazards. This is a year for learning the value of inner wealth.

Month-by-month Forecasts

January

Best Days Overall: 8th, 9th, 17th, 18th, 25th, 26th

Most Stressful Days Overall: 5th, 6th, 7th, 13th, 14th, 19th, 20th

Best Days for Love: 3rd, 4th, 10th, 11th, 13th, 14th, 19th, 20th, 22nd, 28th, 29th

Best Days for Money: 1st, 2nd, 3rd, 4th, 13th, 14th, 21st, 22nd, 28th, 29th, 30th, 31st

Between 70 and 80 per cent of the planetary power is below the Horizon of your chart this month. Thus, you can let career issues ride and work on finding your emotional comfort zone and strengthening family relationships. Feeling right is the prelude to doing right. Job offers which disturb your emotional harmony – no matter how lucrative – are not appealing to you right now. This mood will change later in the year, but for now it is so.

Last month the planets made an important shift into the Western, social sector of your chart – your favourite sector. The month begins with 70 to 80 per cent of them there. By the 24th the percentage increases to 80 to 90 per cent. A very social month. Your natural social genius will carry you to the heights of success now. You get a good chance to exercise your gifts this month.

As 90 to 100 per cent of the planets are moving forward, this indicates that your life moves forward – and pretty speedily at that. This is a month of achievement.

The Lunar Eclipse of the 21st deals kindly with you. It shows a long-term career change or perhaps a shake-up in the company you work for. But this shake-up works in your favour. A friend could be changing careers as well. Relations with a professional organization undergo disruptive change.

Your important areas of interest this month are sales, marketing, and intellectual interests, the home, family and the pursuit of emotional harmony, love affairs, parties, entertainment, creativity and children.

The new Moon of the 5th brings clarity and insight into emotional issues, the family and matters involving the home. Saturn's forward motion on the 12th (it has been retrograde for many months) also brings clarity, confidence and astute judgement to these areas.

Though your long-term health is excellent, rest and relax more until the 20th.

Finances are strong all month, but a happy windfall comes around the 9th. Money comes from sales, marketing, writing, teaching, and the use of the mental faculties. Telecommunications and transportation make good investments – either to buy or sell.

Your Love Planet makes an important move from Aquarius into Pisces on the 4th. This shows a shift in love attitudes. Love is more serious now. More idealistic. Experimentalism is out, spirituality is in. Where late last year love had to be a big honeymoon to make you happy, now love is expressed through service – through deeds rather than mere words. There is a stronger need for a spiritual compatibility rather than a mere physical or sexual compatibility. Nice if you can have both, though.

February

Best Days Overall: 4th, 5th, 13th, 14th, 22nd, 23rd

Most Stressful Days Overall: 2nd, 3rd, 9th, 10th, 15th, 16th, 29th

Best Days for Love: 2nd, 3rd, 7th, 8th, 9th, 10th, 11th, 12th, 17th, 18th, 22nd, 26th, 27th

Best Days for Money: 9th, 10th, 17th, 18th, 19th, 24th, 25th, 26th, 27th, 28th, 29th

Though you will be working hard this month, you will also be playing hard. This is a happy month in a happy year.

Between 80 and 90 per cent of the planets are still in the Western, social sector of your chart. Mars, your Love Planet, moves into your 7th House of Love on the 12th. Venus, your Ruling Planet, is gliding ever more westwards as well. This is another month where you get to exercise your social genius. Other people come first and your good comes to you through them.

The planetary power is still mostly in the bottom half of your chart, so you can safely let your career and 'outer' life coast as you focus on family and domestic issues. Inner harmony will lead, in due course, to outer harmony.

With 90 to 100 per cent of the planets moving forward this month, like last month, you are in a period of forward momentum, progress and achievement. Only you must allow things to come to you rather than trying to make them happen.

The Solar Eclipse of the 5th deals kindly with you and the disruptions and changes it creates bring opportunity to you. It occurs in your 5th House of Children, Love Affairs and Creativity. Thus there are long-term – and happy – changes going on in these areas. A child could go off to university or get married. Flaws in a current love affair are revealed so that they can be dealt with. A weak love affair dissolves. A new love affair comes in. Creative people take a new approach to their careers. The Sun is also the Lord of your Solar 11th House, thus there could be disruptions in a friendship or in an organization to which you belong. Those looking towards a third marriage could meet with a significant opportunity now – but it won't be a smooth ride.

Health is excellent all month. Finances are stable. Jupiter's move into your 8th House on the 15th signals prosperity for your spouse and partner – who has perhaps been struggling over the past year or so. He or she is getting a lot of help now. If you are seeking outside capital – loans or investors – the next few months will be a prime period for this. Debts will be more easily paid now.

Love is still active and happy. Jupiter leaves your 7th House for good on the 15th and by now has probably finished its work there – most of you have found that significant other in the past year. But if not, Mars in your 7th House is still bringing opportunities your way. Singles have many options in love – there are many fun-and-games type opportunities and many serious opportunities. Take your pick.

March

Best Days Overall: 3rd, 4th, 12th, 20th, 21st, 30th, 31st

Most Stressful Days Overall: 1st, 7th, 8th, 14th, 15th, 27th, 28th, 29th

Best Days for Love: 3rd, 4th, 7th, 8th, 12th, 13th, 22nd, 23rd, 27th, 28th

Best Days for Money: 1st, 7th, 8th, 9th, 10th, 16th, 17th, 18th, 19th, 22nd, 23rd, 24th, 25th, 26th, 27th, 28th

With 80 to 90 per cent of the planets in the Western hemisphere of your chart and with your 7th House of Love being an important House of Power, your social genius is getting a real workout this month. Though you will work hard, this is basically a party period.

Mercury's retrograde shows a need for caution when dealing with university administrators, university admissions officers or when planning foreign trips. Make sure all the facts are clear – on both sides – before taking decisive action. Neither good news nor bad news is all that it seems. Mercury is also your Planet of Spirituality, thus dreams and psychic readings need further study and confirmation. A dream or reading could be misinterpreted.

The planetary power is still mostly below the Horizon of your chart, but the balance of power is getting ready to shift. In the meantime, de-emphasize family and domestic concerns and focus on your career and worldly activities. It is not always necessary to be 'there' with the family to be a good family person. Sometimes we show our love by being good providers or making worldly breakthroughs that strengthen the family's position in other ways.

Pluto's retrograde on the 15th is significant for you as it is your Financial Planet. This suggests a need to study financial commitments, investments and major purchases more carefully for the next six months or so. Pluto's retrograde will not stop earnings, but could introduce complications if you are hasty or inattentive. Happily, Pluto is very well aspected during the latter part of the month and earnings should be strong.

Love is probably the most important area of your life during this period. Mars moving through your House of Love makes you more aggressive and socially confident. You go after what you want with great courage. Love-at-first-sight experiences are more common now – very normal. Mars will conjunct Jupiter after the 23rd in your 8th House, suggesting that sex appeal is the major consideration in love during this period. Good communication is important too, but there must be an underlying sexual attraction. Mars conjunct Jupiter suggests a significant love meeting – perhaps with a neighbour or through the introduction of a sibling. A friend or acquaintance wants to be more than that. There are many love opportunities this month; the problem is making up your mind.

Health is basically good, but rest and relax more after the 20th.

April

Best Days Overall: 8th, 9th, 16th, 17th, 18th, 26th, 27th

Most Stressful Days Overall: 4th, 5th, 10th, 11th, 24th, 25th

Best Days for Love: 1st, 2nd, 4th, 5th, 6th, 7th, 12th, 13th, 14th, 15th, 21st, 22nd, 24th, 25th

Best Days for Money: 4th, 5th, 6th, 7th, 14th, 15th, 19th, 20th, 21st, 22nd, 24th, 25th

You are at the height of social popularity this month. Between 80 and 90 per cent of the planets are in the West and your 7th House of Love is an important House of Power. You are on a charm offensive and succeeding. You are in Libra heaven. Good will come to you through other people – just the way you like things – and quickly at that.

By the 13th, the balance of planetary power shifts decisively to the top of half of your Horoscope. Career and outer, worldly activities are becoming ever more important. By now you should have found your point of inner harmony; it's time to leverage that into constructive service to the world. You can safely start to de-emphasize home and family issues now. Home and family issues will still be important this month as Saturn receives intense stimulation – but it is more of a winding-down activity.

Your important areas of interest this month are children, parties, entertainments, love affairs, creativity, health and work, love and romance, personal transformation, borrowing or paying off debt, helping others to prosper, tax issues, the deeper things of life and the libido.

Health is excellent, but rest and relax more until the 19th. Try not to burn the candle at both ends.

You are in one of the social peaks of the current year. Singles meet significant others now. New and creative types of friends come into the picture. Love is honeymoonish now. A fun-and-games type of relationship can end, in favour of something more serious. Love opportunities come at parties and social gatherings, in the neighbourhood, close to home or through the introduction of family members. Your Love Planet in the 8th House shows that love is passionate, sexual and intense. Jealousy and possessiveness can be a problem, but are really signs of intense love.

With so many love opportunities happening now, confusion would be normal. Too many love opportunities are as bad as too few. But the new Moon of the 4th is going to clarify the whole situation, and the by the time the month is over you will know who is who and where everyone fits in your life.

Even Pluto's retrograde cannot stop explosive financial growth during this period. Still, you need to research investments and purchases more closely. Earnings are not the problem, it's the little – but often annoying – glitches and side issues that cause the problems. Avoid speculations all month – but especially after the 19th.

May

Best Days Overall: 5th, 6th, 14th, 15th, 24th, 25th

Most Stressful Days Overall: 1st, 2nd, 7th, 8th, 21st, 22nd, 28th, 29th

Best Days for Love: 1st, 2nd, 3rd, 4th, 5th, 12th, 13th, 14th, 15th, 22nd, 23rd, 24th, 25th, 28th, 29th

Best Days for Money: 1st, 2nd, 3rd, 4th, 9th, 10th, 12th, 13th, 16th, 17th, 18th, 19th, 21st, 22nd, 28th, 29th, 31st

Though there are important developments happening at home, with most of the planets above the Horizon you need to give your career as much attention as possible.

The planetary power is still mostly in the West, so your social genius is still very much the instrument of your good.

This balance of power is soon to change, but for now attain your ends through compromise, negotiation and putting other people first.

Your important areas of interest this month are children, parties, entertainments, love affairs and creativity, debts and their repayment, personal transformation, the deeper things of life, the income of a partner, making money for other people, and libido, and religion, philosophy, foreign travel and higher education.

Retrograde activity is increasing this month. This doesn't stop the progress and forward momentum in your life, but only delays things somewhat. The main effect of the retrogrades seem to be on finances. There are delays and obstructions this month – especially after the 20th. Conflicts over finances could occur, and you must work harder for earnings than you are used to. This is a temporary, short-term situation. Knowing that your supply comes from above – from a Higher Power – and was predestined for you will be a big help in weathering this temporary condition.

The retrograde of Neptune on the 8th affects both job-seekers and employers. Finding work might be difficult or delayed until the 20th. The same with finding staff. Even after the 20th, when the aspects for work are sensational, there is a need for more research – job offers might not be what they seem. The details are everything.

The retrograde of Uranus begins late in the month and occurs with fabulous aspects to it. It signals a need for more patience with children, especially when communicating with them. Aside from this, children are a pleasure and a joy now. Even speculations will go well from the 20th onwards – but there could be delays when it comes to collecting on them.

Health is fabulous all month – but especially after the 20th.

Your partner is prospering beyond all belief and the Jupiter–Saturn conjunction on the 28th signals a long-term trend of prosperity. Debts are more easily made and more easily paid. A good idea brings outside investors to your projects – you can't keep them away.

There are many planets in the Air element from the 20th onwards – mind what you say and keep an eye on your phone bill. The tendency is to get long winded at times like this.

June

Best Days Overall: 2nd, 10th, 11th, 20th, 21st, 29th, 30th

Most Stressful Days Overall: 4th, 17th, 18th, 19th, 25th, 26th

Best Days for Love: 2nd, 3rd, 10th, 11th, 22nd, 23rd, 25th, 26th

Best Days for Money: 6th, 7th, 8th, 9th, 12th, 13th, 14th, 15th, 16th, 17th, 18th, 19th, 25th, 26th, 27th, 28th

The planets make an important shift from the West to the East this month. This represents a psychological shift within yourself. As the months go by you will become more and more independent and self-reliant. Though other people will always be important to you, there is greater freedom now to create conditions as you desire them to be.

The planetary power is very strongly above the Horizon, and your 10th House of Career is an important House of Power. Focus on career and let home and domestic issues slide for a while. Your career is a top priority and major breakthroughs are happening. You have the favour of 'higher-ups', but they demand action. The career environment is unusually competitive but your social grace gives you the edge.

Retrograde activity increases this month – after the 23rd, 40 per cent of the planets are retrograde – but you are not unduly affected. Work and finance are the main areas affected by the retrogrades. For the most part you are still in a period of progress and achievement.

Finances are stressful and stormy and you need to work harder for earnings than usual. The retrograde of your Money Planet is not helping matters. Payments and projects seem stalled and need more thought. A foreign trip now could be ill-conceived and may put a dent in your bank balance. A friend makes unreasonable financial demands. Your spouse or partner disagrees with your financial plans or otherwise causes a needless expense. Hang in there and do what's possible – you are not required to do or give more than you are able. Financial stress eases up after the 21st. But things on this front won't really be back to normal until next month.

With many planets in the 9th House stressing your Money Planet, financial problems now could have their origin in religious or philosophical beliefs. This is a good opportunity to examine these things and revamp them if necessary. Financial issues are causing a crisis of conscience.

Health is excellent most of the month but rest and relax more after the 21st. While career is a priority during this period you still need to discern which activities are really going to further your career and which are only sapping your energy.

Love is happy during this period – though it can be expensive. New friends come into the picture. Singles are turned on by someone who can teach them things early in the month. Later there is an attraction for someone who can help your career. There is much socializing with the 'high and mighty' after the 21st.

July

Best Days Overall: 7th, 8th, 17th, 18th, 26th, 27th

Most Stressful Days Overall: 1st, 2nd, 15th, 16th, 22nd, 23rd, 29th

LIBRA

Best Days for Love: 1st, 2nd, 10th, 11th, 20th, 21st, 22nd, 23rd, 29th, 30th, 31st

Best Days for Money: 3rd, 4th, 6th, 7th, 10th, 11th, 12th, 13th, 14th, 15th, 22nd, 23rd, 25th, 26th, 31st

Hang in there this month and keep the faith. You are entering a very happy and successful period, but first the obstructions to your happiness need to be blasted away. The higher your aspirations in life, the more profound will the disruptions of the Eclipses (three this month) be.

On the 1st, Jupiter moves into Gemini – a beautiful alignment for you. It joins two other powerful long-term planets, Uranus and Neptune, in helping you to your goals. Next month Saturn will also join this heavenly conspiracy of good. Prosperity, happiness and health are yours now.

In general rest and relax more until the 22nd. Especially rest more around the 1st and the 16th – the periods of the first Solar and the Lunar Eclipse. Vitality will be much stronger after the 22nd, and the second Solar Eclipse (on the 30th) is much kinder to you.

The Solar Eclipse of the 1st occurs in your 10th House of Career, signalling important career and/or job changes. These changes are happy. You are probably getting a pay rise, promotion or some honours. Relations with a parent could change around this time as well. Bosses could resign, leaving an opening for you. Shake-ups in the corporate structure create opportunities for you.

The Lunar Eclipse of the 16th seems complementary to the one on the 1st, as it shows a move or major renovation of the home. Since the Moon is also your Career Planet, its Eclipse has career implications as well. Thus, you could move or buy your dream home because of a new career development. Perhaps your move changes a relationship with family members. Family members could also move house around this time. (Remember that Eclipses are in effect for six months or so – so these events could manifest in delayed ways too.)

The Solar Eclipse of the 30th occurs in your 11th House of Friends and Group Activities. Thus there could be a disruption with a friend or an upheaval in a professional organization to which you belong. For those of you working towards a third marriage, it could signal a change in the marital status.

Finances are stronger after the 22nd, but you still need to research purchase, investments and financial commitments very closely. Friends, networking and the use of high-tech equipment are boosting your bank balance.

Singles find love as they pursue career goals or with someone involved in their career. Looks to be someone older.

August

Best Days Overall: 4th, 5th, 13th, 14th, 15th, 23rd, 24th, 31st

Most Stressful Days Overall: 11th, 12th, 18th, 19th, 25th, 26th

Best Days for Love: 8th, 9th, 11th, 12th, 18th, 19th, 20th, 21st, 27th, 28th, 29th, 30th

Best Days for Money: 3rd, 4th, 6th, 7th, 8th, 9th, 13th, 14th, 18th, 19th, 23rd, 24th, 27th, 28th

Your health, happiness and prosperity improved dramatically last month, and this month improve even more. You are entering one of the happiest and most productive periods of your life.

Saturn's move into Gemini on the 11th is a fortunate transit both for you and your family. Your emotional life is optimistic and upbeat. The family circle enlarges through births or marriage. People who are like family to you come into the picture. Foreign travel plans can now include the family as well. Educational opportunities merge harmoniously with family life. There are numerous opportunities for foreign journeys coming up.

LIBRA

Though career activities are less hectic than in previous months, career is still important and still needs your focus. Most of the planets are still above the Horizon.

The majority of planets are now in the Eastern sector of your chart, and though social activities are always important there is a greater sense of freedom, independence and self-reliance now. It is time to create conditions and not merely adapt or react to them.

Health is super this month as virtually all of the planets – long- and short-term – are in harmonious aspect to you. Health problems of the past dissolve miraculously. Your self-confidence and self-esteem are strong and growing stronger day by day.

Your important areas of interest this month are children, creativity, amusement, love affairs, religion, philosophy, foreign travel and higher education, friends, groups, group activities, organizations, platonic relationships, science and astrology, and spirituality and charitable activities.

Finances will be strong this month, but stronger before the 22nd than afterwards. After the 22nd you have to work harder for earnings than before. The forward motion of Pluto, your Money Planet, on the 20th is a positive financial signal as it indicates that your financial confidence and judgement are much stronger. There is a conflict between altruistic concerns and financial concerns after the 22nd. Certain financial arrangements or opportunities violate your sense of ethics and you must make hard choices. Your ethics will probably win out. But have no fear, new opportunities will come very shortly.

Love is happy and playful this month, but far from stable. Love can come suddenly and go just as quickly. Romantic moods run ultra-high and then ultra-low. Affections can change at the drop of a hat. In one week you can experience the range of emotions that it often takes 10 years to experience. Enjoy the roller-coaster!

September

Best Days Overall: 1st, 10th, 11th, 19th, 20th, 27th, 28th

Most Stressful Days Overall: 7th, 8th, 14th, 15th, 16th, 21st, 22nd

Best Days for Love: 1st, 5th, 6th, 10th, 11th, 14th, 15th, 16th, 17th, 19th, 20th, 25th, 26th, 30th

Best Days for Money: 1st, 2nd, 3rd, 5th, 6th, 10th, 11th, 14th, 15th, 19th, 20th, 23rd, 24th, 27th, 28th, 30th

Though your social grace will never allow you to become overly assertive or self-willed, with many planets in the Eastern sector (including Venus, your Ruler) you are more so now than usual. And you should be. You can have things your way. You can and will make things happen. People will start adapting to you. Build the life of your dreams now, Libra – keep your eyes on the prize.

Though there is an increase in retrograde activity and the pace of change and progress has slowed down in the world at large, it doesn't seem to affect you – you are making quick and rapid progress towards your goals.

The planets make an important shift to the bottom half of your Horoscope on the 22nd. Thus, the importance of outer ambitions and worldly success begins to get weaker and the need for emotional harmony and domestic stability increases. This trend will become more pronounced as the months go by.

With virtually all of the long-term planets making wonderful aspects to you, and with many planets in your own Sign, you are in one of the happiest and most successful periods of your life. This is a time for reaping the rewards of past good actions. You will see that every good deed you've done, every thoughtful action and thought, was not wasted but was 'deposited' in a universal bank account, earning interest and dividends. You are collecting on this bank roll now.

Health is super. Health problems of the past are simply vaporized by the influx of omnipotent planetary power. Many of you discover that so-called 'incurable' diseases are not as incurable as you'd thought. They were merely energy problems and not organic problems. Your physical appearance shines all month. Venus in your own Sign gives you beauty, glamour and flair. The Sun in your Sign after the 22nd gives you energy and personal magnetism – true star quality.

There are many planets in the Air element during this period. Be careful not to waste all of this beautiful mental energy on idle speech or destructive gossip or thoughts. Use the power constructively. Write those letters you need to write. Advertise or market your goods or services. Keep a notebook of your constructive ideas for later reference, as there is much gold here. And then switch your mind off. Mind that phone bill now.

Finances are strong all month.

Love is chasing you ardently and is about to catch up with you. You don't need to do anything special to attract it.

October

Best Days Overall: 7th, 8th, 16th, 17th, 25th, 26th

Most Stressful Days Overall: 4th, 5th, 6th, 12th, 13th, 18th, 19th

Best Days for Love: 1st, 4th, 5th, 6th, 9th, 10th, 11th, 12th, 13th, 14th, 15th, 20th, 21st, 23rd, 24th, 29th, 30th

Best Days for Money: 1st, 2nd, 3rd, 7th, 8th, 12th, 13th, 16th, 17th, 20th, 21st, 25th, 26th, 27th, 28th, 29th, 30th

You are still in one of the happiest periods in your year and in your life. Almost all the long-term planets are aligned in your favour. You are surrounded by visible and invisible friends and helpers.

Until the 23rd you are very much in a party mood. There is much personal and sensual pleasure happening. Sensual fantasies are being fulfilled. Personal desires, likewise. Health is super and your image and appearance shine. You have star quality this month.

After the 23rd the emphasis shifts to finance, where things get a little rockier. Earnings will be strong but you will work harder – overcome more obstacles – in their attainment. When all is said and done, and all the dust settles, we expect that you will be much richer when the month ends than when it began.

Though you are catching the lucky breaks this month, speculations should be controlled and done after due deliberation, not blindly and automatically. Reckless speculation can dent your bank balance. Overspending on useless health products or regimes can likewise dent your bank balance. You probably don't need these things as your vitality is super now. Mercury's retrograde in your Money House can create annoying financial delays – though the earnings will still come. Miscommunication about financial issues can also cause glitches.

Fun-and-games types of love affairs are plentiful and happy. The more serious types of love are happening behind the scenes. Many of you are creating a new, more spiritual romantic ideal. Others are working inwardly – through spiritual or metaphysical methods – to manifest your romantic ideal. Serious love is not to be found at parties, discos or nightclubs, but at religious functions, the ashram, church or charitable function. Get involved in a humanitarian cause you believe in (and that is important to you) and love will find you. Many of you are being cured of faulty love attitudes by getting involved in stressful relationships. These are not a punishment but therapy. Some of you need the mirror of another person to see clearly the error of your ways. Once these flaws are corrected, your romantic ideal will manifest very easily.

November

Best Days Overall: 3rd, 4th, 13th, 21st, 22nd

Most Stressful Days Overall: 1st, 2nd, 8th, 9th, 15th, 28th, 29th

Best Days for Love: 2nd, 8th, 9th, 12th, 13th, 19th, 20th, 21st, 22nd, 28th, 29th, 30th

Best Days for Money: 3rd, 4th, 8th, 9th, 12th, 13th, 17th, 18th, 21st, 22nd, 23rd, 24th, 26th, 27th, 30th

A happy month in a happy year, Libra. Enjoy! A Grand Trine in the element of Air after the 4th puts you right in your own element – in synch with the Cosmos. People are light, airy, friendly and detached. Your mental and communication faculties have never been stronger. Sales and marketing efforts are successful. Students do well. The phone lines hum. People are receptive to your message. Mind your phone bills. Use that extra mental energy constructively to write those letters or papers that need to be written or to make constructive plans for the future. Avoid idle or needless gossip.

Most of the planets are in the East and Mars is in your own Sign, increasing your self-confidence, independence and self-reliance. Though you like doing things with other people you have more choices and options these days. You can go your own way if you like or if situations don't suit you.

Mars in your own Sign – and very well aspected – brings many good things. It brings sex appeal, personal magnetism and energy to your body and image. You get things done quickly. You excel in exercise and sport. You are in a 'doing' mode. Mars is also your Love Planet and it indicates that you are involved in a serious relationship – and a happy one. Your lover cannot do enough for you. You get your way in love. Love runs after you rather than vice versa. Your personal style and glamour are stronger than usual.

With most of the planets still below the Horizon you can safely de-emphasize career goals and focus on home, family and psychological issues. Venus, your Ruler, moves into your 4th House of Home and Family on the 13th, reinforcing the above. This is a great time for redecorating and beautifying the home, and for entertaining from home. Venus will be 'out of bounds' all month, indicating that you are going way out of your normal orbit in search of personal pleasure, personal accessories and psychological fulfilment.

Finances will be strong all month. Perhaps the most important financial signal is the power in your Money House most of the month. This indicates a driving urge to achieve financial goals – a fire in the belly that will easily carry you through any difficulties or obstructions. Mercury moving forward in your Money House on the 8th shows that a blocked deal or project now goes forward again.

Health is good all month.

December

Best Days Overall: 1st, 2nd, 10th, 11th, 18th, 19th, 28th, 29th

Most Stressful Days Overall: 6th, 7th, 12th, 13th, 25th, 26th, 27th

Best Days for Love: 1st, 2nd, 6th, 7th, 10th, 11th, 18th, 19th, 28th, 29th, 30th, 31st

Best Days for Money: 1st, 6th, 7th, 10th, 11th, 14th, 15th, 18th, 20th, 21st, 22nd, 23rd, 24th, 28th

Now that Venus moves back into its normal orbit, your life becomes more like normal. This is still a happy month in a happy year, though you should rest and relax more after the 21st.

There is still a loose Grand Trine in Air for most of the month, so the advice given last month still applies: Use your extra mental energy to further your studies, to write those letters you need to write and boost your bank balance through advertising and marketing. Avoid idle gossip and especially avoid negative, destructive types of gossip. It is much too easy to fall into these things now. Use your mind and then switch it off.

Most of the planets are still below the Horizon, showing your need to find your emotional comfort zone and to shore up your home base. The Solar Eclipse of the 25th occurs in your 4th House of Home and Family, further reinforcing this urge.

Though Mars – the planet of aggressive action and self-will – is still in your own Sign, the planetary power is shifting westward this month. Though you may think your way is the best, and may be unduly self-assertive, you are better off being your normal Libra self – charming your way into good, rather than forcing good to happen.

Use the Mars energy for exercise and sport regimes. Use it to strengthen your physical body and not to impose your will on others. Continue to mind your temper until the 23rd.

The Solar Eclipse of the 25th is strong on you, Libra – take a reduced schedule for two days before and a day after. Try to schedule holiday travel around this period. It's not a good idea to be taking a long journey during an Eclipse period – especially one that affects your travel indicators.

The Eclipse will bring up flaws in the home, family relationships and your daily domestic pattern. These will come up so that you can take corrective action. In many cases the corrective action will be a move or a major repair. Deep psychological complexes you were previously unaware of are likely to get stimulated by this Eclipse, and those of you in therapy or who have an active inner life will find this very valuable. There could also be disruptions with friends, and with a professional or religious organization to which you belong.

But this Eclipse takes place in the context of an easy month, and we expect best-case scenarios to happen. The end result is better than what went before.

Scorpio

♏︎

THE SCORPION

Birthdays from
23rd October
to 22nd November

Personality Profile

SCORPIO AT A GLANCE

Element – Water

Ruling Planet – Pluto
   Co-ruling Planet – Mars
   Career Planet – Sun
   Love Planet – Venus
   Money Planet – Jupiter
   Planet of Health and Work – Mars
   Planet of Home and Family Life – Uranus

Colour – red-violet

Colour that promotes love, romance and social harmony – green

Colour that promotes earning power – blue

Gems – bloodstone, malachite, topaz

Metals – iron, radium, steel

Scents – cherry blossom, coconut, sandalwood, watermelon

Quality – fixed (= stability)

Quality most needed for balance – a wider view of things

Strongest virtues – loyalty, concentration, determination, courage, depth

Deepest needs – to penetrate and transform

Characteristics to avoid – jealousy, vindictiveness, fanaticism

Signs of greatest overall compatibility – Cancer, Pisces

Signs of greatest overall incompatibility – Taurus, Leo, Aquarius

Sign most helpful to career – Leo

Sign most helpful for emotional support – Aquarius

Sign most helpful financially – Sagittarius

Sign best for marriage and/or partnerships – Taurus

Sign most helpful for creative projects – Pisces

Best Sign to have fun with – Pisces

Signs most helpful in spiritual matters – Cancer, Libra

Best day of the week – Tuesday

Understanding the Scorpio Personality

One symbol of the Sign of Scorpio is the phoenix. If you meditate upon the legend of the phoenix you will begin to understand the Scorpio character – his or her powers and abilities, interests and deepest urges.

The phoenix of mythology was a bird that could recreate and reproduce itself. It did so in a most intriguing way: it would seek a fire – usually in a religious temple – fly into it, consume itself in the flames and then emerge a new bird. If this is not the ultimate, most profound transformation, then what is?

Transformation is what Scorpios are all about – in their minds, bodies, affairs and relationships (Scorpios are also society's transformers). To change something in a natural, not an artificial, way involves a transformation from within. This type of change is a radical change as opposed to a mere cosmetic make-over. Some people think that change means altering just their appearance, but this is not the kind of change that interests a Scorpio. Scorpios seek deep, fundamental change. Since real change always proceeds from within, a Scorpio is very interested in – and usually accustomed to – the inner, intimate and philosophical side of life.

Scorpios are people of depth and intellect. If you want to interest them you must present them with more than just a superficial image. You and your interests, projects or business deals must have real substance to them in order to stimulate a Scorpio. If they haven't, he or she will find you out – and that will be the end of the story.

If we observe life – the processes of growth and decay – we see the transformational powers of Scorpio at work all the time. The caterpillar changes itself into a butterfly, the infant grows into a child and then an adult. To Scorpios this definite and perpetual transformation is not something to be feared. They see it as a normal part of life. This acceptance of transformation gives Scorpios the key to understanding the true meaning of life.

Scorpios' understanding of life (including life's weaknesses) makes them powerful warriors – in all senses of the word. Add to this their depth, patience and endurance and you have a powerful personality. Scorpios have good, long memories and can at times be quite vindictive – they can wait years to get their revenge. As a friend, though, there is no one more loyal and true than a Scorpio. Few are willing to make the sacrifices that a Scorpio will make for a true friend.

The results of a transformation are quite obvious, although the process of transformation is invisible and secret. This is why Scorpios are considered secretive in nature. A seed will not grow properly if you keep digging it up and exposing it to the light of day. It must stay buried – invisible – until it starts to grow. In the same manner, Scorpios fear revealing too much about themselves or their hopes to other people. However, they will be more than happy to let you see the finished product – but only when it is completely wrapped up. On the other hand, Scorpios like knowing everyone else's secrets as much as they dislike anyone knowing theirs.

Finance

Love, birth, life as well as death are Nature's most potent transformations; Scorpios are interested in all of these. In our society money is a transforming power, too, and a Scorpio is interested in money for that reason. To a Scorpio money is power, money causes change, money controls. It is the power of money that fascinates them. But Scorpios can be too materialistic if they are not careful. They can be overly awed by the power of money, to a point where they think that money rules the world.

Even the term *plutocrat* comes from Pluto, the Ruler of the Sign of Scorpio. Scorpios will – in one way or another –

achieve the financial status they strive for. When they do so they are careful in the way they handle their wealth. Part of this financial carefulness is really a kind of honesty, for Scorpios are usually involved with other people's money – as accountants, lawyers, stockbrokers or corporate managers – and when you handle other people's money you have to be more cautious than when you handle your own.

In order to fulfil their financial goals, Scorpios have important lessons to learn. They need to develop qualities that do not come naturally to them, such as breadth of vision, optimism, faith, trust and, above all, generosity. They need to see the wealth in Nature and in life, as well as in its more obvious forms of money and power. When they develop generosity their financial potential reaches great heights, for Jupiter, the Lord of Opulence and Good Fortune, is Scorpio's Money Planet.

Career and Public Image

Scorpio's greatest aspiration in life is to be considered by society as a source of light and life. They want to be leaders, to be stars. But they follow a very different road than do Leos, the other stars of the Zodiac. A Scorpio arrives at the goal secretly, without ostentation; a Leo pursues it openly. Scorpios seek the glamour and fun of the rich and famous in a restrained, discreet way.

Scorpios are by nature introverted and tend to avoid the limelight. But if they want to attain their highest career goals they need to open up a bit and to express themselves more. They need to stop hiding their light under a bushel and let it shine. Above all, they need to let go of any vindictiveness and small-mindedness. All their gifts and insights were given to them for one important reason – to serve life and to increase the joy of living for others.

Love and Relationships

Scorpio is another Zodiac Sign that likes committed, clearly defined, structured relationships. They are cautious about marriage, but when they do commit to a relationship they tend to be faithful – and heaven help the mate caught or even suspected of infidelity! The jealousy of the Scorpio is legendary. They can be so intense in their jealousy that even the thought or intention of infidelity will be detected and is likely to cause as much of a storm as if the deed had actually been done.

Scorpios tend to settle down with those who are wealthier than they are. They usually have enough intensity for two, so in their partners they seek someone pleasant, hard-working, amiable, stable and easy-going. They want someone they can lean on, someone loyal behind them as they fight the battles of life. To a Scorpio a partner, be it a lover or a friend, is a real partner – not an adversary. Most of all a Scorpio is looking for an ally, not a competitor.

If you are in love with a Scorpio you will need a lot of patience. It takes a long time to get to know Scorpios, because they do not reveal themselves readily. But if you persist and your motives are honourable, you will gradually be allowed into a Scorpio's inner chambers of the mind and heart.

Home and Domestic Life

Uranus is Ruler of Scorpio's 4th Solar House of Home and Family. Uranus is the Planet of Science, Technology, Changes and Democracy. This tells us a lot about a Scorpio's conduct in the home and what he or she needs in order to have a happy, harmonious home life.

Scorpios can sometimes bring their passion, intensity and wilfulness into the home and family, which is not always the place for these qualities. These traits are good for the warrior and the transformer, but not so good for the nurturer and family member. Because of this (and also because of their need for change and transformation) the Scorpio may be prone to sudden changes of residence. If not carefully constrained, the sometimes inflexible Scorpio can produce turmoil and sudden upheavals within the family.

Scorpios need to develop some of the virtues of Aquarius in order to cope better with domestic matters. There is a need to build a team spirit at home, to treat family activities as truly group activities – family members should all have a say in what does and does not get done. For at times a Scorpio can be most dictatorial. When a Scorpio gets dictatorial it is much worse than if a Leo or Capricorn (the two other power Signs in the Zodiac) does. For the dictatorship of a Scorpio is applied with more zeal, passion, intensity and concentration than is true of either a Leo or Capricorn. Obviously this can be unbearable to family members – especially if they are sensitive types.

In order for a Scorpio to get the full benefit of the emotional support that a family can give, he or she needs to let go of conservatism and be a bit more experimental, to explore new techniques in child-rearing, be more democratic with family members and to try to manage things by consensus rather than by autocratic edict.

Horoscope for 2000

Major Trends

1999 was a challenging year, Scorpio. Your health could have been better. Moods and emotions were volatile. Love was stressful and money was earned through hard work. Coming through all of this has made you a stronger, more enlightened person. When the going gets tough the tough get going. No one handles adversity better than you. The adversity brought out your true genius, which relishes new worlds to conquer.

Though many of these trends are continuing in the year 2000, things are getting somewhat easier. If you handled 1999, you'll handle the year 2000.

The important areas of interest in the coming year are finance, home and family, work, love and romance – and, later in the year, transformation, regeneration and the reinvention of yourself.

A once-in-20-years conjunction of Jupiter and Saturn in May shows a whole new financial cycle happening for you, and perhaps a business partnership. More on this later.

Important Eclipses in your 3rd and 9th Houses are indicating changes in your educational status and is most significant for students and those headed for university. The university that you wanted to get into turns you down, and perhaps you get accepted into a better one. Your educational plans get disrupted by the Eclipse as the Higher Power has a different plan for you. A teacher engaged to teach primary school students gets transferred or replaced. Perhaps there is a change of school.

Your paths to greatest fulfilment this year are the career, higher education, religion and philosophy, work, love and the constructive expression of libido.

Health

Like last year there are many long-term planets stressfully aspected to you. Vitality is not up to its usual standards. You have enough energy to handle your true responsibilities, but not enough to waste on the frivolous things, or on things that are not really yours to do. Like last year, the advice is sharp discernment between what you really need to do and what is mere people-pleasing.

Again we urge you to wear the gems, scents, colours and metals of your Sign as these will strengthen you on the subtlest levels. Regular visits to a reflexologist, masseuse, acupuncturist or chiropractor are also excellent. Therapies that strengthen your overall system – which enhance rather than deplete your energy – are recommended.

Many of the things we wrote of last year still apply. Master techniques that will maximize your energy. Avoid people who leave you tired or depleted. Avoid situations that are draining. Cultivate friendships with people who uplift and inspire you – who add to your energy. Work rhythmically and alternate activities. Brain work should be followed by something physical or creative and vice versa. This allows your various faculties to rest and recoup. Learn the art of relaxation – there are many books and tapes on these subjects out on the market. Learn to sleep efficiently in a thoroughly relaxed way. Bring a sense of ease and relaxation into your work – for example, instead of gripping the phone or pencil as if it weighs 100 pounds, hold it lightly. Stretch when you feel tension building up in the neck and shoulders. Talk less and avoid idle gossip. Listen to your body and rest when you feel tired. Take more catnaps during the day.

Learn to meditate. Learn to harness the power of your mind to create health for yourself. In a relaxed state, visualize all the cells and organs of your body filled with white or golden light. Visualize your body as perfect in every way.

Mars is your Health Planet. This shows that brisk physical exercise enhances your health. It also shows that balanced and constructive expression of the libido is healthful. Repression can harm you. The herbs and scents of Mars are good health tonics – ruby, pineapple, garlic, cayenne pepper, onions and honeysuckle are excellent. If you wear a ruby, start on a Tuesday when the Moon is waxing.

Jupiter is still in your 6th House of Health until 15th February. For some of you – those born later in the Sign of Scorpio – it will be there for a few more months. Study the philosophy of health and disease. Educate yourself on these things.

Your most vulnerable health periods this year are from 24th March to 20th May and 22nd July to 22nd August. Be sure to rest and relax more during these periods.

If you maintain your energy levels you should come through the year 2000 with flying colours.

Home and Domestic Life

Like last year this is another volatile and powerful area. Not only is your 4th House being stirred up by two powerful planetary forces, but three Eclipses during the year are also shaking up family and domestic patterns.

Thus there are moves, repairs, radical renovations of the home. Multiple house-moves wouldn't surprise me, as there is a great urge to experiment in the home – an urge to upgrade and improve the home constantly. Thus, when you think you've found your dream home and just settle in, something nicer and 'dreamier' comes along and you want the new one. Just when you thought you had the house or flat decorated the 'right' way, a new concept occurs to you that is even better. The birth of children could also prompt a move.

The urge for high technology in the home continues. You are not satisfied until you have every possible gadget – and since these things are soon rendered obsolete by newer gadgets, you seem to be always upgrading your technology. A little research here can save much expense.

Many of you are experimenting with unconventional domestic patterns – live-in relationships and the like. Child-rearing is also experimental these days.

On an emotional level, mood swings are very intense. The highs are very high and the lows can be ultra-low. And while this brings great psychological insight and growth, it can be very trying both on yourself and those you live with. Your moods can change at the drop of a hat. You can be totally loving and friendly to a family member or flatmate one moment and snarl at them the next. No one knows what to expect from you.

Now, it is normal for the emotions to wax and wane. In a healthy individual moods will change gradually and rhythmically like the phases of the Moon. But you go through all the lunar phases in a day – perhaps even in an hour! The need is to cultivate emotional balance and equilibrium – to stay somewhere in the middle. We will discuss this later on.

Love and Social Life

1999 was a difficult year for love and there was a sense of isolation and perhaps disappointment here. But things are changing rapidly for the better. On 15th February Jupiter enters your 7th House of Marriage and stays there until 1st July. Love is much happier and easier.

Two important and opposing forces are at work in your love life this year. Saturn, like last year, is still mostly in your 7th House. It is urging you to be more selective and choosy about love. There is an urge to test love overmuch. There is a tendency to be too dour, serious and perhaps cynical about it. The feeling of true romance is hard to capture. Jupiter, on the other hand, is totally optimistic and happy. It wants to make everyone your friend. Love is a given and doesn't need to be tested. Jupiter urges you to make friends instantly and quickly – to enter into romance instantly and quickly. For many of you, the year 2000 will be an alternation between pessimism and optimism about love. You will alternate between periods of love at first sight and boundless romance, and periods of sober evaluation and testing. There will be periods of indiscriminate mingling and periods where you weed out the sincere from the insincere. My feeling is that someone is coming into your life who will understand these things and will not be threatened by your trials and tests.

The message of the stars is to let love grow and develop

slowly. Let the circumstances of life test love – you don't need to.

Singles are likely to marry or begin a serious relationship this year – though there will be delays to deal with. Married people will have an easier time in the marriage than last year.

The road to the altar has a few pitfalls that should be mentioned. Before Mr or Ms Right comes along, there is an addictive romantic relationship. Very intense. Very compulsive. It totally swallows you up. You have seldom experienced the power of such sexuality. It dominates your mind and overpowers all other concerns. It threatens to disrupt your whole life, but you don't care. Real love should enhance mental and emotional ease and clarity. But this does just the opposite. It is thrilling on a certain level, but probably won't end up in marriage. (For married people, this relationship threatens to break up the marriage.) Mr or Ms Right will be more well-rounded and will make you feel elevated.

There is also a problem of getting the family to accept your new love and vice versa. There seems to be tension here. Again, the advice is to let love grow and develop naturally. Don't foist the family on the beloved and don't foist the beloved on the family.

Those of you looking towards a second or third marriage need to be patient this year. The status quo is likely.

New and prominent friends come into the picture this year. Business partnerships are also likely – but do the necessary research before you enter into any such arrangement.

Career and Finance

Your 2nd House of Money is still powerful this year and will be so for many years to come. Pluto, your Ruler, is camped out here, indicating that you are taking personal responsibility for finance rather than delegating it to others. You are mastering money. Focused on it. Solving its mysteries. 1999 should have been a good financial year, and this trend continues.

Jupiter, your Money Planet, moves unusually fast this year. It moves through three Signs and Houses of your Horoscope, and gets involved in a rare conjunction with Saturn. This is a year of major financial developments.

Jupiter's speedy motion shows a new confidence in money issues. You make speedy progress towards your goals. You cover a lot of financial territory. Its move through three different Signs and Houses indicates that earnings and earnings opportunities will come in a variety of ways and through a variety of people. Spending and investment habits will change more than you are used to.

While Jupiter is in your 6th House (from 1st January to 15th February) money will come from work and from being productive. Co-workers can bring important financial ideas. Job-seekers meet with good fortune and employers expand the workforce in happy ways. You spend on health, health foods, vitamins and exercise or sports equipment. Investment in these industries also seems profitable.

When Jupiter moves into your 7th House, earnings opportunities will come through fortunate business partnerships or alliances. Friends and perhaps your spouse are instrumental in increasing your earnings. Your social skills and social contacts enhance the bottom line. Good friends are like money in the bank during this period.

When Jupiter moves into your 8th House on 1st July, your thoughts will turn to the prosperity of others. You will prosper by helping others to prosper, and in many cases putting their financial interests ahead of your own. You will find it easy to raise outside capital – either through borrowing or through investors. Debts will be made and paid off much more easily. If debt has been a problem, during this period it will be solved. If an inability to borrow money has been a problem, then this too will be solved. Investments in telecommunications and transportation seem lucrative, but of course you must do the necessary research. Bonds and the bond market also seem good. Married people will prosper due to the prosperity of their spouse.

Jupiter in Gemini (1st July to 31st December) also indicates that earnings come through communication, sales, marketing, mailshots and the like. There is a need to get your message out to others.

Jupiter in Aries (1st January to 15th February) brings sports and exercise equipment to you. Jupiter in Taurus brings objects of beauty and perhaps a new home. Jupiter in Gemini will bring new phones, computers, communication equipment – and perhaps a new car – to you.

Two Eclipses in your House of Career – a Lunar Eclipse on 21st January, a Solar one on 30th July – indicate career changes – perhaps even a whole new career path.

Self-improvement

With volatile emotions and wild mood swings going on, you face a need to strive for balance and equilibrium. Many people don't understand how this is done. The first step is to distance yourself from your feelings. You are an Immortal Spiritual Being who feels, but you are not the feeling. Do you see the distinction here? You feel, but are not the feeling or the state. This separation, first in thought, will allow you to view your states more dispassionately. Observe how your feelings now go one way and now another. This will prevent you from doing rash things under the influence of a particular state. The second step is to express your states in a positive and non-destructive way. Write out your bad moods, or talk them out on to a tape. This will spare those you love from these outbursts. You are much, much more than your feelings. Explore these other areas when you are in a mood. You have a mind, a physical being, a will, a heart. Physical exercise often dissipates a bad mood. Doing something creative such as painting or playing a musical instrument also helps. Meditation on the Divinity within will always make you feel better. Stop feeding a bad mood and it will soon pass. Avoid being too enthusiastic about a good mood, either. Centre in the place where absolute good – eternal and unchangeable good – lies. This is in the Divine aspect of yourself. The knowledge of enduring good will make you more sanguine about 'fleeting', changeable good.

Month-by-month Forecasts

January

> Best Days Overall: 1st, 2nd, 10th, 11th, 19th, 20th, 28th, 29th

> Most Stressful Days Overall: 8th, 9th, 15th, 16th, 21st, 22nd

> Best Days for Love: 3rd, 4th, 13th, 14th, 15th, 16th, 22nd

> Best Days for Money: 3rd, 4th, 13th, 14th, 21st, 22nd, 30th, 31st

The planets are evenly dispersed between the Eastern and Western halves of your chart this month. Thus there is a need to balance the interests of others with your own. You have power to create conditions as you like them but you still need the co-operation of others. On the other hand, you don't need to put yourself last.

Between 80 and 90 per cent of the planets are below the Horizon of your chart – even your Career Planet, the Sun, is there. You can safely let your career coast and focus on home and family issues. Further your career by supporting the career aspirations of others – especially family members. Great psychological insight and progress is attainable now.

With 90 to 100 per cent of the planets moving forward this month, this indicates great change in the world around you and forward momentum in your life. It is an exciting month.

The important areas of interest this month are finance, sales, marketing, intellectual interests, siblings, and home and family.

The Lunar Eclipse of the 21st is strong on you, Scorpio, so do take a reduced schedule during that period – two days before and about a day after. This Eclipse occurs in your Career House, showing a possible job change, change of career direction and perhaps a shake-up in the hierarchy of the company you work for. There will be disruption in your career, but when the dust settles the new pattern will be better than the old.

Your love life is very happy this month. Singles meet someone significant around the 9th. There is much dating and going out. Love finds you as you pursue your financial goals – at the workplace, the bank, etc. Lovers and partners are supportive of your financial goals. Your lover is wealthier during this period. New friends come into the picture as well. Love is physical during this period. Material gifts, financial support or opportunities are romantic turn-ons.

Finances are also strong during this period. Venus travelling with your Financial Planet is helping earnings – be careful of expensive and 'miracle' health cures after the 4th. Earnings still come from work – but work is happy and you are being paid for overtime.

Be sure to rest and relax more after the 20th. Remember the earlier discussion about maximizing energy and focusing on essentials.

Your home life is turbulent and exciting now – there could be a move or major renovation. Practise emotional equilibrium.

February

Best Days Overall: 7th, 8th, 15th, 16th, 24th, 25th

Most Stressful Days Overall: 4th, 5th, 11th, 12th, 17th, 18th

Best Days for Love: 2nd, 3rd, 11th, 12th, 22nd

Best Days for Money: 9th, 10th, 19th, 26th, 27th, 28th, 29th

The planets are marching ever more westward in your chart. By the 18th, 90 to 100 per cent of them will be there. Jupiter makes an important move into your House of Love on the 15th. The message is clear: Love and romance are in the air. Your social grace, not self-will or self-assertion, will carry you to your heart's desire. Friends are like money in the bank. Whom you know is just as important as what you have.

Having 70 to 80 per cent of the planets below the Horizon of your chart this month indicates that you need to focus on the emotional life – psychological progress, finding emotional harmony, mending fences with family members and setting up a stable home base. Let your career coast. But you won't be able to ignore your career completely, as the Solar Eclipse of the 5th is shaking things up.

With 90 to 100 per cent of the planets moving forward, this is an exciting, action-filled month – a month of great achievement, forward momentum and change.

Mercury's retrograde from the 21st onwards suggests caution when borrowing money. Cheap loans might not be as cheap as they seem. Your partner might face more financial complications during this period, though earnings will still be strong. Be more careful of how you communicate to friends.

The Solar Eclipse of the 5th is a very powerful one for you, Scorpio – please take a reduced schedule. Family members and elders should also take a reduced schedule. This Eclipse shakes up the foundations of your life – the pillars upon which you are building. Both your career and the home life get disrupted. Perhaps one is related to the other. A career change causes a move or vice versa. Major, long-term career changes are going on. When the dust settles the new pattern will be better than what went before.

Important financial and social changes are happening as well. Jupiter's move into your House of Love not only expands your social sphere, but brings someone wealthy into your life. Singles might not be single for long. Money is now earned through social networking and connections. Sheer hard work will not cut it any more.

Health is delicate until the 20th. Rest and relax more and remember the health discussion in the Health section, above.

March

Best Days Overall: 5th, 6th, 14th, 15th, 22nd, 23rd, 24th

Most Stressful Days Overall: 3rd, 4th, 9th, 10th, 16th, 17th, 30th, 31st

Best Days for Love: 3rd, 4th, 9th, 10th, 12th, 13th, 22nd, 23rd

Best Days for Money: 1st, 9th, 10th, 18th, 19th, 25th, 26th, 27th, 28th

A happy month, but don't overdo things. Never allow yourself to get overly fatigued – though others pressurize you.

Between 80 and 90 per cent of the planets are in the West and your 7th House of Love is a major House of Power. This is a strong and active social month, with many, many romantic options. With Pluto, your Ruler, going retrograde on the 15th you must avoid power struggles and undue self-assertion. Put others first and your own good will come to you in due course, quite effortlessly.

You are still in a period of psychological progress and getting in touch with your deepest feelings and desires. Living and working from your emotional comfort zone is still more important than worldly success. If you have found your emotional comfort zone, then worldly success will happen very naturally – and the success will be more gratifying.

Your important areas of interest this month are the home, family and domestic concerns, children, love affairs, creativity, entertainment, health and work, and love and social activities.

Though home and family issues are still important, they are nowhere near as frenetic and demanding as they were last month. Now the focus is on having fun, enjoying life and expressing your creativity. Even senior citizens have a childlike quality about them this month which makes them relate to children better.

Job-seekers will meet with good success during this period. Elders and parents (after the 20th) and your spouse or social contacts (after the 23rd) are likely sources for work. Work seems more a question of brawn than brain during this period.

Finances will be strong but volatile. Domestic expenses hamper your bank balance. Perhaps there are conflicts with family members over money. Money comes from work, your spouse or partner, and from social connections. You really shine at work during this period, probably doing the work of two or three people. Increased productivity (and perhaps overtime) boost your bank balance. Scorpio investors are ultra-conservative during most of this period – but after the 23rd there is increased risk-taking, speculation and profit-taking. Property seems like the best investment – but do your research.

With both your 5th House of Love Affairs and your 7th House of Marriage very powerful during this period, singles are faced with a choice. They can opt for fun and games (5th House) or serious commitment (7th House). On a long-term level, the more serious relationship will win out, but it wouldn't surprise us if you dallied a while during this period.

April

Best Days Overall: 1st, 2nd, 10th, 11th, 19th, 20th, 29th, 30th

Most Stressful Days Overall: 6th, 7th, 12th, 13th, 26th, 27th

Best Days for Love: 1st, 2nd, 6th, 7th, 12th, 13th, 21st, 22nd

Best Days for Money: 6th, 7th, 14th, 15th, 21st, 22nd, 24th, 25th

Between 80 and 90 per cent of the planets are in the West, and Pluto, your Ruler, is retrograde all month. Once again this is not a time for self-assertion or power struggles, but for co-operation, adaptability and the development of social skills. Your self-confidence is not as strong as it usually is – and perhaps it's a good thing that this is the case – too much bravado could spoil things. Your good is coming from other people rather than from your own efforts. Put the interests of others first and your own interests will be fulfilled – very naturally.

Most of the planets are still below the Horizon of your chart, so home, family and emotional issues are still very important. And, though your career gets stimulated during this period, most of your energy should go into finding and functioning from your emotional comfort zone. Finding that zone is not as difficult as it seems – it is more an issue of eliminating obstructions rather than adding new things. This is a volatile, emotional month – especially after the 19th – so you will have ample opportunity to observe your emotional 'hot spots'.

With 90 per cent of the planets moving forward, this is another month of great progress and achievement. Many planets in the element of Fire until the 19th show that progress is swift – perhaps too swift. From the 13th onwards there is almost no power in your native Water element. Thus, people can seem unconsciously cruel, unfeeling and insensitive. Bear with this. In most cases it is non-malicious – just the astrological weather.

The North Node of the Moon makes an important shift from your 10th House of Career to your 9th House. It will be in your 9th House for the rest of the year. This shows that personal happiness and fulfilment come from higher education, religion, philosophy and foreign travel. Pursuit of these interests will lift your spirits and banish depression.

Your 7th House of Love is a major House of Power this month, and by the 19th April 40 per cent of the total planetary power there. Thus there are more parties and social gatherings now. Romance is in the air. Singles are either involved, or getting involved in significant relationships. Love can come from all sorts of places – the workplace being an important one. It can also come through the matchmaking of elders or authority figures. Many people are competing – and perhaps having a power struggle among themselves – for your charms. The main problem in love is family conflict. Domestic responsibilities vie with your social life for your attention – your social life will probably win. Family members don't seem thrilled with your spouse, lover or new relationship – and this tension comes to a head after the 19th.

Rest and relax more after the 19th. Remember the health discussion in the Health section, above.

Earnings are soaring, and as mentioned come from social contacts and/or your spouse or partner. Work, too, brings extra earnings and job-seekers meet with good success now.

May

Best Days Overall: 7th, 8th, 16th, 17th, 26th, 27th

Most Stressful Days Overall: 3rd, 4th, 9th, 10th, 24th, 25th, 31st

Best Days for Love: 3rd, 4th, 12th, 13th, 22nd, 23rd, 31st

Best Days for Money: 3rd, 4th, 12th, 13th, 18th, 19th, 20th, 21st, 22nd, 31st

Pluto, your Ruler is still retrograde and 80 to 90 per cent of the planets are in the Western sector. Your self-confidence and self-esteem are not as strong as usual, and your plans for personal happiness might not be realistic. Attain your ends through charm and social skills. Allow good to happen through others. Your way might not be the best way during this period.

Though home and family issues will be important during this period – and for the rest of the year – with many planets now above the Horizon you can shift some energy to your career and ambitions in the world.

Your emotional life is still very stormy and volatile until the 20th. Family members and home projects seem frustrated, but things improve after the 20th.

Your important areas of interest this month are home and family, love, marriage and social activities, personal transformation, debt and its repayment, the deeper things of life, the libido, eliminating the unproductive and useless from your life.

Your 7th House of Love and Marriage is ultra-powerful during this period. Many a Scorpio will be walking down the aisle this month. If not right now, you will be preparing for a walk down the aisle later on. An important social and financial cycle is beginning. Business partnerships are happening. There is a need to defer present gratification until the future. Money management is very important. Love and money are connected right now. When this is expressed positively it shows a wealthy spouse, earnings from social contacts, a business partnership, the financial support of your spouse. When negatively expressed it can show that you feel unworthy of love unless you are earning money. Financial considerations overly impact on the expression of love. There's a tendency to enter into love relationships for financial motives. Conflicts with family members – who seem to oppose your choices in love – are complicating your love life.

Your social life is unusually active. Not only are you dating more, but also attending more parties and social gatherings. Singles have abundant romantic opportunities and happily the new Moon of the 4th is going to clarify this area – the new Moon will provide information that will narrow down the field of choice.

Health still very delicate until the 20th. Rest and relax more and remember previous discussions. This is not a time for burning the candle at both ends. Vitality will improve after the 20th.

June

Best Days Overall: 4th, 12th, 13th, 14th, 22nd, 23rd

Most Stressful Days Overall: 6th, 7th, 20th, 21st, 27th, 28th

Best Days for Love: 2nd, 10th, 11th, 22nd, 23rd, 27th, 28th

Best Days for Money: 8th, 9th, 15th, 16th, 17th, 18th, 19th, 27th, 28th

The planets are still mostly in the West and Pluto, your Ruler, is still retrograde. Continue to take a low profile, adapt to situations, avoid power struggles and allow your good to come to you. This is still very much a good period for re-evaluating and reviewing your personal goals.

Pluto, your Ruler, comes under unusual stress during this period showing that your self-esteem and self-confidence are not what they should be and are being tested now. It is easy to be confident and self-assured when the sun is shining and one is surrounded by admirers and adulation. True self-confidence is shown when we are dealing with adversity and opposition. Opposition has its Cosmic uses. It enables a person to view his or her own weaknesses and correct them. You will come through with flying colours.

By the 21st you are entering one of the happiest and optimistic periods of your year. Past conflicts are forgotten and all seems right with the world. Happy travel and educational opportunities come and you should take them. There will be an enlargement of your perspective on things – both in love and career. Your understanding of the world and of different cultures will widen.

Love and social activities are still very prominent. Jupiter and Saturn conjunct in your 7th House of Love indicates both an expansion and a contraction of your social life at the same time. It shows a need to focus on the quality of your relationships as well as their quantity. Your spouse or partner is very much involved in your finances – and you with theirs. Debts could be a problem early in the month, but this is short term. By the 21st debt issues are resolved one way or another. For singles, serious love is still happening.

Until the 21st it would be good to spend time getting rid of the unnecessary from your life – this could be useless possessions, clothing, furniture – or character traits. The overcoming of addictions will meet with success during this period.

Finances are strong all period. Health is stronger after the 21st. Health is enhanced through detoxification regimes until the 21st, and by metaphysical means thereafter. Prayer is a potent healing tool after the 21st.

July

Best Days Overall: 1st, 2nd, 10th, 11th, 20th, 21st, 29th

Most Stressful Days Overall: 3rd, 4th, 17th, 18th, 24th, 25th, 31st

Best Days for Love: 1st, 2nd, 10th, 11th, 22nd, 23rd, 24th, 25th, 30th, 31st

ARIES

Best Days for Money: 6th, 7th, 12th, 13th, 14th, 15th, 25th, 26th

A happy but tumultuous month, Scorpio. Health is improving day by day but you should still rest and relax more after the 22nd. Those of you with health problems should be hearing good news on this front.

Three Eclipses occur this month, an unusual number. Of the three, only one seems stressful.

The Solar Eclipse of the 1st occurs in your 9th House. It is quite kind to you. It shows long-term changes in your religious life and in your personal philosophy of life. Shake-ups could occur at a church or other religious institution which you frequent. Students change their academic status. One university or graduate school might disappoint while another, better one accepts you. Since the Sun is also your Career Planet, this Eclipse is showing happy career and job changes – probably with higher pay and better working conditions. Venus, your Love Planet, is affected by this Eclipse. Thus there could be shake-ups or disruptions in a current relationship – hidden flaws come out so they can be dealt with. Some flaws could be so great that they can't be corrected, in which case the relationship will end. Singles could decide to marry. (With Jupiter moving out of your 7th House, many singles are already involved in serious relationships – marriage would only be the next step.)

The Lunar Eclipse of the 16th occurs in your 3rd House of Neighbours, Siblings and Intellectual interests. This Eclipse is also kind to you. Since the Moon is also your Planet of Religion, Philosophy and Higher Education, this Eclipse confirms and strengthens the previous one. Long-term changes are occurring in educational and academic status. Students can change schools. School administrators change. Disruptions occur in the neighbourhood or with neighbours. Communication equipment and cars are likely to malfunction – especially if they had hidden flaws to begin with.

273

The Solar Eclipse of the 30th is the strongest one on you. Take a reduced schedule two days before and day after. This Eclipse also affects the career and is indicating career change. If you didn't change jobs after the Solar Eclipse of the 1st, you will certainly do so after this one.

Jupiter, your Money Planet, makes a major move into Gemini on the 1st. Thus there is a strong financial shift going on. Your spouse or partner is prospering and is very generous with you. You prosper as you help others to prosper. Debts will be easily paid. If outside capital is needed – whether as a loan or investment – it is easily attracted.

Love is high on the agenda this month, and though there will be disruptions it seems basically happy. There is much socializing with people of high status after the 13th. Singles are attracted to those who can help their career.

August

Best Days Overall: 6th, 7th, 16th, 17th, 25th, 26th

Most Stressful Days Overall: 13th, 14th, 15th, 20th, 21st, 22nd, 27th, 28th

Best Days for Love: 11th, 12th, 20th, 21st, 22nd, 29th, 30th

Best Days for Money: 3rd, 4th, 8th, 9th, 13th, 14th, 23rd, 24th

Saturn's move into Gemini on the 11th is a very happy transit for you. Not only does it relieve much of the health stress that you've been feeling, it also plays to your natural strengths. Saturn, now with Jupiter in your 8th House, makes you a Super Scorpio. Issues of personal transformation, life, death and rebirth, past lives, life on the other side of the veil – all become important now. Many of you will now deal with addictions (we all have them in some form or another) and will convert them to preferences. Many of you will be working at getting rid of the unnecessary in your lives – whether this means physical possessions, people you find draining, or inner character traits. You are cleaning house on deep spiritual levels. You are reinventing yourself as the person you want to be and were meant to be. As mentioned, this is happy work for a Scorpio – though not so happy for other types.

Most of the planets are above the Horizon, and your 10th House of Career is an important House of Power. You can let go of family and domestic concerns and give your full attention to your career. Much career progress is happening this month. You shine here. Higher-ups are still granting their favours. Love finds you as you pursue your career path, and there is much personal satisfaction happening in the career as well. There is no conflict between the demands of the career and your personal desires. They are very much in synch.

Finances are stronger before the 22nd than afterwards. After the 22nd you must work harder for earnings. With Jupiter in your 8th House there is a need to balance your personal financial interests with those of your partner or shareholders. You prosper by helping them to prosper – but don't ignore your own interests completely. You are in a period where you can pay off debt and attract outside capital. Tax and estate issues are bittersweet this month. Your spouse or partner is prospering but needs financial management and organization.

Love can happen with bosses or underlings during this period. After the 6th love is more platonic. Singles find love at organizations or through group activities. Your Love Planet is in Virgo – a mixed blessing. On the one hand there is a drive for purity in love and an intense examination of the beloved's motives – every word and gesture gets analysed. You want pure love unmixed with anything else. On the other hand, destructive criticism and pickiness – the focus on small, insignificant things – is major romantic turn-off. Avoid destructive criticism like the plague now.

September

Best Days Overall: 7th, 8th, 17th, 18th, 25th, 26th, 30th

Most Stressful Days Overall: 10th, 11th, 17th, 18th, 23rd, 24th

Best Days for Love: 1st, 10th, 11th, 17th, 18th, 19th, 20th, 30th

Best Days for Money: 1st, 5th, 6th, 10th, 11th, 19th, 20th, 27th, 28th

Pluto, your Ruler, is now moving forward. The planetary power is now in your Eastern sector. Your own Sign of Scorpio grows more powerful day by day. Go for it, Scorpio. Create the lifestyle you dream of living. If circumstances don't suit you, withdraw and create new ones. Your self-confidence is strong. Personal power is strong. You have secret help in all your projects.

Though home and family issues have been and continue to be important, with many planets above the Horizon this is still an important career period. Mars in your 10th House (Career) until the 17th indicates that you are working hard in this area – perhaps there are career changes and upheavals – perhaps you are shifted within your corporate structure – perhaps you are dealing with powerful competition. No matter, all of this will be resolved after the 17th – and positively at that.

When Mars leaves Leo on the 17th, your health (which has been improving dramatically these past few months) gets even better. Venus' move into your own Sign on the 24th, followed by Mercury on the 28th, enhances your health even further. Many health problems of the past are disappearing from your life now.

Your major interests this month are home and family, personal transformation, debt and its repayment, making money for others, the deeper things of life and the libido, friends, groups and organizations, spirituality, and the body, image and personal appearance.

Your love and social life really shines this month, Scorpio, but you need to look for opportunities where the spiritual connection is strong. Even your social life – the parties you attend – should have a spiritual or charitable flavour to them. The people you are meeting now are connected to you by deeper bonds than mere flesh. In some cases you are paying back past karma; in other cases you are being paid. Watch the dynamic of the relationships and you will know who is who. Serious love is definitely in the air. You might have a few false starts (karmic connections) but the end result is good. Love is chasing you ardently – all you need to do is allow it to happen.

Finances, though strong, become more complicated towards the end of the month, as your Money Planet, Jupiter, starts to retrograde. But Jupiter is receiving so many good aspects that I doubt it will stop earnings, only delay things a bit. In this case, I read Jupiter's retrograde as positive – there is so much financial progress happening that you need to take a breather and take stock of things.

October

Best Days Overall: 1st, 9th, 10th, 11th, 18th, 19th, 27th, 28th

Most Stressful Days Overall: 7th, 8th, 14th, 15th, 20th, 21st

Best Days for Love: 1st, 9th, 10th, 11th, 14th, 15th, 20th, 21st, 29th, 30th

Best Days for Money: 2nd, 3rd, 7th, 8th, 16th, 17th, 25th, 26th, 29th, 30th

Saturn's retrograde back into Taurus on the 16th increases the health stress on you. On the other hand, many planets in your own Sign are helping you. Health is a neutral this month.

Pluto is moving forward and most of the planets are in your Eastern sector. This is excellent for self-confidence and self-esteem. There's less of a need now to adapt to situations as you can create conditions as you desire them to be. With the Sun in your 12th House until the 23rd, it's a good time to take a solitary breather and work out your goals for the coming year – especially in the career. It's important to attain mental clarity on these issues.

By the 23rd, 70 to 80 per cent of the planets will be in the lower half of your Horoscope, making career and ambitions less of a priority while emotional issues – home and family concerns – are more of a priority. Still, with your Career Planet in your own Sign this month you will be making important career progress. Balancing your career with a happy home life is a major challenge this month. The conflict is very dramatic. There is also a need to balance personal inclinations with your home and domestic duties. They are in sharp contrast at present.

Your most important interests this month are the body, personal pleasure and the image, finances, home and family, personal transformation, the deeper things of life, debts and their repayment, and spirituality.

The Sun in your own Sign shows greater ambition and star quality. You don the image of the person you long to be. You appropriate the 'look' of the status that you seek – even before you have it. You dress more conservatively and with an eye to how superiors and bosses will look at you. Venus in your own Sign lends beauty and glamour to your image.

Venus, your Love Planet, in your own Sign shows that love is there with you. You are not chasing after it, but enjoying it now. Perhaps this is why you are reducing your social activities – you want to focus on that one special someone. Love is physical and sensual these days – expressed through the body and not so much through talk.

After the 19th it is expressed materially – through material gifts and financial support.

Finances are getting stronger every day. But Jupiter's retrograde shows the need for more research and caution regarding purchases and investments. Your Financial Planet continues to receive wonderful aspects, so its retrograde is not stopping earnings, only creating minor and short-term glitches.

November

Best Days Overall: 6th, 7th, 15th, 23rd, 24th

Most Stressful Days Overall: 3rd, 4th, 10th, 11th, 17th, 18th

Best Days for Love: 8th, 9th, 10th, 11th, 19th, 20th, 28th, 29th

Best Days for Money: 3rd, 4th, 12th, 13th, 21st, 22nd, 26th, 27th, 30th

Be patient with gossips and overly talkative people this month. They can't help themselves now, as there is a Grand Trine in the Air element after the 4th. As you are normally a strong, silent, introverted type, this kind of behaviour can irritate you. You too might do more talking than you are used to – and inadvertently reveal things which, under normal circumstances, would keep hidden. This is the astrological weather this month.

Most of the planets are in the East, and Pluto (your Ruler) is firmly forward. Compromise and adaptability are not that important now. You are independent, self-confident and self-reliant. You can have things your way and create conditions as you desire them to be. Go for it.

Career is important this month and seems successful. But with most of the planets below the Horizon, shift your attention to the home and family. Work to create a more stable home base. You must work to get family support for your career goals now – especially early in the month.

This is a banner financial month. Career success is measured in pounds and pence. You consider yourself successful in proportion to the amount of money you earn. Status and prestige in and of themselves carry little weight. Your good reputation and professional status propel earnings and bring new (and happy) earnings opportunities to you. Your bosses or parents might have different ideas of where your true financial interest lies. They basically want to help you, though you might not see it that way. You might have to make a short-term sacrifice for a longer-term gain. Partners and lovers are going way out of their way – doing strange things – to boost your earnings.

Those of you involved in committed or serious relationships are seeing the relationship go into unexplored territory. Relationships are very unconventional now. Those of you not involved are going off to strange places – way out of your normal orbit – in search of love. Your deepest fantasies do exist somewhere out there and you are searching ardently for them.

Health is reasonable this month. You still need to focus on essentials and manage your energy.

December

Best Days Overall: 3rd, 4th, 12th, 13th, 20th, 21st, 22nd, 30th, 31st

Most Stressful Days Overall: 1st, 2nd, 8th, 9th, 14th, 15th, 28th, 29th

Best Days for Love: 8th, 9th, 10th, 11th, 18th, 19th, 28th, 29th

Best Days for Money: 1st, 10th, 11th, 18th, 23rd, 24th, 28th

Mars in your 12th House for most of the month shows a secret war you are waging. This is not a war of bullets or fists, but a psychological war of psychic energy and 'button pushing'. The way to victory is to let go and focus on your good – easy to say, but not so easy to do. Keep your eyes on the prize emotionally and spiritually.

Mars moves into your own Sign on the 23rd and the short-term planets are making harmonious aspects to you – a positive health indicator. Mars in your own Sign makes you a Super Scorpio these days. Your normally acute psychic perceptions are even stronger. Sex appeal and libido are increased. Your temper can be short and your outbursts can be devastating. Keep them in check.

Though most of the planets are below the Horizon there will be much career activity during this period as the Solar Eclipse of the 25th stirs things up. This shows a career or job change for many of you. Some of you will take a completely different career track; others will move on to new companies; others will take different jobs within the same company. Your corporate hierarchy gets shaken up and for a while the rules and your status are different. But since this Eclipse deals kindly with you, we expect best-case scenarios.

The Eclipse occurs in your 3rd House, showing disruptions with siblings and neighbours – and perhaps within your actual locality. Mercury, Lord of Communication and Secondary Education, is also affected by the Eclipse. Thus students experience changes in their education or with their teachers. Perhaps they change schools or curricula.

The Eclipse on the Lord of your 8th and 11th Houses shows financial changes with your spouse or partner. Flaws in their investments or investment strategies are revealed so that they can be corrected. There could be a falling out with a professional organization to which you belong. Attitudes to debt – one way or another – get dramatically changed.

Finances are strong during this period though there is some conflict between you and your spouse or partner over financial issues. But this is a good conflict – it comes from love and from a desire for mutual improvement.

Love is happy and active during this period. It is close to home – perhaps with someone from your past or someone introduced to you by your family. The 12th and 24th are excellent periods for meeting that special someone.

Sagittarius

♐

THE ARCHER
Birthdays from
23rd November
to 20th December

Personality Profile

SAGITTARIUS AT A GLANCE

Element – Fire

Ruling Planet – Jupiter
  Career Planet – Mercury
  Love Planet – Mercury
  Money Planet – Saturn
  Planet of Health and Work – Venus
  Planet of Home and Family Life – Neptune
  Planet of Spirituality – Pluto

Colours – blue, dark blue

Colours that promote love, romance and social harmony – yellow, yellow-orange

Colours that promote earning power – black, indigo

Gems – carbuncle, turquoise

Metal – tin

Scents – carnation, jasmine, myrrh

Quality – mutable (= flexibility)

Qualities most needed for balance – attention to detail, administrative and organizational skills

Strongest virtues – generosity, honesty, broad-mindedness, tremendous vision

Deepest need – to expand mentally

Characteristics to avoid – over-optimism, exaggeration, being too generous with other people's money

Signs of greatest overall compatibility – Aries, Leo

Signs of greatest overall incompatibility – Gemini, Virgo, Pisces

Sign most helpful to career – Virgo

Sign most helpful for emotional support – Pisces

Sign most helpful financially – Capricorn

Sign best for marriage and/or partnerships – Gemini

Sign most helpful for creative projects – Aries

Best Sign to have fun with – Aries

Signs most helpful in spiritual matters – Leo, Scorpio

Best day of the week – Thursday

SAGITTARIUS

Understanding the Sagittarius Personality

If you look at the symbol of the archer you will gain a good, intuitive understanding of a person born under this astrological Sign. The development of archery was humanity's first refinement of the power to hunt and wage war. The ability to shoot an arrow far beyond the ordinary range of a spear extended humanity's horizons, wealth, personal will and power.

Today, instead of using bows and arrows we project our power with fuels and mighty engines, but the essential reason for using these new powers remains the same. These powers represent our ability to extend our personal sphere of influence – and this is what Sagittarius is all about. Sagittarians are always seeking to expand their horizons, to cover more territory and increase their range and scope. This applies to all aspects of their lives: economic, social and intellectual.

Sagittarians are noted for the development of the mind – the higher intellect – which understands philosophical, metaphysical and spiritual concepts. This mind represents the higher part of the psychic nature and is motivated not by self-centred considerations but by the light and grace of a Higher Power. Thus, Sagittarians love higher education of all kinds. They might be bored with formal schooling but they love to study on their own and in their own way. A love of foreign travel and interest in places far away from home are also noteworthy characteristics of the Sagittarian type.

If you give some thought to all these Sagittarian attributes you will see that they spring from the inner Sagittarian desire to develop. To travel more is to know more, to know more is to be more, to cultivate the higher mind is to grow and to reach more. All these traits tend to broaden the intellectual – and indirectly, the economic and material – horizons of the Sagittarian.

The generosity of the Sagittarian is legendary. There are many reasons for this. One is that Sagittarians seem to have an inborn consciousness of wealth. They feel that they are rich, that they are lucky, that they can attain any financial goal – and so they feel that they can afford to be generous. Sagittarians do not carry the burdens of want and limitation – which stop most other people from giving generously. Another reason for their generosity is their religious and philosophical idealism, derived from the higher mind. This higher mind is by nature generous because it is unaffected by material circumstances. Still another reason is that the act of giving tends to enhance their emotional nature. Every act of giving seems to be enriching, and this is reward enough for the Sagittarian.

Finance

Sagittarians generally entice wealth. They either attract it or create it. They have the ideas, energy and talent to make their vision of paradise on Earth a reality. However, mere wealth is not enough. Sagittarians want luxury – earning a comfortable living seems small and insignificant to them.

In order for Sagittarians to attain their true earning potential they must develop better managerial and organizational skills. They must learn to set limits, to arrive at their goals through a series of attainable sub-goals or objectives. It is very rare that a person goes from rags to riches overnight. But a long, drawn-out process is difficult for Sagittarians. Like Leos, they want to achieve wealth and success quickly and impressively. They must be aware, however, that this over-optimism can lead to unrealistic financial ventures and disappointing losses. Of course, no Zodiac Sign can bounce back as quickly as Sagittarius, but only needless heartache will be caused by this attitude. Sagittarians need to maintain their vision – never letting it go – but must also work towards it in practical and efficient ways.

SAGITTARIUS

Career and Public Image

Sagittarians are big thinkers. They want it all: money, fame, glamour, prestige, public acclaim and a place in history. They often go after all these goals. Some attain them, some do not – much depends on each individual's personal horoscope. But if Sagittarians want to attain public and professional status they must understand that these things are not conferred to enhance one's ego but as rewards for the amount of service that one does for the whole of humanity. If and when they figure out ways to serve more, Sagittarians can rise to the top.

The ego of the Sagittarian is gigantic – and perhaps rightly so. They have much to be proud of. If they want public acclaim, however, they will have to learn to tone down the ego a bit, to become more humble and self-effacing, without falling into the trap of self-denial and self-abasement. They must also learn to master the details of life, which can sometimes elude them.

At their jobs Sagittarians are hard workers who like to please their bosses and co-workers. They are dependable, trustworthy and enjoy a challenge. Sagittarians are friendly to work with and helpful to their colleagues. They usually contribute intelligent ideas or new methods that improve the work environment for everyone. Sagittarians always look for challenging positions and careers that develop their intellect, even if they have to work very hard in order to succeed. They also work well under the supervision of others, although by nature they would rather be the supervisors and increase their sphere of influence. Sagittarians excel at professions that allow them to be in contact with many different people and to travel to new and exciting locations.

Love and Relationships

Sagittarians love freedom for themselves and will readily grant it to their partners. They like their relationships to be fluid and ever-changing. Sagittarians tend to be fickle in love and to change their minds about their partners quite frequently.

Sagittarians feel threatened by a clearly defined, well-structured relationship, as they feel this limits their freedom. The Sagittarian tends to marry more than once in life.

Sagittarians in love are passionate, generous, open, benevolent and very active. They demonstrate their affections very openly. However, just like an Aries they tend to be egocentric in the way they relate to their partners. Sagittarians should develop the ability to see others' points of view, not just their own. They need to develop some objectivity and cool intellectual clarity in their relationships so that they can develop better two-way communication with their partners. Sagittarians tend to be overly idealistic about their partners and about love in general. A cool and rational attitude will help them to perceive reality more clearly and enable them to avoid disappointment.

Home and Domestic Life

Sagittarians tend to grant a lot of freedom to their family. They like big homes and many children and are one of the most fertile Signs of the Zodiac. However, when it comes to their children Sagittarians generally err on the side of allowing them too much freedom. Sometimes their children get the idea that there are no limits. However, allowing freedom in the home is basically a positive thing – so long as some measure of balance is maintained – for it enables all family members to develop as they should.

Horoscope for 2000

Major Trends

With all the long-term planets in harmonious aspect to you, 1999 should have been a fabulous year. True, you worked hard at your job, but there was a lot of fun too. It was a strong party year. Some of these trends are continuing in 2000, some are changing.

The party life continues until mid-February, and then its down to more serious business – work.

In the summer love blooms, and the year 2000 is shaping up to be a major romantic year.

The long-term process of reinventing yourself, improving yourself in terms of your health and physical appearance seems to be paying dividends. Others take notice, and curiously, your success could obstruct the further efforts you need to do in this area. Love can be distracting to the work of transformation and regeneration. More on this later.

Your Houses of Power this year are the 1st House (the Image and the Body), the 3rd House (Communication, Siblings, Neighbours and Intellectual Interests), the 5th House – until 15th February – (Parties, Children, Entertainment, Creativity, Love Affairs Outside of Marriage), the 6th House (Health and Work), and the 7th House – after 1st July – (Love, Romance, Marriage, Committed Relationships). These are the areas that will be most important to you in the coming year – the areas where you will spend most of your time, attention and energy.

Your paths to fulfilment this year are higher education, religion, philosophy and foreign travel, helping others to prosper, the constructive expression of libido, paying off debt, reinvention and transformation, parties and love affairs (until 15th February), health and work, and (after 1st July) love and romance.

Health

Your 6th House of Health is an important House of Power this year – yet, with almost all of the long-term planets in wonderful aspect to you, this is a curious circumstance. Your health looks wonderful. Vitality is strong. Your self-esteem is so strong you could look down at the sky. Perhaps merely feeling good is not enough for you – you want ultimate health – the highest ideal of health.

Saturn, your Money Planet, has been in your 6th House of Health for over a year now and will spend most of this coming year there. This indicates that you are spending money on health items – diets, miracle foods, exercise equipment, health gadgets and the like. With your physical health so good I also read this as being more concerned with financial health. You embark on a search for purity in the financial life. There's a weeding out of ideas, people and concepts which impede your earnings and overall financial health.

Saturn in your 6th House indicates a conservatism in health matters. You lean towards the traditional orthodoxy in these issues. You want methods and regimes that are tried and have withstood the test of time. New fads are anathema to you. This position also shows a desire for enduring, long-term health.

Jupiter moving through your 6th House (15th February to 1st July) shows a personal interest in health issues – not just a financial one. During this period good health also means 'looking good'. Health means physical beauty and not just feeling good. There is a strong desire to cultivate the image of health.

Both Saturn and Jupiter in your 6th House suggest a disciplined and sustained health regime – strictly adhered to.

Saturn rules the spine and the teeth, thus health can be enhanced even further by taking special care of these parts of the body.

Jupiter rules the thighs; these too enhance the health and should be massaged regularly.

Your most vulnerable health period in the coming year is from 22nd August to 4th November. There is a temporary line-up of planets in inharmonious aspect to you; rest and relax more during this period.

Home and Domestic Life

Your 4th House of Home and Family is not a House of Power this year, so you have a lot of freedom to create this area as you wish it to be. In general the Cosmos neither denies nor affirms your efforts. The home and family pattern seems much as you want it to be and you have no need to focus here.

But Neptune, your Family Planet, moves in strange company early in the year – and is affected by a Solar Eclipse on 5th February. This shows a shake-up in the home and domestic pattern. A parent behaves compulsively and automatically in a given area, and you find this behaviour irksome. Compulsive habits in the home need to be dealt with. Compulsive emotional patterns are revealed to you. The addictions of family members are highlighted so that they can be dealt with. Flaws in the home, which you didn't know existed, surface and must be repaired. A new neighbour turns out to be a pest – though he or she is not necessarily an evil person. Drunks or addicts invade the neighbourhood and cause you to re-evaluate your home. All of these scenarios involve 'underworld, deeply subconscious' forces that were always there but of which you were unaware. The first few months of 2000 will provide you with an opportunity to deal with these things in a creative way. There will be great psychological progress during this period.

Neptune in the Sign of Aquarius for many years to come makes you more expressive emotionally – there is new freedom to express how you feel, which you haven't had for many years. The communication of feeling is important now. It shows a need for freedom in the home and a special disdain for routine. It could show many moves in the coming years.

Neptune in your 3rd House indicates that when you buy a home or move house, you tend to buy the neighbourhood rather than the home. The area is more important to you. An OK home in a good residential area is preferred to an excellent home in a less fashionable neighbourhood.

The domestic life (as well as the overall life) of a sibling is very unsettled. A move, perhaps multiple moves, are in store this year.

Love and Social Life

As the year begins you are in a party mood. You don't seem inclined to 'get serious' or look for committed relationships. Fun and games seem to suffice for you. But as the year progresses your attitudes change. By the summer – perhaps after a disappointment in love – you are ready for a real and significant relationship. You are ready to meet your Divine Selection, and you will.

Thus, love is status quo for the first half of the year, but really rockets after this.

Jupiter moving into your 7th House of Love on 1st July not only brings serious romance, but also new and important friends and social connections. Your social life expands and is happy.

This, of course, doesn't happen by itself. You are making it happen. You are very aggressive socially, reaching out to others, putting the interests of others ahead of your own, working to become popular, developing your social graces and skills.

Typically Sagittarian, you are not sitting at home waiting for the Divine Selection to come to you. You are out there, on the hunt, on the prowl, attending one party after another, attending seminars and lectures, looking, searching ... until it happens. Ostensibly, you are networking for your business, but this is not the true agenda.

But love is not a smooth ride this year. Saturn will move into your 7th House on 11th August, and rest assured it will test the current love. Saturn is a genius at this and you should rejoice in this testing. For Saturn will winnow out the real from the unreal, the true from the counterfeit. If your love is true, it will not only withstand the tests and pressures placed upon it (they seem financial in nature) but actually grow stronger.

Saturn in your 7th House suggests patience in love, the need to focus on quality rather than quantity, the need to recognize the burdens and responsibilities that come with a relationship. It also shows a few false starts in the love area.

On the positive end, this will bring you someone who can further your financial goals. Perhaps the intended will be someone wealthy or from a wealthy family. It could indicate someone much older and more settled than yourself.

Jupiter conjuncts Saturn in May of 2000. This heralds a business partnership for you. Both Jupiter and Saturn in your 7th House from 11th August to 27th October also suggests a business partnership.

Those of you looking towards a second marriage (or who are currently in a second marriage) have a few crisis on their hands – these are brought up by the Lunar Eclipse of 21st January and the Solar Eclipse of 30th July. For the unattached it shows dissatisfaction with the present condition and perhaps a decision to change the marital status. For the attached, it shows a crisis in the relationship and a need either to correct the flaws or dissolve the partnership.

Those of you looking towards a third marriage (or who are married for the third time) can expect to maintain the status quo. But even you will have an expanded social life this year, and perhaps embark upon a business partnership.

Career and Finance

Neither your 2nd House of Money nor your 10th House of Career is a House of Power this year, Sagittarius, so these areas are not that important to you. Other things take priority. Things are pretty much the way you want them and you have a lot of freedom here. No compulsions one way or another.

Yet there are interesting developments happening on the financial front – almost on their own. Saturn, your Money Planet, will change Signs in August and will enter a rare and unusual (once in 20 years) conjunction with Jupiter in May.

For most of the year your Money Planet will be in Taurus, your 6th House of Health and Work. We've discussed the health implications of this earlier. Financially, this indicates that the bulk of your income is being earned – it comes from work and productive service. Saturn in Taurus suggests earnings from property, agriculture, beef and the beef industry, builders, and sugar and the sugar industry. This could come from working for these kinds of companies, getting these kinds of companies as clients or customers for your business, or from investments here.

Though you are playful and speculative in your personal life in the early part of the year, when it comes to finances you seem unusually conservative. You are thinking long term. You avoid risks. You take a steady, day-to-day approach to amassing wealth – attaining to financial goals in steady steps rather than all at once. You are saving more these days, which is uncharacteristic of you. You are more careful of how you spend, checking prices and looking for the best deals – also uncharacteristic of you. Sagittarian investors are value investors these days rather than momentum players. They are more havers-and-holders rather than traders.

But Saturn will move into Gemini on 11th August, signalling a shift in financial attitudes and strategies. Investors will perhaps shift into areas like telecommunications, transportation and the media. They will become more active traders. Financial windfalls will come from mergers and acquisitions. Non-investors will earn money from social contacts, from the marriage, from networking and perhaps through landing jobs or clients in the above-mentioned industries. Sales and communication become important to your bank balance.

Jupiter is your personal planet – your Ruler. Saturn is your Money Planet. When they come together in May (they will travel together during May and June, but will be exactly conjunct on the 28th May) the symbolism is very clear. You come into money. You take control of earnings. There is an important financial windfall or financial opportunity. Perhaps a business partnership is forming. You dress for success and get a new and expensive wardrobe. You take on the image of wealth and lead a more opulent lifestyle. This is a very happy and fortunate financial period.

Self-improvement

In August two important planets oppose Pluto in your own Sign. As mentioned earlier, Pluto is the force that is transforming your image, personality and body. It is the force that is helping you to reinvent yourself as the person you want to be – the ideal you. This summer love enters the picture and seems to distract you from this project. This is natural. In all probability the kind of love you attract will show you – very graphically – how far you've come. For the lover is a mirror of yourself. Social urges in general can distract you as you have a need to be out there and be socially popular. The process of transformation is often, on the other hand, a lonely process – best done away from the crowd, in the secret chambers of the mind and heart. By all means have a happy social life, but don't let it swallow you up to the point where you neglect the important work of personal transformation. Give time to both.

Your 3rd House of Communication and Intellectual Interests is very powerful this year – and for years to come. Your intellectual life is in ferment. Your mind is working overtime. Keep a diary and record your thoughts and ideas. Take classes in things that interest you. Keep your mind occupied on constructive rather than destructive projects. If you channel this extra mental energy into studies, you will have less time for idle gossip, idle thinking and other energy-wasters. And you will become a better, more interesting person.

Month-by-month Forecasts

January

Best Days Overall: 3rd, 4th, 13th, 14th, 21st, 22nd, 30th, 31st

Most Stressful Days Overall: 10th, 11th, 17th, 18th, 23rd, 24th

Best Days for Love: 3rd, 4th, 5th, 6th, 7th, 13th, 14th, 15th, 16th, 17th, 18th, 22nd, 25th, 26th

Best Days for Money: 3rd, 4th, 5th, 6th, 7th, 13th, 14th, 15th, 16th, 21st, 22nd, 23rd, 24th, 30th, 31st

Though the percentage lessens somewhat this month, the planetary power is still mostly in the Eastern sector of your chart – the sector of self. Thus there is less of a need for social toadying, or catering to other people. Of course you shouldn't be nasty to them, but you are more independent now, and if things are not the way you want them you have power to create your own conditions.

With 90 to 100 per cent of the planets moving forward this month, you will enjoy great success in your projects and creations. There is much (and fast-paced) forward momentum in your life and in the world around you – just the way you like things, Sagittarius.

Between 90 and 100 per cent of the planets are below the Horizon of your chart, indicating that you can safely let career issues and worldly affairs go and focus on your inner life – the finding of your emotional comfort zone, mending relations with family members, setting up a stable home base and making psychological progress within yourself. Those of you in therapy will enjoy great success during this period.

The important areas of interest this month are the body, the image, personal pleasures, finance, sales, marketing, siblings and intellectual interests, and home and family.

The Lunar Eclipse of the 21st deals kindly with you but it wouldn't hurt to take a reduced schedule that day anyway. The disruptions it causes in the world work in your favour. For you, this Eclipse brings a change in your partner's income and financial strategies. He or she might have had unrealistic financial goals (either too low or too high) and the Eclipse will straighten things out. For students it shows a change in academic status or some disruption at school. Perhaps you had your heart set on one school and another, better one opens up for you. Perhaps you change what subject you wish to focus on. Religious attitudes change for the long term.

Love seems very happy during this period. With Venus in your own Sign until the 24th you have seldom looked better. Your aesthetic taste and sense of style are ultra-high. This is a good time to buy clothing and accessories. Until the 19th love is physical and materialistic. You are turned on by worldly attributes – material gifts or by someone wealthy and successful – someone who can help you financially. After the 19th love becomes much more interesting and exciting. Abstract qualities like glamour, unconventionality and genius appeal to you. Love comes suddenly – probably in your neighbourhood or close to home.

Health is excellent and finances are very powerful. When your Money Planet moves forward on the 12th, long-stalled deals will start moving forward.

February

Best Days Overall: 9th, 10th, 17th, 18th, 26th, 27th, 28th

Most Stressful Days Overall: 7th, 8th, 13th, 14th, 19th, 20th

Best Days for Love: 2nd, 3rd, 6th, 11th, 12th, 13th, 14th, 15th, 16th, 22nd, 24th, 25th

Best Days for Money: 2nd, 3rd, 9th, 10th, 11th, 12th, 19th, 20th, 29th

By the 20th the planetary power will shift decisively to the Western sector of your chart. Thus, you need to let go of self-assertion, wilfulness and a 'my way' attitude and embrace the social graces – negotiation, charm, compromise and the seeking of consensus. Good will come through the grace of others now.

With 90 to 100 per cent of the planets still below the Horizon, you need to continue to focus on emotional, inner issues, rather than outer, worldly issues. Continue to search for, and function from, your emotional comfort zone. Find your point of inner happiness and work from there. Family relations can be stormy early in the month, but from a psychological point of view these storms are valuable as they aid in your understanding of your emotional trigger points. With all these planets below the Horizon and with Mercury, your Career Planet, retrograde from the 21st onwards, you can safely let career issues go for a while. Your career judgement is not realistic until then and important decisions shouldn't be taken.

Aside from the fact that the planetary momentum is overwhelmingly forward, there are other signals showing this to be a month of momentous change, progress and achievement. Jupiter, your Ruling Planet (the planet that depicts you personally) makes a major move from your 5th House to your 6th House. Thus you are becoming more serious in life. Work and service are becoming more important than the party life. Personal health is also becoming more important and you are starting on a serious, disciplined regime.

The Solar Eclipse of the 5th deals kindly with you. For students it shows changes in educational status. In many cases these are natural (though disruptive) changes – you graduate from one school and enter another one. You go off to university. One university turns you down but another, better one accepts you. The Eclipse also shows changes in philosophy and religious beliefs. There could be a shake-up in your church, mosque or synagogue that is disruptive to your religious life. Relations with a sibling or a neighbour get stormy for a brief period. But remember that the Eclipses serve a Higher Plan, and these disruptions are merely the agents of positive change.

Finances are stormy during this period. Perhaps you have to work harder for earnings than you are used to. But this is short term. Over the long term the financial picture is bright indeed. Jupiter is moving ever closer to your Financial Planet, and by May will catch up with it. Personal wealth and financial freedom are close at hand.

March

Best Days Overall: 7th, 8th, 16th, 17th, 25th, 26th

Most Stressful Days Overall: 5th, 6th, 12th, 18th, 19th

Best Days for Love: 3rd, 4th, 5th, 6th, 12th, 13th, 14th, 15th, 22nd, 23rd, 24th

Best Days for Money: 1st, 9th, 10th, 18th, 19th, 27th, 28th, 29th

By the 13th the planetary power will be firmly in your Western sector, the sector of other people. It's time to develop social skills and enjoy the conditions you've created for yourself in the past few months. Presumably you have what you want and it is now time to put other people first.

With 90 to 100 per cent of the planets still below the Horizon you can safely let go of career activities and focus on psychological progress and home and family issues. With your Career Planet (Mercury) still retrograde, career issues are at a standstill anyway, so you may as well mend fences at home.

With 90 per cent of the planets forward all month this is still a period of progress, achievement and forward momentum in most areas of your life.

Your important areas of interest this month are local travel, communication, intellectual interests, neighbours and siblings, home, family and psychological issues, children, creativity, entertainment and love affairs, and health and work.

This month favours redecorating or otherwise beautifying the home, having family gatherings and get togethers, and entertaining from the home. The new Moon of the 6th is going to clarify all of these issues as the month progresses.

The full Moon of the 20th occurs right on the cusp of your 10th and 11th Houses and gives you extra energy to deal with group activities and your career. (Though career matters are de-emphasized this month, that doesn't mean they are non-existent.)

Health is basically good but rest and relax more until the 20th. After the 20th you have the energy of 10 people. Health can be enhanced by taking care of your ankles, feet and stomach.

Committed types of love are complicated until the 14th, as your Love Planet is retrograde. But non-serious love affairs seem plentiful all month. Love is enhanced by giving the beloved space and by nurturing. A home-cooked meal or a quiet evening at home suits the beloved just fine. Love is close to home and can come through the introduction of family members or parents. There is much love nostalgia now and many of you are yearning for things that belong to the past. You are not being very realistic. Look to the future.

Finances are getting stronger day by day. Beware of excessive risk-taking after the 23rd.

April

Best Days Overall: 4th, 5th, 12th, 13th, 21st, 22nd

Most Stressful Days Overall: 1st, 2nd, 8th, 9th, 14th, 15th, 29th, 30th

Best Days for Love: 1st, 2nd, 8th, 9th, 10th, 11th, 12th, 13th, 21st, 22nd

Best Days for Money: 6th, 7th, 14th, 15th, 24th, 25th

This is one of the happiest, most carefree months of your year, so enjoy, Sagittarius.

With 60 to 70 per cent of the planets in the Western sector there's a need for less self-assertion and more co-operation and social grace. Other people are becoming ever more vital to your good and you must cultivate their grace.

With 90 to 100 per cent of the planets still below the Horizon you are in a period of psychological rather than career growth.

Your important areas of interest this month are local travel, intellectual interests, sales, marketing and communication, neighbours and siblings, the home, family and domestic issues, children, parties, love affairs, creativity and entertainment, and health and work.

The North Node of the Moon shifts (on the 10th) from your 9th House to your 8th House. Thus there is great emotional fulfilment to be gained from dealing with personal transformation, the deeper things of life, in-depth psychology, dealing with addictions, helping others to prosper and getting rid of the unnecessary from your life. Pluto in your own Sign has been spurring these interests for some years now – but now these interests are even stronger. You have the Cosmic opportunity to create a whole new body and image for yourself – to give birth to the person you want to be and were meant to be.

Health, though good, is a major focus this month – especially after the 19th. Health regimes, diets and disciplines go well. You are very motivated here. You are attending health seminars, reading books on health and otherwise increasing your knowledge in these areas. You have decided – and rightly so – to take personal responsibility for your health and not delegate the job to others.

Job-seekers meet with good fortune now. Employers are taking on more people. The pace at work is hectic. Personal productivity soars. There are more opportunities for overtime work and for the extra earnings this brings. Co-workers come up with interesting financial propositions or ideas.

Finances are improving day by day. A happy windfall (perhaps through a speculation or through some creative project) comes around the 16th–17th. Your Money Planet is receiving powerful benefic influences. There is a conspiracy of good in your financial life.

Now that Mercury is moving forward, love is happier. But the focus this month is on love affairs and not committed, serious relationships. Married people are more 'honeymoonish' and playful during this period.

May

Best Days Overall: 1st, 2nd, 9th, 10th, 18th, 19th, 20th, 28th, 29th

Most Stressful Days Overall: 5th, 6th, 12th, 13th, 26th, 27th

SAGITTARIUS

Best Days for Love: 3rd, 4th, 5th, 6th, 12th, 13th, 14th, 22nd, 23rd, 24th, 25th

Best Days for Money: 3rd, 4th, 12th, 13th, 21st, 22nd, 31st

Though retrograde activity increases this month, this is still a very momentous month for you – both socially and financially. Long-term changes are going on in these areas, with perhaps some delayed reactions.

The planetary power is now mostly in the West and your 7th House of Social Activities is a major House of Power for most of the month. Though in general you are an independent, self-reliant person, this month you are much less so. You need the grace and the co-operation of other people now and must adapt to their needs. This is no time to go it alone. Happily, your social grace and charm are strong and very much up to the tasks ahead. Your popularity will soar as the month progresses.

The short-term planets are shifting to the upper half of your Horoscope by the 20th. And though the bottom half is still powerful, it is less emphasized than last month. You've got to balance career and family, inner progress with outer progress – you can't lean too far in either direction.

Your important areas of interest now are siblings, neighbours, intellectual pursuits, sales, marketing and communication, local travel, health and work, and love and romance.

Job-seekers continue to enjoy good fortune. Those already at jobs are working harder and being more productive. Overtime opportunities seem plentiful. Employers too are expanding their staff.

Love seems stormy early in the month as there can be a power struggle with your spouse or current love. Your ego and self-esteem will be tested. A lover from your past comes back into the picture and will test the spiritual work you've been doing on your image and personality. But love gradually improves as the month progresses. Mercury (your Love Planet) moves into your House of Love on the 14th, bringing true romance into the picture. There is much intellectual communion with the beloved – and much talk in general. Mind those phone bills. The Sun enters your House of Love on the 20th, making love more honeymoonish and fun. A current relationship becomes more like a love affair than a marriage. For single women this indicates an Adonis-type coming into your life. There are more parties and entertainments with the beloved. Venus enters your House of Love on the 25th. Again this increases romance and party-going. For single men it indicates a young, beautiful person entering the picture.

Health is delicate after the 20th; rest and relax more.

Finances are very powerful during this period. Long-term prosperity is happening. A happy financial windfall comes towards the end of the month.

June

Best Days Overall: 6th, 7th, 15th, 16th, 25th, 26th

Most Stressful Days Overall: 2nd, 8th, 9th, 22nd, 23rd, 29th, 30th

Best Days for Love: 2nd, 3rd, 4th, 5th, 10th, 11th, 12th, 13th, 14th, 22nd, 23rd, 29th, 30th

Best Days for Money: 8th, 9th, 17th, 18th, 19th, 27th, 28th

With many planets in the West and with retrograde activity increasing, there is little you can do to hasten the pace of change and progress. Things will happen when they should and not a moment sooner. Patience is a great virtue during this period. Coast along now, adapt to situations, develop your social skills and put other people first. Your good will come to you very naturally.

The planets have firmly shifted to the upper half of your Horoscope now, making you more ambitious and worldly than usual. It's a good time to focus on your career, but try to wrap up major career projects or changes before the 23rd. Mercury's retrograde doesn't stop career progress, but slows it down somewhat. Career offers and job changes need more research after the 23rd. Your judgement in these issues is not as keen as usual. Don't jump into anything without a full understanding of the details.

Mercury's retrograde on the 23rd complicates love issues for a while – but considering the hectic pace and activity of your love life during this period, the retrograde seems like a good thing. It creates a pause – a breather from which you can further develop a current relationship or your love life in general.

You are still unusually aggressive in love until the 16th. Venus in your 7th House (happily) is preventing you from indulging in caveman tactics and helps you to be aggressive in charming, non-offensive ways. Power struggles are playful and not malicious. There is an abundance of romantic opportunity during this period, and the new Moon of the 2nd will help you sort things out.

Health and vitality will improve after the 21st. Rest and relax more until then.

Social demands have put a temporary halt on your project to revamp your image and body. But after the 21st these issues go well again. Now is the time to give birth to your true and ideal self.

After the 21st the deeper things in life call to you. Psychic ability increases and you are more interested in life, death, and life after death.

Major financial developments are still taking place – and they are happy and prosperous. Pay off debt after the 21st, or refinance existing debt where possible. Your partner or spouse is prospering and is more generous with you. Job-seekers are successful and co-workers are a source of financial opportunity.

July

Best Days Overall: 3rd, 4th, 12th, 13th, 22nd, 23rd, 31st

Most Stressful Days Overall: 5th, 6th, 20th, 21st, 26th, 27th

Best Days for Love: 1st, 2nd, 10th, 11th, 20th, 21st, 22nd, 23rd, 26th, 27th, 29th, 30th, 31st

Best Days for Money: 6th, 7th, 14th, 15th, 16th, 25th, 26th

An eventful but happy month. Major developments are happening in love, finance and in academic status.

Three Eclipses disrupt the world around you this month, Sagittarius, but none of this disruption really touches you. Disruptions are actually opportunities. They clear the way to higher happiness.

The Solar Eclipse of the 1st occurs in your 8th House, affecting the income and finances of your spouse or partner. Flaws in their investments or with investment strategies will be revealed so that corrective action can be taken. A loan or mortgage you covet could fall through or be temporarily delayed – but it will happen eventually either with the same bank or with another – and probably at better terms. An investor can change his or her mind – but the needed funds will come one way or another. Changes in sexual attitudes are occurring as well.

The Lunar Eclipse of the 16th occurs in your Money House, causing you to change investments, investment advisors, banks or brokers. Flaws in your finances or financial planning will be revealed so you can fix them. Finances for the month are basically strong.

The Solar Eclipse of the 30th occurs in your 9th House of Religion, Higher Education and Philosophy. For students this shows changes in academic status. You are moving on to university or graduate school or graduating from these institutions. In many cases the Eclipse produces a hiatus in education. You think you're going to one school but end up in another. You think you will have one teacher and end up with another. While the change is happening you feel in limbo. Many of you will shift religious and philosophical attitudes during this period, as their hidden flaws are revealed. Those of you looking to make a second marriage could decide to change your marital status.

Jupiter, your Ruling Planet, makes a major move from Taurus into Gemini on the 1st. This is your 7th House of Love and Marriage. It indicates an intense interest in these things now. You are chasing after love aggressively, cultivating the social graces and in general shoring up your popularity. Love is important for the rest of the year. Right now most of the planets are in the West, so this new social popularity (which you are working hard to attain) is going to help you. But this interest will remain strong even when the planets move eastward. Marriage or a significant relationship is very likely in the coming months.

Health is excellent all month – but especially after the 22nd.

August

Best Days Overall: 8th, 9th, 18th, 19th, 27th, 28th

Most Stressful Days Overall: 1st, 2nd, 16th, 17th, 23rd, 24th, 29th, 30th

Best Days for Love: 8th, 9th, 11th, 12th, 18th, 19th, 20th, 21st, 23rd, 24th, 29th, 30th

Best Days for Money: 2nd, 3rd, 4th, 11th, 12th, 13th, 14th, 22nd, 23rd, 24th

Saturn's move into Gemini on the 11th complicates the love life and increases the health stress on you. By all means rest and relax more after the 22nd. Focus on essentials and maximize your energy. This is a time for making hard choices, as you can't be everywhere and do everything.

Though love is happy and active most of the month, Saturn's move into your House of Love shows a need for testing love. It shows caution in relationships and a tendency to follow your mind rather than your heart. Relationships have a practical angle to them – mostly financial. Financial issues are important in love compatibility now – they either enhance or detract from a relationship – perhaps unduly. You find yourself attracted to those who can help elevate your financial status.

Saturn in your House of Love also indicates a need to focus on the quality of your relationships rather than their quantity. Jupiter in your House of Love urges you to make friends indiscriminately – the more friends the better. Saturn urges you to the opposite – to weed out the flawed and insincere ones. So this is how your love life will go for a while. There will be periods where you socialize indiscriminately – social bingeing – and there will be periods where you go on a social diet.

For sure you are attracting the wealthy into your social sphere these days. Many of you are marrying wealthy people, or entering into business partnerships and alliances.

Finances are strong until the 22nd. Earnings increase; there is a sense of financial optimism, a widening of your financial horizons and an easy-come-easy-go attitude. After the 22nd finances become somewhat more difficult – of course you earn, but the earnings will come through more work and effort. There is a conflict between the urge for status and the urge for wealth. Financial deals or arrangements that detract from your professional status or public prestige bother you. You may be involved in some such deals, and resolving the conflict is difficult.

Power in your 9th House until the 22nd ensures that this is basically a happy month. The Cosmos plays to your natural strengths – there is an urge to higher education, foreign travel and to explore the deeper mysteries of religion and philosophy.

September

Best Days Overall: 5th, 6th, 14th, 15th, 16th, 23rd, 24th

Most Stressful Days Overall: 12th, 13th, 19th, 20th, 25th, 26th

Best Days for Love: 1st, 10th, 11th, 19th, 20th, 29th, 30th

Best Days for Money: 1st, 7th, 8th, 10th, 11th, 19th, 20th, 27th, 28th

By the 17th, 70 to 80 per cent of the planets will be in the Eastern sector. And, though your love and social life will still be very important, you are much more independent and self-reliant than you have been of late. You are not going to withdraw completely from society and go it alone, but you will have greater control of conditions and circumstances. You seem to have a knack for knowing where you can go it alone without offending others – to be independent and still maintain popularity.

With the 10th House of Career a major House of Power all month, and with most of the planets above the Horizon, this is an important career month. De-emphasize home and domestic issues and push forward towards your worldly goals. Career will go great guns as there are many benefic planets in your 10th House. The Sun (Lord of your 9th House) in your Career House until the 22nd shows you are a star at work. Professional and public esteem are high and expansive. Career horizons are expanded. A pay rise or pro-motion is likely. Mars in your Career House after the 17th shows hard work but also fun at work. Career gambles pay off. Many of you are doing more entertaining and partying related to your career – perhaps entertaining clients or prospects. Your children's careers become important. The achievements of children (for those of you with children) boost your public prestige.

Your important areas of interest this month are neighbours, siblings, communication, local travel and intellectual interests, love and romance, career, friends, groups and organizations, and spirituality.

Your Financial Planet, Saturn, goes retrograde on the 12th. Major purchases, investments and financial commitments need more study. Your financial judgement is not as sharp as usual, and financial deals and projects may not be what you think they are. Still this will be a powerful earnings month as Saturn receives beautiful aspects from most of the planets. Saturn's opposition to Pluto shows a financial disagreement with a friend. It will abate in the coming months but it is not over yet. Hopefully you consummated business partnerships last month. Now things are more delicate and partnerships need to be studied more carefully.

Love is still happy, but the retrograde of Jupiter in your House of Love shows that you are ready for a breather from all this social activity. As written in preceding months – focus on quality, not quantity. This applies to relationships and to going out. Pick and choose your friends and social activities more carefully.

Rest and relax more until the 22nd. Health is basically good.

October

Best Days Overall: 2nd, 3rd, 12th, 13th, 20th, 21st, 29th, 30th

Most Stressful Days Overall: 2nd, 3rd, 9th, 10th, 11th, 16th, 17th, 23rd, 24th

Best Days for Love: 1st, 9th, 10th, 11th, 16th, 17th, 18th, 19th, 20th, 21st, 27th, 28th, 29th, 30th

SAGITTARIUS

Best Days for Money: 4th, 5th, 6th, 7th, 8th, 15th, 16th, 17th, 24th, 25th, 26th

Many planets in the East and the retrograde of two important social planets suggest a need for getting into your own thing and de-emphasizing your social life. Social activities are still very important, but seem aimless and confused. Work to create your own happiness.

The planets are evenly distributed between the upper and lower halves of your Horoscope – there is a need to balance career and family – don't go too far one way or the other. With Mars in your 10th House you are working hard, fending off the competition, defending your position in the world. But don't ignore your home base.

Though your love life is basically happy, and your social circle is undergoing a big expansion, this is a time for taking a breather – for taking stock of the situation and seeing where you want to go next. The situation is like a pause in a rising bull market.

The retrograde of Jupiter, your Ruler, along with many planets in your 10th House after the 23rd suggest that taking stock should be done in other areas of your life aside from the social side of things. This is a good period for more solitude and introspection – to review the past year and make plans for the next. This is a good period for seeking counsel from astrologers, gurus or ministers. Give some thought to what is being said, as the intent of the message can be different from what you may think superficially. When clarity is attained you will be in a better position to create happy conditions.

Finances become more delicate during this period as Saturn, your Money Planet, goes retrograde on the 16th. Major purchases, investments and financial deals need more study and homework. Big deals are subject to various delays. This is not a time for thinking about quick money, but about wealth over the long term. Saturn's shift back into Taurus suggests a shift in financial attitudes as well. Money comes from work and service and not so much from partners and social contacts.

Health is basically good, but you need to be careful of overwork. The driving urges of your ambitions can lead you to overtax your body. Venus moves into your own Sign on the 19th which brings you love and glamour. It's a good time to buy clothing and personal accessories – if you need them – as your sense of style will be good.

November

Best Days Overall: 8th, 9th, 17th, 18th, 26th, 27th

Most Stressful Days Overall: 6th, 7th, 13th, 19th, 20th

Best Days for Love: 6th, 7th, 8th, 9th, 13th, 15th, 16th, 19th, 20th, 23rd, 24th, 28th, 29th

Best Days for Money: 1st, 2nd, 3rd, 4th, 11th, 12th, 13th, 20th, 21st, 22nd, 28th, 29th, 30th

Though your social life continues to shine, you are having second thoughts about it as it leads you into situations that you can't control. Many planets in the East and power in your own Sign after the 22nd are reinforcing your natural independence and self-will. There is great ambivalence about social issues during this period. You want an active social life but you find the limitations irksome. On the other hand, though you know you can have things your own way you are reluctant to abandon the friendships and love relationships you've developed. You will have to pick and choose the areas of life in which you want to be independent.

By the 22nd the planetary power shifts to the bottom half of your chart and you enter a period of increased emphasis on emotional harmony and home and family issues. Mars leaves your 10th House of Career on the 4th, which also de-emphasizes career matters. You've been working hard lately; take a break now.

Job-seekers are venturing into strange and unknown places in search of work – perhaps indulging in shocking and attention-getting behaviour in the process. It seems to work.

A weird and unconventional health regime or diet could work though it seems outlandish to you. This is a month for stretching the borders of your health concepts. Health is basically good, though – especially after the 22nd – but your urge is to enhance it further.

Though your Ruler is retrograde, your self-confidence and self-esteem is unaffected. Jupiter is receiving such wonderful aspects all month that nothing can daunt it. Your personal appearance shines. Personal and sensual pleasures are abundant. The Cosmos, and those around you, are working overtime to keep you happy.

Mercury moves forward on the 8th and the Lord of your 9th House moves into your own Sign on the 22nd. Combine this with a Grand Trine in the Air element for most of the month and you have one of the best periods in the year for students, teachers, and sales and marketing people. Grades should be extra good now. Learning comes easily. There is good news about university. Foreign travel opportunities come your way.

Finances are powerful all month. You can't help making money now. Friends and lovers are powerful on your behalf.

Love is improving with Mercury's forward motion on the 8th. Still, a marriage or divorce should not be scheduled now.

December

Best Days Overall: 6th, 7th, 14th, 15th, 23rd, 24th

Most Stressful Days Overall: 3rd, 4th, 10th, 11th, 16th, 17th, 30th, 31st

Best Days for Love: 6th, 7th, 10th, 11th, 14th, 15th, 18th, 19th, 25th, 26th, 28th, 29th

Best Days for Money: 1st, 8th, 9th, 10th, 11th, 16th, 17th, 18th, 25th, 26th, 27th, 28th

Both Mercury and the Lord of your 9th House (indicating long-distance travel) are affected by the Solar Eclipse of the 25th. Many of you will not be able to avoid travelling during this holiday season, but try to schedule your flights or driving around this period. Otherwise this Eclipse is basically kind to you.

Dynamic Mars moves into the intense Sign of Scorpio on the 23rd. This is your 12th Solar House. Thus there will be a tendency to fight a secret war. This is a psychological war and not a physical one – yet it can be just as deadly in a different way. It will be an excellent period for letting go of anger and resentment and cultivating inner peace. It won't be easy, but it is worth doing.

Health is fabulous all month. The Sun, Pluto and Mercury in your own Sign bring energy, social grace and joviality to your image. You can walk into a room and banish depression from everyone there. Love is pursuing you ardently and your lover is doing everything possible to please you. (You are also going out of your way to please your lover, so the arrangement seems to work out fine.) The Solar Eclipse has a major impact on your love life – a marriage could be in store now. The urge is to change or turn your current status around.

Finances, too, are strong all month, though the Solar Eclipse of the 25th is going to shake things up a bit. Since the Eclipse is kind to you I read this as a good shake-up. Obstructions to your financial goals and good must be cleared away in order for you to achieve them. Your investment strategy will change. Brokers, bankers, financial advisors, etc. are also likely to be changed. When the dust settles you will be in better financial shape than before.

Capricorn

♑

THE GOAT

*Birthdays from
21st December
to 19th January*

Personality Profile

CAPRICORN AT A GLANCE

Element – Earth

Ruling Planet – Saturn
   Career Planet – Venus
   Love Planet – Moon
   Money Planet – Uranus
   Planet of Communications – Neptune
   Planet of Health and Work – Mercury
   Planet of Home and Family Life – Mars
   Planet of Spirituality – Jupiter

Colours – black, indigo

*Colours that promote love, romance and social
harmony* – puce, silver

Colour that promotes earning power – ultramarine blue

Gem – black onyx

Metal – lead

Scents – magnolia, pine, sweet pea, wintergreen

Quality – cardinal (= activity)

Qualities most needed for balance – warmth, spontaneity, a sense of fun

Strongest virtues – sense of duty, organization, perseverance, patience, ability to take the long-term view

Deepest needs – to manage, take charge and administrate

Characteristics to avoid – pessimism, depression, undue materialism and undue conservatism

Signs of greatest overall compatibility – Taurus, Virgo

Signs of greatest overall incompatibility – Aries, Cancer, Libra

Sign most helpful to career – Libra

Sign most helpful for emotional support – Aries

Sign most helpful financially – Aquarius

Sign best for marriage and/or partnerships – Cancer

Sign most helpful for creative projects – Taurus

Best Sign to have fun with – Taurus

Signs most helpful in spiritual matters – Virgo, Sagittarius

Best day of the week – Saturday

Understanding the Capricorn Personality

The virtues of Capricorns are such that there will always be people for and against them. Many admire them, many dislike them. Why? It seems to be because of Capricorn's power urges. A well-developed Capricorn has his or her eyes set on the heights of power, prestige and authority. In the Sign of Capricorn ambition is not a fatal flaw, but rather the highest virtue.

Capricorns are not frightened by the resentment their authority may sometimes breed. In Capricorn's cool, calculated, organized mind all the dangers are already factored into the equation – the unpopularity, the animosity, the misunderstandings, even the outright slander – and a plan is always in place for dealing with these things in the most efficient way. To the Capricorn, situations that would terrify an ordinary mind are merely problems to be managed, bumps on the road to ever-growing power, effectiveness and prestige.

Some people attribute pessimism to the Capricorn Sign, but this is a bit deceptive. It is true that Capricorns like to take into account the negative side of things. It is also true that they love to imagine the worst possible scenario in every undertaking. Other people might find such analyses depressing, but Capricorns only do these things so that they can formulate a way out – an escape route.

Capricorns will argue with success. They will show you that you are not doing as well as you think you are. Capricorns do this to themselves as well as to others. They do not mean to discourage you but rather to root out any impediments to your greater success. A Capricorn boss or supervisor feels that no matter how good the performance there is always room for improvement. This explains why Capricorn supervisors are difficult to handle and even infuriating at times. Their actions are, however, quite often effective – they can get their subordinates to improve and become better at their jobs.

Capricorn is a born manager and administrator. Leo is better at being king or queen, but Capricorn is better at being prime minister – the person actually wielding power.

Capricorn is interested in the virtues that last, in the things that will stand the test of time and trials of circumstance. Temporary fads and fashions mean little to a Capricorn – except as things to be used for profit or power. Capricorns apply this attitude to business, love, to their thinking and even to their philosophy and religion.

Finance

Capricorns generally attain wealth and they usually earn it. They are willing to work long and hard for what they want. They are quite amenable to foregoing a short-term gain in favour of long-term benefits. Financially, they come into their own later in life.

However, if Capricorns are to attain their financial goals they must shed some of their strong conservatism. Perhaps this is the least desirable trait of the Capricorn. They can resist anything new merely because it *is* new and untried. They are afraid of experimentation. Capricorns need to be willing to take a few risks. They should be more eager to market new products or explore different managerial techniques. Otherwise, progress will leave them behind. If necessary, Capricorns must be ready to change with the times, to discard old methods that no longer work.

Very often this experimentation will mean that Capricorns have to break with existing authority. They might even consider changing their present position or starting their own ventures. If so, they should be willing to accept all the risks and just get on with it. Only then will a Capricorn be on the road to highest financial gain.

CAPRICORN

Career and Public Image

A Capricorn's ambition and quest for power are evident. It is perhaps the most ambitious Sign of the Zodiac – and usually the most successful in a worldly sense. However, there are lessons Capricorns need to learn in order to fulfil their highest aspirations.

Intelligence, hard work, cool efficiency and organization will take them a certain distance, but will not carry them to the very top. Capricorns need to cultivate their social graces, to develop a social style, along with charm and an ability to get along with people. They need to bring beauty into their lives and to cultivate the right social contacts. They must learn to wield power gracefully, so that people love them for it – a very delicate art. They also need to learn how to bring people together in order to fulfil certain objectives. In short, Capricorns require some of the gifts – the social grace – of the Libra to get to the top.

Once they have learned this, Capricorns will be successful in their careers. They are ambitious hard workers who are not afraid of putting in the required time and effort. Capricorns take their time in getting the job done – in order to do it well – and they like moving up the corporate ladder slowly but surely. Being so driven by success, Capricorns are generally liked by their bosses, who respect and trust them.

Love and Relationships

Like Scorpio and Pisces, Capricorn is a difficult Sign to get to know. They are deep, introverted and like to keep their own counsel. Capricorns do not like to reveal their innermost thoughts. If you are in love with a Capricorn, be patient and take your time. Little by little you will get to understand him or her.

Capricorns have a deep romantic nature, but they do not show it straight away. They are cool, matter of fact and not

319

especially emotional. They will often show their love in practical ways.

It takes time for a Capricorn – male or female – to fall in love. They are not the love-at-first-sight kind. If a Capricorn is involved with a Leo or Aries, these Fire types will be totally mystified – to them the Capricorn will seem cold, unfeeling, unaffectionate and not very spontaneous. Of course none of this is true, it is just that Capricorn likes to take things slowly. They like to be sure of their ground before making any demonstrations of love or commitment.

Even in love affairs Capricorns are deliberate. They need more time to make decisions than is true of the other Signs of the Zodiac, but given this time they become just as passionate. Capricorns like a relationship to be structured, committed, well regulated, well defined, predictable and even routine. They prefer partners who are nurturers, and they in turn like to nurture their partners. This is their basic psychology. Whether such a relationship is good for them is another issue altogether. Capricorns have enough routine in their lives as it is. They might be better off in relationships that are a bit more stimulating, changeable and fluctuating.

Home and Domestic Life

The home of a Capricorn – as with a Virgo – is going to be tidy and well organized. Capricorns tend to manage their families in the same way they manage their businesses. Capricorns are often so career-driven that they find little time for the home and family. They should try to get more actively involved in their family and domestic life. Capricorns do, however, take their children very seriously and are very proud parents, particularly should their children grow up to become respected members of society.

Horoscope for 2000

Major Trends

1999 was a year of spiritual and psychological growth, with a lot of fun thrown in. And though your finances were erratic – sometimes ultra-high and sometimes ultra-low – there was a basic stability and feeling of security about things. You were sailing on clear seas towards your long-term goals.

Many of these trends are continuing in the year 2000. There will be shake-ups and surprises – three Eclipses are going to supply that – but your boat is strong enough to weather the storm. The long-term trends are positive.

With Jupiter moving into Taurus on 15th February there is much good fortune ahead of you. More money, happiness, speculative success, pay rises and promotions, love affairs and parties – and for those of you of childbearing age, a new addition to the family.

The year 2000 is a year of great personal happiness. There is much sensual and personal pleasure. The mood is upbeat and optimistic. And early in the year you will want to play. But when both Jupiter and Saturn enter your 6th House in the summer, the mood becomes more serious. Work becomes important. And what Capricorn doesn't like work?

Your Houses of Power (areas of greatest interest) in the coming year are the home and family, finances, fun, love affairs, children and speculations, work and health (from 1st July onwards), and spirituality and charity.

Your paths of greatest fulfilment in the coming year are debt and the payment of debt, the libido, the reinvention of the self, helping others to prosper, love and romance, the home and family (until 15th February), personal and sensual pleasures, children and creativity (15th February to 1st July), and health and work (1st July onwards).

Health

Your 6th House of Health doesn't become important until the latter half of the year – the summer. The major long-term planets are kind to you, and get even kinder as the year progresses. So your health is going to be fabulous.

This is not to say that there won't be cleansings and detoxification periods this year. Two Eclipses in your own Sign – a Lunar Eclipse on 16th July and a Solar one on 25th December – will tend to bring these on. But those of you who are careful about dietary issues will experience only a redefinition of your personality and perhaps a change in your image. Those who are not careful about dietary issues will probably experience a physical detoxification programme. Impurities in the body will come up for cleansing. Sometimes this happens voluntarily. In any event, it would be a good idea to take a reduced schedule during these Eclipse periods.

The power in your 6th House of Health must be evaluated in the context of beautiful health aspects. So this power is not indicating health problems, but a greater interest in health. You are more motivated to watch your diet, to study the laws (especially the metaphysical laws) of health and disease, to exercise and to undertake a disciplined health regime.

Jupiter enters your 6th House on 1st July and will stay there for the duration of the year. Jupiter rules the thighs. Thus regular massage of the thighs (inner and outer) will enhance your health. As Lord of the 12th House, Jupiter is associated with the feet. Thus regular foot massage is also a good health preventative.

Saturn, your Ruling Planet, enters your 6th House on 11th August. It makes only a brief visit there, but is a signal of things to come. It indicates an important shift in health attitudes. Health is more than just feeling good – it involves looking good. The image of health becomes very important to you. Health is physical fitness as well as the absence of disease.

Saturn in your 6th House also shows a conservatism in health matters. You stick to the orthodoxy in these issues – to techniques that are tried and true. Fads and experimentation are anathema to you.

The health of your spouse or partner could be a concern later in the year. Your partner needs to cultivate feelings of joy. Creative hobbies are good therapy.

Two Eclipses – a Lunar one on 21st January and Solar one on 30th July – cause some physical detoxification in a parent. Let the parent co-operate with the process rather than resist it. Physical impurities need to come out – their coming out is actually a good sign.

The health of children and grandchildren is stable.

Home and Domestic Life

Your 4th House of Home and Family was very important last year, and continues to be important in the early part of this year. Many of you moved to larger quarters last year, and if you haven't yet moved house or found your dream home, the aspects are still good now. This is especially so for those of you born late in the Sign of Capricorn – from 15th to 19th January. There is still good fortune in property, and a tendency to enlarge the home and to acquire second and third homes. Family support and relationships still seem excellent.

Jupiter moving through the 4th and 5th Houses for the first half of the year suggests heightened fertility among Capricorns of childbearing age. For those not of childbearing age it suggests new additions to the family through birth or marriage.

Saturn, your Ruling Planet, has been in your 5th House of Children for over a year now. It will be in this House for most of this year as well. Thus there is great interest in children, their upbringing and their welfare. Those of you who have children are spending more time with them – enjoying them more. Those who haven't got children are perhaps thinking of adopting some, or are becoming more involved in children's issues nationally or globally. Children's issues are dear to your heart now.

You Capricorns are always mature beyond your years. Yet now there is a playful, more childlike quality about you which enables you to relate better to children. Your tendency is to be authoritarian with them, but now you discover that when you are more like them you can reach them more easily.

Jupiter moving through your 5th House from 15th February to 1st July increases your joy with children. There is great pleasure gained from them. They are doing well now – happy and optimistic. Those who are adults are prospering and shining in their fields. They are travelling more, leading the high life. Those who are students are doing well at school, and perhaps being accepted to the university of their choice.

Jupiter is still moving through your 4th House early in the year, indicating that there is great psychological expansion and understanding this year. This was so last year and the trend continues. Those of you undergoing counselling or therapy are making important breakthroughs.

Love and Social Life

Neither your 7th House of Love and Marriage nor your 11th House of Friendships is a House of Power this year, Capricorn. Thus these issues take a back seat to other things. The year 2000 seems more like a 'play' year rather than a marriage year. I expect that the status quo will be the result. Singles will remain single and married people will remain married.

An Eclipse in your 7th House on 1st July could shake your love life up a bit. And while it might not lead to an immediate change in marital status, it could lead to changes in attitudes about marriage (or about being single). Married people will have a chance to correct flaws in the relationship. Singles will perhaps contemplate a more serious involvement.

But the main thrust of the year, especially for singles, regards uncommitted love affairs. There will be plenty of these – especially from 15th February to 1st July. Not only is this kind of love plentiful, but it seems very enjoyable and happy as well. We can well understand why you express no interest in marriage this year!

Two kinds of lovers come into the picture. The first type is a mirror image of yourself. This person is sober, practical, businesslike and ambitious. Very worldly. You are comfortable with this type. But another type comes into the picture as well. This type is spiritual, spontaneous, spends money like water, is educated and creative – and probably not very worldly. This type you find not as 'comfortable' but very fascinating. You could waver between the two for months.

The Moon is your Love Planet. And since the Moon moves through your entire Horoscope very quickly, love and romantic opportunities tend to come to you in a many different ways. Your needs and attitudes to love change quickly. When the Moon waxes, your social magnetism will tend to be strongest. When it wanes, your social magnetism (and enthusiasm) also tends to wane. Thus if you are scheduling parties or dates you can adjust your schedule accordingly. See the month-by-month forecasts for more details.

Career and Finance

Your 2nd House of Money has been a House of Power for some years now, and continues to be one this year. Your 6th House of Work will become a House of Power in the summer. So there is great focus on these two areas.

As in previous years, your financial life is very exciting now. This is a great period to be a Capricorn. Rarely have you had as much personal control over your financial destiny as you have of late. Earnings are volatile, and earnings momentum can change at the drop of a hat. The financial highs are super-high and the lows can be super-lows. Sometimes you feel you go from rags to riches in a week – and vice versa. But underneath all this volatility is a steady growth in earnings – a steady accumulation of wealth.

Capricorns are not known for being risk-takers or innovators in finance. In general they like the tried, the true and the conservative. Old-line blue-chip companies appeal to them – both as investments and as employers. But these days you are very entrepreneurial. Start-up companies appeal to you – and many of you are starting your own business or have recently started one. New and avant-garde industries appeal to you. Capricorn investors are profiting from speculation – especially in property and agricultural companies. There is a great interest in high-tech businesses – and Capricorns are profiting either as investors, by being employed in these types of companies, or by having these types of businesses as clients. Likewise with media companies.

Neptune recently (1998–9) moved into your Money House, indicating the importance of sales, marketing and communications in your financial life. Whatever your business is, sales and marketing will be the driving force. It also indicates investments in oil, natural gas, hospitals, retirement homes, pharmaceutical companies, music, film and photography. Some of you might not invest in these companies but will profit from them in other ways – by working for them or having them as customers or clients.

Neptune is the planet of intuition. Thus, intuition becomes important in your financial life. Now, Capricorn is not noted for intuition. By nature you are hard-headed and rational. So the next 13 to 14 years or so will be very interesting and illuminating. Operating intuitively will feel strange at first, but once you get the hang of it riches will come faster than you can spend them.

Job-seekers have good fortune from 1st July onwards. Employers will be taking on new help – expanding the workforce during this period too. Those of you already employed will find more pleasant working conditions during this period.

Self-improvement

We mentioned earlier about Neptune's move into your Money House. This is an important long-term transit and thus a long-term trend in your life. Neptune is the planet of intuition and spirituality. Thus these things are being brought to bear in your financial life. The Cosmos is going to train your intuition through financial affairs. Finances are going to be a road through which you grow spiritually. One of the first things you need to understand is that the financial problems which could arise are not what they seem. These will only be the way that the Higher Power uses to get your attention. They are calls to prayer and meditation. Once the Higher Power succeeds, the financial problem will dissolve of its own accord. The second thing to understand is that true intuition never negates logic. It complements logic, though it transcends it. When you have a true intuition you will always find that it is eminently logical. Intuition never screams, is never panicky, never upset, violent or loud. It is quiet, confident, at peace. Often you have to be very still to hear it. Loud panicky voices in your head are not intuitive voices. Sometimes it comes as a feeling – but not what is commonly called a 'gut' feeling. Gut feelings are instinct, not intuition. Intuition often comes from the chance remark of a stranger, or something in a book or newspaper that leaps out at you. It can happen anywhere at any time. It is a most marvellous faculty to develop.

Pluto in your 12th House of Spirituality for many years to come is also training your intuition. The friends you make and the groups you join – probably ministerial or of a spiritual nature – are going to lead you deeper into the magical world of intuitive living.

Month-by-month Forecasts

January

Best Days Overall: 5th, 6th, 7th, 15th, 16th, 23rd, 24th

Most Stressful Days Overall: 13th, 14th, 19th, 20th, 25th, 26th

Best Days for Love: 3rd, 4th, 5th, 6th, 7th, 13th, 14th, 15th, 16th, 19th, 20th, 22nd, 25th, 26th

Best Days for Money: 3rd, 4th, 8th, 9th, 13th, 14th, 17th, 18th, 21st, 22nd, 25th, 26th, 30th, 31st

A happy month in a happy year, but the best is yet to come.

With 70 to 80 per cent of the planets in the Eastern sector of your chart, you have great independence now and unusual power to create conditions as you like them. No need for gaining other people's co-operation, you have the power to go it alone for now. You are unusually self-assertive and you get your way in life – people will adapt to you. Just be careful not to overdo it and cause long-term resentment.

With 90 to 100 per cent of the planets moving forward your creations will succeed, and the changes that you desire will happen – and rather quickly at that. Saturn (your Ruling Planet) goes forward on the 12th, adding a new sense of self-confidence and of direction to your life. Saturn's forward motion is also a positive health indicator.

With 70 to 80 per cent of the planets below the Horizon of your chart there's a focus on the inner life and the need to attain inner harmony. When this is attained worldly affairs will go better.

The new Moon of the 5th occurs in your own Sign and makes beautiful aspects to your Ruling Planet – new ways to find personal pleasure and sensual fulfilment are revealed to you. New ways to enhance your image come your way.

The most important areas of interest this month are the body, the image, personal pleasure, finance and spirituality.

The Lunar Eclipse of the 21st is basically kind to you. The disruptions it causes in the world work in your favour. It occurs in your 8th House, indicating that important, and long-term, changes are occurring in the income and financial strategies of your spouse or partner. Flaws in the marriage or in a current relationship come out so that they can be dealt with.

Many planets are in your own Sign this month so you are feeling your oats. There is much energy, self-confidence, sex appeal and personal magnetism. You look and feel great and others are sure to sit up and take notice. Venus will enter your Sign on the 24th, adding a sense of style and glamour to your image. This is a good period to buy clothing or personal accessories.

Though you look great, love seems unimportant to you. You are willing to let love come to you rather than chasing after it.

Finances are strong all month, but especially after the 20th. Your credit line increases, as does access to other people's money. Debts are easily made and easily paid. Money can come suddenly out of the blue – when you least expect it – and assets that you own are suddenly worth more. Sales and marketing will enhance earnings.

February

Best Days Overall: 2nd, 3rd, 11th, 12th, 19th, 20th, 29th

Most Stressful Days Overall: 9th, 10th, 15th, 16th, 22nd, 23rd

Best Days for Love: 2nd, 3rd, 4th, 5th, 11th, 12th, 13th, 14th, 15th, 16th, 22nd, 24th, 25th

Best Days for Money: 4th, 5th, 9th, 10th, 13th, 14th, 19th, 22nd, 23rd, 29th

An important and very happy month, Capricorn. Enjoy.

Between 80 and 90 per cent of the planets are still below the Horizon. Though nothing will ever stop or thwart your ambitions, you can safely put them on a hold for a while and get your home and domestic situation in order. Mars, your Family Planet, moves into your 4th House of Home and Family on the 12th. This is a great period for doing major repairs, renovations, rearranging furniture, or engaging in other heavy, demanding work around the house. On a psychological level this is a great period for getting in touch with your deepest feelings and giving them the nourishment they need.

The planetary power is still mostly in the Eastern sector of the self – making you more independent and more able to stand alone and do your own thing than usual. You are getting your way in life and the Cosmos supports you.

With 90 to 100 per cent of the planets moving forward now, like last month you are in a period of change, progress and achievement. Your creations, urges and desires manifest quickly.

Mercury goes retrograde from the 21st onwards. Thus job-seekers and employers must exercise more caution and do more research either when looking for work or when hiring. A foreign journey might not be what you think.

The important areas of interest this month are finance, intellectual interests, sales, marketing and relations with siblings, and the home and family.

Health is excellent and will get even better after the 15th.

CAPRICORN

Earnings are powerful all month. The Solar Eclipse of the 5th has a dramatic affect on earnings. It signals a turning point in your financial life. Major change – positive change – is happening, but in order for the positive to happen the 'flotsam and jetsam' – the obstructions – need to be blasted away. This is what the Eclipse will do for you. Flaws, unreasonable assumptions, and mistaken strategies or plans in finance will be revealed and you will be able to take corrective action. Your financial heart's desire is coming to pass.

Serious love maintains the status quo. But 'entertainment' types of love (love affairs) are plentiful and readily available. You are entering a party period of the year.

March

Best Days Overall: 1st, 9th, 10th, 18th, 19th, 27th, 28th, 29th

Most Stressful Days Overall: 7th, 8th, 14th, 15th, 20th, 21st

Best Days for Love: 3rd, 4th, 5th, 6th, 12th, 13th, 14th, 15th, 22nd, 23rd, 25th, 26th

Best Days for Money: 1st, 3rd, 4th, 9th, 10th, 12th, 18th, 19th, 20th, 21st, 27th, 28th, 30th, 31st

The planets make a decisive shift into the Western sector of your chart late in the month, thus there is a shifting of gears in your life – from super-independence and self-assertion to co-operation and the search for consensus. Other people's interests start to come ahead of your own. Since you've just gone through a phase of having things your way, now you can see how well you've created. Your creations will get road-tested.

With 80 to 90 per cent of the planets still below the Horizon it is still safe to downplay career issues and worldly ambitions and focus on getting your home and emotional life in order. Of course you won't completely stop career activities, only de-emphasize them somewhat. Everything is a matter of degree.

The overwhelming forward motion of the planets indicates that this is a month of action, change, achievement and progress – especially after the 20th. The pace of life is quick. People tend to be rash and impulsive – often hotheaded. You stay cool and focus on the tasks at hand.

Your important areas of interest this month are finance, intellectual interests, sales and marketing projects, siblings and neighbours, local travel, the home, family and psychological issues, and children, creativity, love affairs and entertainment.

Intellectual interests, sales and marketing projects dominate the month until the 20th. The new Moon of the 6th is helping you out by bringing clarity and illumination to all these areas. Your next steps are clearly revealed.

This remains a good period to do heavy work at home – like last month. It's also a good time to get rid of old furniture or household items that are no longer necessary. Get rid of clutter now.

Health is excellent all month, but rest and relax more after the 20th. Health can be enhanced through relaxation techniques and through special attention to the lungs and nervous system.

Serious love seems unimportant this month – either you are happy with your present relationship or happy with your current status. Non-committal love affairs are plentiful, though. These are all close to home.

Job-seekers need more caution before accepting job offers before the 14th. Study these offers carefully as things are not what they seem. Likewise with employers who are hiring. It's OK to interview before the 14th, but leave any final decisions until later on.

Finances are still very strong, and even some sudden expenses concerning the home, or some family member, cannot dent your enthusiasm or your bank balance.

April

Best Days Overall: 6th, 7th, 14th, 15th, 24th, 25th

Most Stressful Days Overall: 4th, 5th, 10th, 11th, 16th, 17th, 18th

Best Days for Love: 1st, 2nd, 4th, 5th, 10th, 11th, 12th, 13th, 21st, 22nd, 24th, 25th

Best Days for Money: 6th, 7th, 8th, 9th, 14th, 15th, 16th, 17th, 24th, 25th, 26th, 27th

Health is good, but rest and relax more until the 19th. You are entering one of the happiest, most prosperous periods of your year – enjoy.

The planetary power is almost completely below the Horizon of your chart, and even your Career Planet is reaching its nadir (low point in the Horoscope) – thus this is a period of psychological and inner progress rather than outer, worldly progress. Home and family issues should be focused on. The emotional infrastructure of future career success should be worked on. Not only are the planets beneath the Horizon but your 4th House of Home and Family is a major House of Power. This is an excellent period for doing work around the house, mending fences with family members, having family gatherings, entertaining from the home and redecorating or buying objects of beauty for the home. Your aesthetic sense is powerful right now.

By the 13th the planetary power will have made an important shift to the Western, social sector of your chart. Thus you are emerging from a period of self-will and self-assertion and entering into an era of co-operation and compromise. Not so easy now to go it alone or have your own way. In fact your way might not be the best way these days. Listen to others, gain their perspectives and the resultant actions and decisions will be a lot better.

Your most important areas of interest this month are finance, intellectual interests, sales, marketing and communication, local travel, neighbours and siblings, the home and family, and children, love affairs, creativity and entertainment.

The North Node of the Moon shifts (on the 10th) from your 8th House to your 7th House. It will be there for the rest of the year. Thus there is great happiness and a sense of fulfilment from love and social activities. When this Node gets stimulated by other planets (not this month, though) you will need to guard against addictive relationships.

Love is basically status quo this month. The Moon (your Love Planet) will wax from the 4th to the 18th, increasing your social magnetism and grace and giving you more enthusiasm for your social life. We are talking about serious, committed kind of love. Fun-and-games types of love – love affairs which have no marriage potential – are plentiful and happy. After the 19th you are in a party mood, so you might enjoy these things.

Finances are choppy after the 19th. Speculations should be avoided. Be careful of overspending on amusement – or on entertaining clients – to the detriment of your bank balance. Avoid the grand gesture during this period.

May

Best Days Overall: 3rd, 4th, 12th, 13th, 21st, 22nd, 31st

Most Stressful Days Overall: 1st, 2nd, 7th, 8th, 14th, 15th, 28th, 29th

Best Days for Love: 3rd, 4th, 7th, 8th, 12th, 13th, 22nd, 23rd, 24th

Best Days for Money: 3rd, 4th, 5th, 6th, 12th, 13th, 14th, 15th, 21st, 22nd, 24th, 25th, 31st

The planetary power is still mostly below the Horizon, so continue to shore up the home base and get in touch with your deepest feelings. Inner growth will lead to outer growth.

The planetary power is still mostly in the West, increasing your need for the social gifts and graces. You can't go it alone right now and must have the co-operation of others to attain your good.

Many planets in the Earth element until the 20th and increasing retrograde activity are slowing down the pace of change. Change is happening in more gradual ways – just the way you like things.

Normally a strong silent type, the power in the Air element after the 20th can be uncomfortable for you. Everyone wants to talk and chatter. You feel as if you are being rude if you are your normal Capricorn self. But if you are involved in sales and marketing, this tendency will boost your bank balance. Sales and marketing projects go extremely well after the 20th. Mass mailshots or telemarketing campaigns will succeed, but with delayed reactions. You might not see the full extent of your success right away.

Your most important interests are parties, children, creativity, love affairs, entertainment, health and work, and finance.

Though you should avoid speculations early in the month, this is a happy-go-lucky period. Your personal creativity is at an all-time high. Parties and entertainment abound. Relations with children are happy – though they can prove expensive. And there are many opportunities for love affairs. Serious love seems to maintain the status quo, though.

The conjunction of Jupiter with Saturn in your 5th House is a happy long-term prosperity indicator. Wealth will come easily to you over the long term. A financial breakthrough occurs.

The spiritual life becomes ever more important. Many of you will meet an important guru, teacher or mentor and form a long-term relationship with him or her.

Earnings are still volatile until the 20th but soar afterwards. Earnings for this period come from work, overtime opportunities and through co-workers. Even Uranus' retrograde won't stop the cash from piling up – though it could slow things down a little.

Job-seekers are aggressively seeking work and enjoying great success after the 20th. Those already employed are working harder.

Health is excellent all month. Exercise and athletic regimes go well after the 20th. Breathing properly will have a dramatic impact on both athletic performance and overall health after the 20th.

June

Best Days Overall: 8th, 9th, 17th, 18th, 19th, 27th, 28th

Most Stressful Days Overall: 4th, 10th, 11th, 25th, 26th

Best Days for Love: 2nd, 3rd, 4th, 10th, 11th, 22nd, 23rd

Best Days for Money: 2nd, 8th, 9th, 10th, 11th, 17th, 18th, 19th, 20th, 21st, 27th, 28th, 29th, 30th

Most of the planets are in the West, your 7th House of Love and Social Activities is very powerful, and retrograde activity is increasing during this period. Avoid self-assertion or rush. Put other people first. Adapt to situations and refuse to get ruffled by delays. Keep your eyes focused on the ultimate goal and don't take too much notice of the bumps in the road. This is an important social period in your year. Singles are more likely to meet a significant other during this period. There are more parties and social gatherings now – and you should take up every social opportunity.

The planets make an important shift from the bottom half of your Horoscope to the top half this month. Thus, by now, you should have the home and family situation well stabilized and can prepare to launch your worldly ambitions.

Though this is still an important psychological and family period, the emphasis is inexorably changing.

Pursue career goals through social means. The right social contacts seem indispensable to career success – and they are happening now.

The pace at work is very hectic – with probably much overtime. Job-seekers are successful early in the month but need to be more cautious after the 23rd. The pace at work slows down after the 23rd as well.

Health and exercise regimes are still strongly emphasized until the 23rd. Afterwards, Mercury's retrograde suggests a breather here and an evaluation of the results before continuing with these things. A review will show where modifications are needed. This is a period for fine-tuning your health regime.

Love is happy and active during this period, as mentioned. There are more social gatherings with the family and with those involved in your career. Singles find hot, passionate love. In fact there is an overabundance of love opportunities which next month's new Moon will clarify.

Finances are strong, though delays can be irksome. Two planets retrograde in your Money House indicate that you need to study all investments and major purchases carefully. Continue to avoid speculations or overspending on children and creative projects. Spend, but proportionally.

Important spiritual developments are taking place. Children are growing in a spiritual way as well – probably dramatically. Children's issues spur your personal spiritual growth. The urge to devote time to charity and to 'getting right with God' conflicts with your financial interests and duties; you must work hard to balance these two aspects of your life.

July

Best Days Overall: 5th, 6th, 15th, 16th, 24th, 25th

Most Stressful Days Overall: 1st, 2nd, 7th, 8th, 22nd, 23rd, 29th

Best Days for Love: 1st, 2nd, 10th, 11th, 20th, 21st, 22nd, 23rd, 29th, 30th, 31st

Best Days for Money: 6th, 7th, 8th, 14th, 15th, 17th, 18th, 25th, 26th, 27th

A tumultuous and stressful period, Capricorn, make sure to rest and relax more until the 22nd – especially reduce activities around the period of the Eclipses on the 1st and the 16th.

The planets are mostly in the West so you will have to wait until the dust settles from the various Eclipses to see what actions need to be taken. You will have to adapt to the various changes going on.

The Solar Eclipse of the 1st occurs in your 7th House of Love and Marriage. Thus flaws in a current relationship come up for cleansing. The relationship can become stormy and disruptive, swallowing much of your time and energy. But it is a good test of a relationship. The good ones will weather this, the seriously flawed ones will disintegrate. This Eclipse, since it affects the Sun, also impact on the income of your partner. Hidden flaws or weaknesses in his or her financial plans or investments will come up. The cause of the disruption between you could be finances. Your partner may change brokers, bankers or financial planners around this time. A mortgage or other loan you need could be denied, leaving you in limbo while you seek another. An investor – one on whom you relied – could change his or her mind at the last minute.

The Lunar Eclipse of the 16th occurs in your own Sign. Thus there is a changing of your image and a redefinition of your personality. You will change your mode and style of dress and work to project a different image. Impurities in the body could come up for cleansing. But since your overall health seems good, this could be only a temporary and minor annoyance. The Moon is also your Love Planet and thus many of the relationship problems we wrote of above could recur. Weak relationships don't stand a chance now, with all this pummelling.

The Solar Eclipse of the 30th occurs in your 8th House and reinforces much of what was written about the Eclipse of the 1st. It impacts on the finances of your partner. If they haven't corrected their previous financial flaws, they will most certainly have to do so now.

Jupiter makes an important move into your 6th House. For job-seekers this is a fortunate transit as it shows happy, fulfilling work – with lucrative pay: a dream job with dream conditions and benefits. For those of you with health problems this brings good news and probably a healing. For employers it shows an expansion of your workforce.

August

Best Days Overall: 1st, 2nd, 11th, 12th, 20th, 21st, 22nd, 29th, 30th

Most Stressful Days Overall: 4th, 5th, 18th, 19th, 25th, 26th, 31st

Best Days for Love: 8th, 9th, 11th, 12th, 18th, 19th, 20th, 21st, 25th, 26th, 29th, 30th

Best Days for Money: 3rd, 4th, 5th, 13th, 14th, 15th, 23rd, 24th, 31st

For the past two years – while Saturn has been in Taurus – you have been in a party mood. Your deepest urge was to enjoy life and help others to enjoy life. Now Saturn moves into Gemini on the 11th – your 6th House. This is a more serious period. You are interested in work and service. You are interested in being more productive in the world.

But Saturn in Gemini has other important effects. It relieves much of the financial stress and blockage on you. Though you have been prospering, you might not have enjoyed the process of prosperity. Now you will. Earnings are getting ready to skyrocket – but you will feel this more after the 22nd.

For many of you Saturn's change of Sign signals a job change, and a new attitude towards work – a stronger work ethic. Many of you landed dream jobs last month, but now you see that, dream job though it is, you still need to produce.

For employers this change indicates greater personal participation in the work place – more direct involvement with employees and their problems. Many of you will take your place beside your employees and share their burdens. You are a worker just like they are.

The planetary power is mostly in the West – including Saturn, your Ruler. Thus there is still a need to adapt to existing circumstances, with less independence and self-reliance. Social skills bring you where you want to go, not self-assertion or self-will.

With most of the planets above the Horizon, and your 6th House of Work an important House of Power, this is a work and career period. You can safely de-emphasize family and psychological issues and focus on your outer work in the world.

Though your health is excellent this month and long term, having Saturn and Jupiter in your 6th House is giving you a stronger focus on health issues. The combination of both a physical and spiritual health regime will really work wonders for you. One or the other by themselves won't have the same effect.

Finances, though improving, are stormy until the 22nd. There are financial conflicts with partners and some stress between your personal financial interests and those of shareholders or partners. Debt could be stressing you out. But hang in there; these issues will be resolved after the 22nd.

September

Best Days Overall: 7th, 8th, 17th, 18th, 25th, 26th

Most Stressful Days Overall: 1st, 14th, 15th, 16th, 21st, 22nd, 27th, 28th

Best Days for Love: 1st, 7th, 8th, 10th, 11th, 17th, 18th, 19th, 20th, 21st, 22nd, 30th

Best Days for Money: 1st, 10th, 11th, 12th, 13th, 19th, 20th, 27th, 28th

Retrograde activity increases this month and Saturn, your Ruler, goes retrograde on the 12th. The pace of change in the world and in your life slows down a bit. You're taking a breather and being more cautious these days.

Most of the planets are above the Horizon and your 10th House of Career is strong after the 22nd. Let emotional and family issues go for a while and focus on your worldly ambitions. Your family is increasingly inclined to support your career progress. This is a banner career month. Pay rises, promotions and other career coups are very likely now. Job-seekers enjoy good success. Your career is as much a fun-type activity as going to the cinema or a nightclub. There is much socializing with people of status and power. Higher-ups are favourably disposed to you and grant your their favours. The achievements of children reflect well on your community standing.

The planets make an important shift to the Eastern sector this month, giving you greater independence and self-reliance than you've had for a while. You can have things your way now, but with Saturn retrograde, you need to figure out just what 'your way' is – or what it should be.

Your important areas of interest are finance, health and work, religion, foreign travel and higher education, career, and friends, groups and organizations.

Even the retrograde of two powerful planets in your Money House can't stop the onrush of prosperity during this period. Wealth aspects are just super – especially after the 22nd. Perhaps you need to take a breather to decide what to do with all your newfound wealth. Big and important financial developments are taking place and it is all positive.

Health is strong until the 22nd, but afterwards rest and relax more.

Love is stable this month and events in this area, both happy and stressful, all seem short term. The Moon waxes from the 1st to the 13th and from the 27th onwards. These will be your periods of greatest social activity and enthusiasm. Friendship and platonic love seem more important than romance right now.

October

Best Days Overall: 4th, 5th, 6th, 14th, 15th, 23rd, 24th

Most Stressful Days Overall: 12th, 13th, 18th, 19th, 25th, 26th

Best Days for Love: 1st, 7th, 8th, 9th, 10th, 11th, 16th, 17th, 18th, 19th, 20th, 21st, 27th, 28th, 29th, 30th

Best Days for Money: 7th, 8th, 16th, 17th, 25th, 26th

Many planets are now in your Eastern sector, giving you self-confidence, independence and self-reliance. But the retrograde of Saturn, your Ruler, detracts somewhat from this. By all means create your own happiness, but do so cautiously and with more thought and planning.

Most of the planets are still above the Horizon of your chart, and your 10th House is still a House of Power – you are still in a period of outer ambition and career success.

CAPRICORN

Handle the family issues that come up, but focus on your career. Career can be enhanced through cost-cutting and the constructive use of debt. Networking, advertising, and charitable activities also enhance your career this month.

Your important areas of interest this month are finance, health and work, children, creativity, amusements and love affairs, career, friends, groups and organizations, and spirituality.

Job-seekers can experience some rough going from the 18th to the 31st, as two retrograde planets delay and confuse things. Job offers may not be what they seem, and contracts need to be studied extra carefully. Better to use this period for evaluating job options rather than starting a new job. Employers, too, need to be careful about hiring during this period.

Finances are improving behind the scenes, though you might not see the effects during this period. They are strong until the 23rd, but afterwards require more work, effort and going the extra mile to maintain. But with two powerful planets now moving forward in your Money House – after months of retrograde motion – your financial direction is getting clearer. Hidden developments over the past few months now take objective shape and form. Financial conflicts with partners need to be smoothed out – and they will be by next month.

Romantic love is not especially emphasized during this period. You have much freedom to shape this area as you will. There is more interest in friendship than in romantic love right now. The Moon will wax from the 1st to the 13th and from the 27th onwards – these should be your strongest romantic periods.

Health is excellent this month, but rest and relax more before the 23rd.

November

Best Days Overall: 1st, 2nd, 10th, 11th, 19th, 20th, 28th, 29th

Most Stressful Days Overall: 8th, 9th, 15th, 21st, 22nd

Best Days for Love: 6th, 7th, 8th, 9th, 15th, 16th, 19th, 20th, 26th, 27th, 28th, 29th

Best Days for Money: 3rd, 4th, 12th, 13th, 21st, 22nd, 30th

A child or parent comes to visit – probably from a long way off and in an unusual way. Creative projects take you way off your beaten path, but lend excitement and glamour to the month. Children's issues can swallow you up towards the end of the month, temporarily eclipsing all your other interests.

By the 4th, 70 to 80 per cent of the planetary power is in the East. Your power to create conditions as you like them and to have things your own way is increasing day by day. Good will come through your own efforts and initiative, by taking the bull by the horns.

By the 13th the planets will be evenly distributed between the upper and lower halves of your Horoscope. Thus, both emotional harmony and worldly ambitions will vie for your attention. Both will be important and you will juggle between the two. The balance you develop will be a dynamic one – now you will lean one way and now another. Mars in your House of Career from the 4th onwards indicates that you are working hard, dealing with the competition and defending your career turf. But Mars is also your Family Planet, and its elevation in the chart shows the importance of home and family issues as well – reinforcing what was said earlier. Push the careers of family members as well as your own now.

Venus in your own Sign after the 13th adds glamour and beauty to your image. This is a great time to shop for clothing and accessories as your sense of style is excellent. You are very attractive, but serious love seems unimportant to you now. Home, work, career and finances all take priority. Singles are attracting love opportunities, but not serious committed ones. Enjoy them for what they are and don't place any major expectations on them.

Job-seekers meet with excellent success during this period – especially after the 8th, when Mercury moves forward. If you are contemplating a job offer, wait until after the 8th to decide. You are not desperate and have many opportunities open to you.

Personal health is excellent during this period. The health of a friend improves after the 8th. Personal health can be enhanced further by maintaining harmony with friends.

Finances are simply spectacular this month – especially after the 22nd. Whatever you touch turns to gold. Almost the entire Cosmos is conspiring to enrich you. A financial conflict with a partner gets resolved harmoniously after the 22nd.

December

Best Days Overall: 8th, 9th, 16th, 17th, 25th, 26th, 27th

Most Stressful Days Overall: 6th, 7th, 12th, 13th, 18th, 19th

Best Days for Love: 6th, 7th, 10th, 11th, 12th, 13th, 14th, 15th, 18th, 19th, 25th, 26th, 28th, 29th

Best Days for Money: 1st, 2nd, 10th, 11th, 18th, 19th, 28th, 29th

Though there are many planets in the East now and you are filled with independence and self-will, better to wait until after Christmas before making important changes or going after major personal goals. The Solar Eclipse of the 25th is going to change the whole landscape of things – you're better off thinking about what you want and what needs to be changed rather than acting on these things right now.

The Solar Eclipse of the 25th is a powerful one on you, Capricorn. Take a reduced schedule two days before and a day afterward. Only you can decide what is necessary and what unnecessary, but reschedule the unnecessary for another time.

The Eclipse occurs in your 1st House of the Body and Image. Thus, personal goals are likely to change – especially if there were flaws in your plans to begin with. You will change your image, your mode of dress and your personality. Those of you who are not careful about diet will probably experience some physical cleansing during this period. This is not sickness but cleansing. Co-operate with it. Many of you will be changing jobs during this period – either with a new company or within the same company. An insurance or legal issue will now start to move forward one way or another. Your spouse or partner will make important financial and investment changes. Their portfolio of assets will get rearranged. An important decision about debt will be taken.

Personal finances are getting stronger day by day. Earnings come easily and happily. Your financial confidence and judgement is strong. A family member who helped you might want paying back after the 23rd. There is also a need to avoid over-spending on the home.

Though the Eclipse stirs things up, your basic health and vitality are strong now. You could change doctors, diets, medication or health regimes now. There is never one way that works for ever. The body's needs change and the Eclipse is revealing this to you.

By the 23rd Mars will be out of your Career House and the planetary power will be overwhelmingly below the Horizon. After your career battles and work of the last two months your need to find your emotional comfort zone is stronger than ever.

Aquarius

~~~

THE WATER-BEARER

Birthdays from
20th January
to 18th February

Personality Profile

AQUARIUS AT A GLANCE

Element – Air

Ruling Planet – Uranus
  Career Planet – Pluto
  Love Planet – Venus
  Money Planet – Neptune
  Planet of Health and Work – Moon
  Planet of Home and Family Life – Venus

Colours – electric blue, grey, ultramarine blue

Colours that promote love, romance and social harmony – gold, orange

Colour that promotes earning power – aqua

Gems – black pearl, obsidian, opal, sapphire

Metal – lead

Scents – azalea, gardenia

Quality – fixed (= stability)

Qualities most needed for balance – warmth, feeling and emotion

Strongest virtues – great intellectual power, the ability to communicate and to form and understand abstract concepts, love for the new and avant-garde

Deepest needs – to know and to bring in the new

Characteristics to avoid – coldness, rebelliousness for its own sake, fixed ideas

Signs of greatest overall compatibility – Gemini, Libra

Signs of greatest overall incompatibility – Taurus, Leo, Scorpio

Sign most helpful to career – Scorpio

Sign most helpful for emotional support – Taurus

Sign most helpful financially – Pisces

Sign best for marriage and/or partnerships – Leo

Sign most helpful for creative projects – Gemini

Best Sign to have fun with – Gemini

Signs most helpful in spiritual matters – Libra, Capricorn

Best day of the week – Saturday

AQUARIUS

Understanding the Aquarius Personality

In the Aquarius-born, intellectual faculties are perhaps the most highly developed of any Sign in the Zodiac. Aquarians are clear, scientific thinkers. They have the ability to think abstractly and to formulate laws, theories and clear concepts from masses of observed facts. Geminis might be very good at gathering information, but Aquarians take this a step further, excelling at interpreting the information gathered.

Practical people – men and women of the world – mistakenly consider abstract thinking as impractical. It is true that the realm of abstract thought takes us out of the physical world, but the discoveries made in this realm generally end up having tremendous practical consequences. All real scientific inventions and breakthroughs come from this abstract realm.

Aquarians, more so than most, are ideally suited to explore these abstract dimensions. Those who have explored these regions know that there is little feeling or emotion there. In fact, emotions are a hindrance to functioning in these dimensions; thus Aquarians seem – at times – cold and emotionless to others. It is not that Aquarians haven't got feelings and deep emotions, it is just that too much feeling clouds their ability to think and invent. The concept of 'too much feeling' cannot be tolerated or even understood by some of the other Signs. Nevertheless, this Aquarian objectivity is ideal for science, communication and friendship.

Aquarians are very friendly people, but they do not make a big show about it. They do the right thing by their friends, even if sometimes they do it without passion or excitement.

Aquarians have a deep passion for clear thinking. Second in importance, but related, is their passion for breaking with the establishment and traditional authority. Aquarians delight in this, because for them rebellion is like a great game or challenge. Very often they will rebel strictly for the fun of rebelling, regardless of whether the authority they defy is right or wrong. Right or wrong has little to do with the rebellious actions of an Aquarian, because to a true Aquarian authority and power must be challenged as a matter of principle.

Where Capricorn or Taurus will err on the side of tradition and the status quo, an Aquarian will err on the side of the new. Without this virtue it is doubtful whether any progress would be made in the world. The conservative-minded would obstruct progress. Originality and invention imply an ability to break barriers; every new discovery represents the toppling of an impediment to thought. Aquarians are very interested in breaking barriers and making walls tumble – scientifically, socially and politically. Other Zodiac Signs, such as Capricorn, also have scientific talents. But Aquarians are particularly excellent in the social sciences and humanities.

Finance

In financial matters Aquarians tend to be idealistic and humanitarian – to the point of self-sacrifice. They are usually generous contributors to social and political causes. When they contribute it differs from when a Capricorn or Taurus contributes. A Capricorn or Taurus may expect some favour or return for a gift; an Aquarian contributes selflessly.

Aquarians tend to be as cool and rational about money as they are about most things in life. Money is something they need and they set about acquiring it scientifically. No need for fuss; they get on with it in the most rational and scientific ways available.

Money to the Aquarian is especially nice for what it can do, not for the status it may bring (as is the case for other Signs). Aquarians are neither big spenders nor penny-pinchers and use their finances in practical ways, for example to facilitate progress for themselves, their families or even strangers.

However, if Aquarians want to reach their fullest financial potential they will have to explore their intuitive nature. If they follow only their financial theories – or what they believe to be theoretically correct – they may suffer some losses and disappointments. Instead, Aquarians should call on their intuition, which knows without thinking. For Aquarians, intuition is the short-cut to financial success.

Career and Public Image

Aquarians like to be perceived not only as the breakers of barriers but also as the transformers of society and the world. They long to be seen in this light and to play this role. They also look up to and respect other people in this position and even expect their superiors to act this way.

Aquarians prefer jobs that have a bit of idealism attached to them – careers with a philosophical basis. Aquarians need to be creative at work, to have access to new techniques and methods. They like to keep busy and enjoy getting down to business straight away, without wasting any time. They are often the quickest workers and usually have suggestions for improvements that will benefit their employers. Aquarians are also very helpful with their co-workers and welcome responsibility, preferring this to having to take orders from others.

If Aquarians want to reach their highest career goals they have to develop more emotional sensitivity, depth of feeling and passion. They need to learn to narrow their focus on the essentials and concentrate more on the job in hand. Aquarians need 'a fire in the belly' – a consuming passion and desire – in order to rise to the very top. Once this passion exists they will succeed easily in whatever they attempt.

Love and Relationships

Aquarians are good at friendships, but a bit weak when it comes to love. Of course they fall in love, but their lovers always get the impression that they are more best friends than paramours.

Like Capricorns, they are cool customers. They are not prone to displays of passion nor to outward demonstrations of their affections. In fact, they feel uncomfortable when their mate hugs and touches them too much. This does not mean that they do not love their partners. They do, only they show it in other ways. Curiously enough, in relationships they tend to attract the very things that they feel uncomfortable with. They seem to attract hot, passionate, romantic, demonstrative people. Perhaps they know instinctively that these people have qualities they lack and so seek them out. In any event, these relationships do seem to work, Aquarius' coolness calming the more passionate partner while the fires of passion warm the cold-blooded Aquarius.

The qualities Aquarians need to develop in their love life are warmth, generosity, passion and fun. Aquarians love relationships of the mind. Here they excel. If the intellectual factor is missing in a relationship an Aquarian will soon become bored or feel unfulfilled.

Home and Domestic Life

In family and domestic matters Aquarians can have a tendency to be too non-conformist, changeable and unstable. They are as willing to break the barriers of family constraints as they are those of other areas of life.

Even so, Aquarians are very sociable people. They like to have a nice home where they can entertain family and friends. Their house is usually decorated modernly and full of state-of-the-art appliances and gadgets – an environment Aquarians find absolutely necessary.

If their home life is to be healthy and fulfilling Aquarians need to inject it with a quality of stability – yes, even some conservatism. They need at least one area of life to be enduring and steady; this area is usually their home and family life.

Venus, the Planet of Love, rules the Aquarian's 4th Solar House of Home and Family as well, which means that when it comes to the family and child-rearing, theories, cool thinking and intellect are not always enough. Aquarians need to bring love into the equation in order to have a great domestic life.

Horoscope for 2000

Major Trends

These are very exciting times to be an Aquarian. 1999 was full of sudden changes, and so it will be in the year 2000.

As in 1999 the thrust will be on personal change – in the image, the body, the diet and how you dress. The tendency to move house at the drop of a hat, to have multiple residences, is still very strong. There is a yearning for a stable home base these days, and this could happen – a few times – this year. More on this later.

Jupiter moves through three different Signs and Houses of your horoscope this year, expanding and bringing pleasure to many areas of life. It begins the year in your 3rd House, bringing more domestic travel, knowledge and enhanced sales and marketing ability. On 15th February it moves into your 4th House of Home and Family, bringing happier family relations, a new home (or a renovation of the old) and more emotional support. On 1st July it moves into your 5th House, bringing parties, fun, amusements and speculative success.

Jupiter in the Sign of Gemini brings all kinds of good fortune to you – foreign travel, increased earnings, personal and sensual pleasure, creativity and general optimism. The second half of the year is going to be much happier than the first half.

Saturn will leave Taurus briefly this year, relieving some of the pressure and stress that you have been feeling over the past year. And though this transit is brief – from 11th August to 27th October – it is an omen of things to come. The hardest part of the Saturn transit is about over.

Your paths of greatest Fulfilment in the coming year are love and romance, health and work, the pursuit of intellectual interests (1st January to 15th February), home and family issues (15th February to 1st July), and children, creativity, love affairs and personal pleasure (1st July onwards).

Health

Though your 6th House of Health is not a House of Power this year, two powerful long-term planets are in stressful aspect to you. Further, there are many Eclipses that impact on you. So, the danger is that you are ignoring health issues when you shouldn't. You are taking things for granted when you should be working harder at them.

Your most vulnerable health period is from 15th February to 1st July, when both Jupiter and Saturn are in stressful aspect to you. After 1st July the pressure will ease up. So be sure to rest and relax more during this period. Listen to your body. Take more naps when you feel tired. Focus on essential activities and either delegate the rest or let it go.

The 1st July is an important date for you in terms of your health, Aquarius. Jupiter leaves its stressful aspect and starts making a harmonious one, and a Solar Eclipse occurs in your 6th House of health. You will be changing doctors or health regimes. (A job change could occur around this time as well.)

Uranus and Neptune in your own Sign for many years to come shows great experimentation with the physical body. The urge is to test its limits – perhaps in reckless ways. This too is a health danger. You can experiment by all means, but in ways that are not physically dangerous.

Neptune in your own Sign shows a more refined physical body. This is going to happen gradually over the years. It shows a need for more dietary purity – though you should not over-refine the diet. This transit brings an almost supernatural beauty and glamour to your image and an ability to visualize your body as you desire it to be. Your body becomes almost chameleon-like – and it reflects your thoughts, moods and will. Thus thought and mood control become very important – not only to your health, but to your physical appearance as well. Praise your body regularly. Visualize it as you desire it to be. Talk to your different organs and tell them that you love them and appreciate them for all the wonderful work that they do. This will improve both your health and physical appearance in dramatic ways.

Uranus in your own Sign shows that many of you have not yet settled on your self-image. You are constantly upgrading and improving it. The interest in 'miracle' foods, diets and health fads continues. Many of you dress to shock – and you succeed, especially with family members.

A word about miracle foods and pills: There is no one miracle food. All are essentially good, and will help some people at certain times. When you understand that the body is only a reflection of your inner state – your psychological and philosophical self – then you will be on the royal road to good health. When you work seriously on your inner states of mind, the necessary foods, pills or diets will come to you as needed – with little effort on your part. You will be attracted to the foods you need on a given day.

Home and Domestic Life

Your 4th House of Home and Family was an important House of Power last year and becomes even more important this year.

Many of you have been moving around a lot in the past few years. You have been wonderers and wanderers. Nomads. The urge for a stable home base – some place you can call home – is becoming ever stronger. The need for family and their support is also strong. Yet this conflicts with your need for freedom – which is equally strong. You want to be independent and free, yet you want family and emotional support. A difficult task to achieve. This year you must give up some personal freedom in exchange for family support. But be careful not to give up too much freedom either. Your family would be glad of this, but you wouldn't.

Saturn moving through your 4th House is making many of you feel cramped in the home. Last year you could get round this by making better use of the existing space. This year you may have to move to larger quarters or expand the present quarters. This should occur from 15th February to 1st July.

Moves could happen suddenly and unexpectedly. Friends could be the catalysts or recommenders of the change. Sharing your home with a friend might be a good option right now, as you can afford larger quarters by splitting expenses.

Some of you will be purchasing second or third homes during this period. There are new additions to the family, through birth or marriage. Aquarians of childbearing age are more fertile this year.

Relations with children start improving this year as well. Those of you who have them will derive much pleasure from them. There is a need to balance 'being their friend and equal' with good discipline. You can't go too far in either direction – especially from 11th August to 27th October.

Adult children are prospering this year. Adult female children are more fertile.

A depressed or stressed-out parent starts to feel happier after 15th February. Parents could move house this year as well.

With both Jupiter and Saturn in your 4th House from 15th February to 1st July, this is a year for psychological progress. Mood swings can be intense. There is a fluctuation between deep pessimism and high optimism. You should stand in the middle. Those of you in therapy or counselling should experience significant breakthroughs.

Love and Social Life

Your 7th House of Love and Marriage is not a House of Power this year, Aquarius. Thus there seems to be little interest in this area. But two Eclipses in your 7th House of Marriage ensure there will be some excitement here. Married people could experience crises in their relationships, and singles could yearn to change their status. For married people the survival of the marriage is far from a sure thing.

The problem in love this year is the same as it was last year – your need for change, your need for absolute freedom, your wanderlust and your changing affections. This makes it very hard for your partner to keep up with you. Your partner feels he or she hardly knows you. No sooner does your partner get accustomed to one type of you than you change into another you – a new and updated version – and so the process has to begin all over.

And since you are changing very rapidly, it is only natural that your affections change as well.

Further complicating things is your personal beauty and glamour. Seldom has it been this strong. Thus you are attracting many others, but baffling them as well. Both you and they are confused by your inconsistencies. Stormy love vibrations are all around you. Even the strongest of relationships will have a rocky road.

For singles, the safest route is uncommitted love affairs. There will be plenty of opportunities for these later on in the year – from the summer onwards. These too seem stormy but will become much more stable after 27th October when Saturn leaves your 5th House.

Saturn in your 5th House of Love Affairs from 11th August to 27th October indicates a clandestine relationship with someone older. This, for various reasons, needs to be kept under wraps.

Jupiter in this House from 1st July onwards suggests love affairs with people who were formerly friends or acquaintances – or perhaps people you meet at professional or social organizations. From 11th August to 27th October you could be dating two people at the same time: one openly and one in secret. After 27th October the field narrows down to one.

Marriage opportunities could come between 13th July and 22nd August, but these seem short lived. Your mood is more romantic and you are perhaps thinking along these lines, but changeable Uranus in your own Sign is sure to assert itself.

There will be many love affairs of the mind as well as the body this year.

A single parent could remarry from 15th February to 1st July. Siblings are doing well and probably attracting interest, but the status quo will prevail on that front (that is, if they are single they are likely to remain so, if married likewise). Children of marriageable age will meet a significant other. Marriage is a strong possibility – but the road is rocky. Grandchildren of marriageable age are involved in a serious relationship early in the year – with marriage very likely.

AQUARIUS

Career and Finance

None of the Houses associated with finance or career is especially powerful this year, so the status quo will probably prevail. The year 2000 is more about personal growth, self-discovery, psychological progress, setting up a home base, finding your emotional 'comfort zone' and having fun – rather than the mundane realities of the world.

Of course, most of you will probably work and pursue a career – but your heart is not in it. Earnings will surely come – this is not a year of lack – but there is little interest in it.

Your Money Planet (Neptune) in your own Sign shows that you are adopting – slowly but surely – the image of wealth. You dress more expensively and elegantly. You spend more on yourself and your personal appearance. You invest in yourself. The image seems very important in your financial life these days. Those of you who are models, salespeople or who in some other way earn their living from their image will do well in the coming years.

The Money Planet in your own Sign reinforces many of your natural gifts. Money comes to you from technology, science, groups and group activities, the media, astrology and organizations. This is a very positive signal. You can earn from your personal strengths.

Jupiter, the planet of abundance, moves through your 3rd House until 15th February, bringing new telecommunications equipment, computers, fax machines and perhaps a car to you. When it moves through your 4th House from 15th February to 1st July it brings the fortunate sale or purchase of a home, big-ticket items for the home, and good fortune through family connections. When it moves through your 5th House from 1st July onwards it brings speculative success and perhaps more 'toys' – VCRs, home entertainment centres, CD players, TVs, sports equipment and the like.

Self-improvement

Your Money Planet, Neptune, recently (1998–9) made a major move into your own Sign. This is giving you the urge for total financial freedom. You don't want to attain financial goals in graduated steps over time, but want it all at once – in one fell swoop. And while the urge for financial freedom is healthy and wholesome, the urge to quick and easy money can be dangerous. All sorts of unethical people lie in wait to exploit this desire – and they mean you no good. Do the necessary research carefully.

Neptune is the planet of intuition and spirituality. So your whole life is about developing intuition through financial affairs. In so far as you trust it and are aware of it, you prosper. This is especially so now, with Neptune in your own Sign. Earnings are only the barometer which shows how well you are developing intuition. The earnings are not the purpose, but the side-effect.

Charitable giving is always important in your financial life, but more so now.

Financial problems need to be understood for what they are: calls to prayer and to deeper unity with the Higher Power within you. They are only ways that the Higher Power uses to get your attention. Once you enter the desired state of unity, the financial problem will disappear.

Month-by-month Forecasts

January

Best Days Overall: 8th, 9th, 17th, 18th, 25th, 26th

Most Stressful Days Overall: 1st, 2nd, 15th, 16th, 21st, 22nd, 28th, 29th

Best Days for Love: 3rd, 4th, 5th, 6th, 7th, 13th, 14th, 15th, 16th, 21st, 22nd, 25th, 26th

Best Days for Money: 3rd, 4th, 8th, 10th, 11th, 13th, 14th, 17th, 21st, 22nd, 25th, 30th, 31st

Most of the month the planets are still more or less evenly distributed between the upper and lower halves of your chart. So there is a need to balance the inner life with the outer life; outer, worldly activities with home and domestic activities; success in the world with a feeling of emotional harmony. But after the 20th a major shift occurs and the planetary power energizes the lower half of your chart – the half that is below the Horizon. Thus, home, family and emotional issues will become increasingly dominant as the months progress. An important shift in attitude is happening now.

Between 80 and 90 per cent of the planets are in the Eastern sector and many planets will be in your own Sign of Aquarius after the 20th. Thus you are unusually independent now (you are always independent, but now more so) – more self-willed – more inclined to want your own way in life – and more inclined to get it. The world will just have to adapt to you now and not vice versa.

With 90 to 100 per cent of the planets moving forward you are zooming ahead towards your goals. This is a month of great progress and achievement.

With so much personal power at your disposal, it would not be a bad idea to spend more time in seclusion early in the month and review the past year. Review your successes and your failures and see where you want to go from here. It's very important to have mental clarity before you start creating conditions and circumstances. Be careful of the goals you set now because you will certainly attain them – along with everything that comes with them.

The Lunar Eclipse of the 21st is a strong one on you, so please take a reduced schedule – two days before and day afterwards would be best. The Eclipse represents a Cosmic power surge – the normal energy that we would get from the Moon is interrupted and we are not up to our usual standards of energy. Avoid stressful activities during this period. Though we don't want you being fired from your job or getting divorced over an Eclipse, short of that anything that doesn't absolutely *have* to be done should be rescheduled.

The Eclipse (along with your sense of independence and self-will) doesn't bode well for a current relationship. A major explosion could occur. A good relationship will probably survive and become even better – but a bad one could be doomed. Singles might decide they are unhappy with their single status and start looking for serious love around this time. Important long-term decisions about a current relationship will have to be made. You can't sit on the fence and delay things anymore.

Health and finances are excellent all month but especially after the 20th.

February

Best Days Overall: 4th, 5th, 13th, 14th, 22nd, 23rd

Most Stressful Days Overall: 11th, 12th, 17th, 18th, 24th, 25th

Best Days for Love: 2nd, 3rd, 4th, 5th, 11th, 12th, 13th, 14th, 17th, 18th, 22nd, 24th, 25th

AQUARIUS

Best Days for Money: 4th, 7th, 8th, 9th, 10th, 13th, 19th, 22nd, 29th

An exciting, eventful and challenging month, Aquarius, but hang in there as the Cosmos blasts away the obstructions to your happiness. I would describe this month as a little like going to the dentist. The dentist needs to do some drilling, sanding and cleaning before she can get the teeth to where they should be. Minute pockets of decay must be drilled away, leaving only that which is healthy. The drilling is not pleasant – it is noisy and perhaps there is some discomfort. But the end result is very good. Trust in the Cosmic Dentist and hold your vision of the happy end result and all will be well.

The Solar Eclipse of the 5th hits you like a smart bomb, so please take a reduced schedule – for two days before and a day after. Not only does it occur in your own Sign of Aquarius, but it occurs right on Uranus, your Ruling Planet. The symbolism is clear – the Cosmos is drilling away decay in your body, image and self-definition – and also in your love life and a current relationship. Those who are careful of their diets will feel minimal physical discomfort, though even these will change their image and mode of dress. Many of you could move house as well. Those who are not careful about their diets could see a major detoxification period coming up. Physical impurities must be flushed out. Singles could decide to marry in the coming months, and married people could decide to divorce. The marital status is changing. Even a stable marriage could undergo a shift in the ground rules – though it survives the Eclipse. Remember the discussion in the Health section, earlier.

Happily, the Highest Wisdom decrees that you will have help during this period. Many planets in your own Sign are giving you strength and stamina to deal with the changes. There is both inner and outer support for you.

Finances too will be strong as friends and partners are financially supportive. Sales and marketing projects go well. Writers sell their manuscripts. Investments in transportation and telecommunications seem strong – though your personal chart (based on your precise date and time of birth) could modify this. Be careful not to get so swallowed up by financial minutiae that you have no time for other things.

And, as if you didn't have enough change with the Eclipse, Jupiter moves into your 4th House on the 15th, showing a possible move or expansion of the current residence. It also shows that the change and upheaval is producing much psychological insight and understanding, and that family members are giving support.

March

Best Days Overall: 3rd, 4th, 12th, 20th, 21st, 30th, 31st

Most Stressful Days Overall: 9th, 10th, 16th, 17th, 22nd, 23rd, 24th

Best Days for Love: 3rd, 4th, 5th, 6th, 12th, 13th, 14th, 15th, 16th, 17th, 22nd, 23rd, 25th, 26th

Best Days for Money: 1st, 3rd, 5th, 6th, 9th, 10th, 12th, 18th, 19th, 20th, 27th, 28th

Presumably the dust has settled from the frenetic activity of last month. And, though things are easier, this is still a fast-paced, active month, with 90 per cent of the planets in forward motion.

Pluto, your Career Planet, goes retrograde on the 15th. Between 80 and 90 per cent of the planets are below the Horizon (in the bottom half) of your chart. The message is very clear: let go of outer, worldly type activities and focus on the home, family and psychological issues. Inner growth is more important – and happier – than outer growth during this period.

AQUARIUS

With 60 to 70 per cent of the planets still in the Eastern sector of your chart, you still have great power to build the life that you want for yourself. No need to worry too much about the reactions of other people as they will adapt to you. You are in a period of progress and achievement.

Mercury's retrograde until the 14th suggests caution – and much patience – with children. Be more careful of how you communicate with them. Many problems are coming from poor communication and simple misunderstanding. Your spouse or partner needs to do more research on financial issues, purchases and investments. He or she is better off executing financial plans after the 14th.

Family life and relations with family members are bitter-sweet during this period. There is much love, but also stormy, volatile emotions – especially after the 23rd. Many old repressions will come up during this period. After the 23rd you are in an excellent period for doing heavy work around the house – moving furniture, doing construction or renovation, ripping out wires or plumbing, etc.

Health is still delicate and you must be ruthless in apportioning your energy. You won't be able to do everything that you 'think' you need to do – or that society expects you to do. Certain things will have to go by the wayside or be delegated. You should even manage your thought life tightly, focusing only on positive, uplifting types of thoughts and letting fear, anger and resentment go. In spite of this, you have seldom looked so good. Venus in your own Sign is adding beauty, glamour and a unique sense of style to your image.

Finances are very strong as your Money House is very active. Your spouse or partner, family members and people from your past are supporting your financial goals. Your personal financial intuition shines.

Love is still unstable. Right now you are looking for someone who can help you financially, or help you to attain your financial goals. Love finds you as you pursue your normal financial business.

April

Best Days Overall: 8th, 9th, 16th, 17th, 18th, 26th, 27th

Most Stressful Days Overall: 6th, 7th, 12th, 13th, 19th, 20th

Best Days for Love: 1st, 2nd, 4th, 5th, 12th, 13th, 21st, 22nd, 24th, 25th

Best Days for Money: 1st, 2nd, 6th, 7th, 8th, 14th, 15th, 16th, 17th, 24th, 25th, 26th, 27th, 29th, 30th

The planets are almost completely below the Horizon of your chart and, after the 19th, your 4th House of Home and Family is a major House of Power (even more than last month). Pluto, your Career Planet, is retrograde. The message is clear: focus on psychological growth rather than outer growth. And there will be psychological growth aplenty. When we are growing inwardly we welcome emotional upheavals and turmoil as they reveal our complexes and deepest feelings. They are not seen as tragedies or disasters but as opportunities to heal and grow. You will get a clear picture of the moods and feelings that have been victimizing you these many years.

And though Pluto is retrograde, there are still career opportunities happening all month. You need to be more careful about them, however, and study them more deeply. Avoid job offers that will interfere with your emotional harmony or family life. Other opportunities will come that are better overall.

Though the planets are still mostly in the East, your self-esteem and self-confidence are not up to their usual standards. You want your way, you feel self-assertive, but family and emotional concerns divert you. This is a month for balancing personal desires with those of family members. Probably, family duties will overwhelm your personal desires.

Health is very delicate now and you must rest and relax more. Read the discussion in the Health section, above. Not only must you maximize your physical energy, but also your mental and psychic energy. Avoid thoughts and words that are non-constructive or that will bring disharmony into your life. Talk less. Think less. Do less. Learn to relax more. Separate from your stormy feelings and emotions. They are not you. You are the Being that feels, not the feeling. From this point of detachment you can exert some direction and control over these moods. As long as you have your spiritual will and mental clarity you will be relatively safe.

This is not a month to be concerned about finances. They are stable. Trust in a Higher Power to supply you and let go of all fear and worry. Riches will come to you in due course, but now you've got to focus on keeping your energy levels as high as possible.

Love is happy until the 19th, but starts getting stormy after then. You and the beloved are not in synch and are pulling in opposite directions. Your family seem more supportive of your partner than of you. But these are short-term issues. A deeper harmony will emerge from all this.

May

Best Days Overall: 5th, 6th, 14th, 15th, 24th, 25th

Most Stressful Days Overall: 3rd, 4th, 9th, 10th, 16th, 17th, 31st

Best Days for Love: 3rd, 4th, 9th, 10th, 12th, 13th, 22nd, 23rd, 24th

Best Days for Money: 3rd, 4th, 5th, 12th, 13th, 14th, 21st, 22nd, 24th, 26th, 27th, 31st

Health is still vulnerable until the 20th, so continue to maximize physical and emotional energy. You can't do everything, be everywhere and fulfil everyone's expectations. Focus on essentials, delegate where possible and let lesser things go. Health will improve dramatically after the 20th. When you emerge from this period – one of the most stressful in the year – you will be a much stronger person.

There will be many planets in your native Air element from the 20th onwards. You are very comfortable in this milieu. People are communicating more, interested in ideas, theories and abstract concepts. You are in Aquarius heaven. The danger comes from too much of a good thing. You might get mentally over-stimulated – have trouble turning your mind off and relaxing. Your phone bill could sky rocket. You also run the risk of wasting vital mental energy on non-essentials – idle gossip or, even worse, negative thoughts and speech. Use the extra mental energy constructively – write, teach, do those mailshots and marketing projects.

The planets are shifting ever more westward day by day. Two powerful planets are retrograde in your own Sign – one of them, Uranus, your Ruler. This is no time to be self-assertive or rebellious. Flow with the crowd now. Adapt to situations. Your way might not be the best way at the moment.

Most of the planets are below the Horizon, and your 4th House of Home and Family is still a major House of Power. Like last month, focus on emotional harmony and inner growth. Finding and functioning from your emotional comfort zone is the most important thing now. Career issues can be safely let go of for a while. This is a period of great psychological progress. Aquarians who are undergoing therapy or counselling will make important breakthroughs.

Love begins to improve after the 20th, though it is stormy before then. The Sun's move into Gemini brings greater synchronicity between you and the beloved. Kiss and make up and go off on a second honeymoon. Love is more playful and honeymoonish. Singles have options for either serious love or for non-committal love affairs.

The retrograde of your Money Planet (Neptune) on the 8th won't stop explosive earnings growth this month – only delay things and make for greater complications. Investments and major purchases need more research. Earnings are very strong after the 20th, and they come rather easily – while you're having fun. Speculations are very favourable then – but be sure you follow your intuition and don't risk more than you can afford to lose.

June

Best Days Overall: 2nd, 10th, 11th, 20th, 21st, 29th, 30th

Most Stressful Days Overall: 6th, 7th, 12th, 13th, 14th, 27th, 28th

Best Days for Love: 2nd, 3rd, 6th, 7th, 10th, 11th, 22nd, 23rd

Best Days for Money: 2nd, 8th, 9th, 10th, 11th, 17th, 18th, 19th, 20th, 21st, 22nd, 23rd, 27th, 28th, 29th, 30th

The conflict between personal desires and ideas of fulfilment, and family duties and family life, continues. It's easier perhaps than it has been in previous months, but is far from over. Each area must be given its due; you must walk the middle way.

Friends are becoming more like family and family like friends – you have some difficulty in drawing distinctions here. Many of you are meeting up with your spiritual families these days and it's a wonderful thing. Everyone has a spiritual family – which usually is different and distinct from the biological family. The biological family is often a karmic thing – a way to cleanse and resolve past life issues. The spiritual family is with you life after life.

With many planets in the West and the retrograde of Uranus, your Ruler, there's once again a need for patience, the avoidance of power struggles and undue self-assertion, the need to adapt to situations and to other people's needs and desires – silly though they sometimes seem. This is a period for developing your social graces and for putting other people's interests ahead of your own.

Power in your 4th House of Moods and Psychological Understanding and many planets in the Sign of Cancer after the 21st indicate that this is a month of psychological progress – of inner growth rather than worldly, career growth. Inner growth is successful this month.

Finances are strong, though there are delays and glitches. Major purchases and investments still need strong scrutiny. Avoid things that you don't completely understand. It's important that you study the fine print of all contracts. Financial intuition needs confirmation from other sources. Psychic guidance likewise.

Love issues are much happier during this period. Until the 21st you want someone who will show you a good time. Love must be honeymoonish and idyllic. But after the 21st you are more serious. Love is expressed through nurturing and service to the beloved. Until the 21st singles find love in the usual places – parties, nightclubs, places of entertainment, resorts, etc. Afterwards love is found at the workplace, the doctor's surgery or in hospital. Love will catch you as you go about your normal health regime.

Health is good this month and you are paying more attention to it.

July

Best Days Overall: 7th, 8th, 17th, 18th, 26th, 27th

Most Stressful Days Overall: 3rd, 4th, 10th, 11th, 24th, 25th, 31st

Best Days for Love: 1st, 2nd, 3rd, 4th, 10th, 11th, 21st, 22nd, 23rd, 30th, 31st

Best Days for Money: 6th, 7th, 14th, 15th, 17th, 18th, 20th, 21st, 25th, 26th

Though health is still delicate after the 22nd, the health stresses of the past year is weakening. Jupiter's move into Gemini on the 1st makes fabulous aspects to you and initiates a long-term period of joy. Aquarians of childbearing age are more fertile now.

There are three Eclipses during this period, indicating major changes in the world around you. Of these three only one is stressful on you – the Solar Eclipse of the 30th. Please take a reduced schedule about two days before and a day after.

The Solar Eclipse of the 1st affects both love and work. (Every Solar Eclipse affects your love life in some way, as the Sun is your Love Planet.) Though this Eclipse will cause hidden flaws in a relationship to come up to the surface it will not be as strong as the Solar Eclipse of the 30th. Perhaps you will see the first rumblings on the horizon now. Since this Eclipse occurs in your 6th House there are job changes or changes in the conditions of the workplace. A health crisis leads to complete healing – and perhaps to a change in doctors or health regimes. Attitudes towards health undergo long-term changes as flaws in previous attitudes are clearly revealed. Venus, which rules both your 4th and 9th Houses, is also affected by this Eclipse – so the areas ruled by these Houses are undergoing long-term change and some disruption. There could be a move, or major renovation or repair of the home. Your academic status undergoes change.

The Lunar Eclipse of the 16th affects health, work and spiritual issues. (Every Lunar Eclipse affects health and work, as the Moon is the ruler of these things in your chart.) Again job changes and changes in the conditions of the workplace are signalled. Again, this heralds good news on the health front but perhaps through a crisis or shift in healing techniques and/or doctors.

The Solar Eclipse of the 30th affects love, marriage, the marital status and a current relationship. Good relationships will only get better when the dust settles. Impurities in the relationship need to come out so they don't fester there.

Weak relationships or friendships could unravel at this time – or within the next few months.

Jupiter's move out of your 4th House of Home and Family and a corresponding shift of the planets above the Horizon show that most of your family issues are resolved and you can start focusing on outer, worldly activities.

Finances are strong before the 22nd, slower afterwards. Before the 22nd speculations are favourable and creative projects boost your bank balance. After the 22nd you need to work harder for earnings than you are used to. Over the long term you need not be concerned, as there are many positive 'behind the scenes' developments taking place.

August

Best Days Overall: 4th, 5th, 13th, 14th, 15th, 23rd, 24th, 31st

Most Stressful Days Overall: 6th, 7th, 20th, 21st, 22nd, 27th, 28th

Best Days for Love: 8th, 9th, 11th, 12th, 18th, 19th, 20th, 21st, 27th, 28th, 29th, 30th

Best Days for Money: 3rd, 4th, 13th, 14th, 16th, 17th, 23rd, 24th, 31st

Though you should still rest and relax more until the 22nd, the health stress on you is lessening day by day and your health is becoming what it should be.

Last month, Jupiter moved away from a stressful alignment with you. This month, Saturn moves away from its stressful alignment. Saturn was the major culprit of any health problems you may have experienced in the past two years. Now these two Cosmic powerhouses are actually helping you.

Saturn and Jupiter in your 5th House indicates that you are in a party mood for next few months. There is an urge to have fun in life and to make other people happy. With many planets in your 7th House until the 22nd, this party atmosphere is reinforced.

The strength in your social sector is reinforced by many planets in the Western sector. This is a time to develop social skills, not those of self-reliance or independence.

Though love and social activities are active and important, committed love affairs seem stormy. You and the beloved seem out of synch. The beloved wants to go to the cinema and you want to stay home, the beloved wants Italian food and you want Chinese, the beloved wants to spend money on jewellery and you want to spend on a new gadget or piece of software. Compromise is essential in holding things together – yet a part of you resents having to give up part of your personality for another person. There is a power struggle – a tug of war – going on.

This tug of war creates some temporary financial stress as well. Perhaps you are spending too much on socializing. Perhaps the beloved is causing needless expenses. Earnings come with greater effort, but they will come. Jupiter and Saturn are making long-term beautiful aspects to your Money Planet, so the long-term outlook is wonderful. Speculations go better before the 22nd than afterwards. Money comes from creative projects or from industries that cater to children. Aquarian investors will profit from calculated risks in telecommunications, entertainment and energy. Casino-type speculations should be avoided – but calculated, well-hedged speculation seems profitable.

After the 22nd there is much power in the 8th House, making this a good period to deal with addictions, explore the deeper things of life, pay off debt, attract investors to your projects, help others to prosper and get rid of the unnecessary from your life.

Health improves dramatically after the 22nd.

September

Best Days Overall: 1st, 10th, 11th, 19th, 20th, 27th, 28th

Most Stressful Days Overall: 2nd, 3rd, 17th, 18th, 23rd, 24th, 30th

Best Days for Love: 1st, 7th, 8th, 10th, 11th, 17th, 18th, 19th, 20th, 23rd, 24th, 30th

Best Days for Money: 1st, 10th, 11th, 12th, 13th, 19th, 20th, 27th, 28th

Though the pace of change in the world is slowing down some because of increased retrograde activity, and though Uranus, your Ruler, retrograde leaves you unsure of your future direction, all of this suits you just fine. You are entering one of the happiest, most successful periods of your life and the *now* is where it's at. The future will take care of itself if you enjoy the now to the fullest.

There are many planets in your native element of Air during this period. Thus, your mental clarity and communication ability have never been better. Writers, teachers, lecturers and marketing people are going to have an awesome month. It's very important that you use this energy constructively – in ways that lead you to your goals. Otherwise, it can easily be frittered away in useless gossip (very difficult to resist now) and over-heated thought. Too much mental stimulation can cause insomnia and nervous depletion – not to mention huge phone bills. Learn to shut your mind off when not in use – meditation and relaxation exercises can help you do this.

Most of the planets are in the West, indicating that you need to continue to adapt to situations and win the grace of other people. This is no time for power struggles or for going it alone. Power struggles are happening in your love life, but work to minimize these things rather than maximize them. Give in where possible – on the small things. Save the big rows for something really important.

Most of the planets are above the Horizon, and your 10th House of Career will be strong for the next few months. Though family, emotional and domestic issues are important, you need to achieve these goals through success in the outer world. Your family seems supportive of your career these days. Great career expansion will happen towards the end of the month.

Your health is super, with the only danger being the one mentioned earlier – too much thinking, too much talking, over-stimulating the mind. But there is great overall vitality.

The retrograde of your Money Planet seems to have little impact on finances during this period. It receives so much positive stimulation that you can't help but make money. Everything you touch turns to gold. It would be wise, though, to give more thought to how you spend and invest it.

Love will vastly improve after the 22nd. Until then it seems stormy. Perhaps you are over-aggressive in love and your partner (or object of your affection) is turned off by this. The challenge until the 22nd is gaining your objectives with charm rather than force.

October

Best Days Overall: 7th, 8th, 16th, 17th, 25th, 26th

Most Stressful Days Overall: 1st, 14th, 15th, 20th, 21st, 27th, 28th

Best Days for Love: 1st, 7th, 8th, 9th, 10th, 11th, 16th, 17th, 20th, 21st, 27th, 28th, 29th, 30th

Best Days for Money: 7th, 8th, 9th, 10th, 11th, 16th, 17th, 25th, 26th

With Saturn's retrograde back into Taurus and many planets in Scorpio there is increased stress on your health during this period. Be sure to rest and relax more – especially after the 23rd. Remember the discussion in the Health section, above. And though your vitality is not up to its usually high standards it is nowhere near as stressed out as it was early in the year. If you got through the early part of the year, this month will be a snap.

In spite of the increased health stress this is a happy and successful month, a party month. Many planets in your own native Air element make you feel right at home. Your mind has never been sharper and your communication skills never keener. People in general are in a more talkative mood. Abstract ideas – your strength – are appreciated and in vogue. Many Aquarians gravitate to sales, marketing and media activities – and these people are having a banner month. Salespeople who cold call – normally a frustrating line of work – have a banner month as well.

With the Sun and other planets moving through your 10th House of Career – and with most of the planets above the Horizon – you are experiencing a yearly career peak. The demands of career are intense but satisfying. You socialize with the high and mighty – with people of prominence and power. Love could happen with a boss, or through the normal pursuit of career success. Your present love will be supportive of career – though he or she might conflict with you in other ways. Your spouse or love is also unusually ambitious during this period. Mercury retrograde in your 10th House suggests caution in how you communicate to bosses or to those involved with your career – take nothing for granted and make sure they understand exactly what you mean. Miscommunication is the major barrier to career happiness now. Another danger is personal desire. Your personal inclinations and desire for freedom could interfere with your career goals.

Finances are beautiful until the 23rd. They will be good afterwards too, but you'll have to work harder for them. The question that confronts you after the 23rd is – which is more important, prestige/titles or cash? A good mix of both would be the ideal.

AQUARIUS

Love is happy until the 23rd, but afterwards gets stormy. Much compromising will be necessary to make things work. A significant other is in your life now.

November

Best Days Overall: 3rd, 4th, 13th, 21st, 22nd

Most Stressful Days Overall: 10th, 11th, 17th, 18th, 23rd, 24th

Best Days for Love: 6th, 7th, 8th, 9th, 15th, 16th, 17th, 18th, 19th, 20th, 26th, 27th, 28th, 29th

Best Days for Money: 3rd, 4th, 6th, 7th, 12th, 13th, 21st, 22nd, 30th

A happy period in a happy year – this in spite of the temporary health stress until the 22nd. Rest and relax more until then. Ease up and focus only on what is important. You'll feel much more vitality after the 22nd.

There is a Grand Trine in your native Air element after the 4th. This sharpens and enhances your already acute mental and communications skills. You learn easily and communicate what you learn even more easily. Seldom have you been this inspired or eloquent in your expression. Ideas come easily out of the air. Students, writers, teachers and marketing people all have a banner month.

This is another month of balancing love, career and personal desires. Each pulls you in a different direction. Your job is to make all these areas support each other. Career will probably take priority now as your 10th House is strong and most of the planets are above the Horizon. But allow time for love and personal pleasure as well. Your career will go well all month. After the 22nd there is more dealing with friends, groups and organizations. Group activities – your great love – become prominent and happy then.

Love is still stormy and conflicted until the 22nd. Some of you are torn by conflicting desires – do I go for the one I truly love or the one who can further my career aspirations? Like last month there is much socializing with people of high status. A romance with a boss or employee is likely – but the road will not be a smooth one. Love issues resolve harmoniously after the 22nd.

Finances are very powerful this month as your Money Planet receives incredibly beautiful aspects. Your financial intuition is keen and you can go to the bank with it. Speculations are favourable. Money comes easily now.

You are venturing into weird and unusual spaces to beautify the home. Your ideas about this are unconventional – even for you, who love unconventionality. Family members are doing unusual things as well. The search for emotional harmony and inner peace takes you into unknown spaces. Spiritual and religious illumination comes in strange garbs. There could be a journey to an exotic land.

December

Best Days Overall: 1st, 2nd, 10th, 11th, 18th, 19th, 28th, 29th

Most Stressful Days Overall: 8th, 9th, 14th, 15th, 20th, 21st, 22nd

Best Days for Love: 6th, 7th, 10th, 11th, 14th, 15th, 18th, 19th, 25th, 26th, 28th, 29th

Best Days for Money: 1st, 3rd, 4th, 10th, 11th, 18th, 28th, 30th, 31st

Health is much improved these days, though you need to be careful of overwork after the 23rd. Most of the planets are above the Horizon and Mars crosses the Midheaven point on the 23rd. Outer ambitions are very important and you're willing to go great lengths to defend your turf. A competitive situation is coming to a head this month.

Most of the planets are in the East and three planets in your 1st House are moving forward. This is a month of change and personal progress. You can and should have things your way. If you don't, you're ready, willing and able to go it alone. This is a month for creating conditions as you like them.

The Solar Eclipse of the 25th is a powerful one for the world at large, but deals rather kindly with you. Relationships, business partnerships and marriages get tested now. Irreparable ones will fall by the wayside, healthy ones will get even better. Job changes are likely during this period. This could be within your present company or with a new company. Health regimes, diets and doctors will probably get changed in the coming months as well – remember that the effects of an Eclipse last for six months.

The Solar Eclipse occurs in your 12th House of Spirituality. Thus there will be changes in your spiritual life and orientation. There are upheavals in a spiritual or charitable organization to which you belong. Meditative paths and spiritual disciplines get changed. Your dreamlife will be very active all month, but especially around the time of the Eclipse. Visions seen around the Eclipse period should not be taken too seriously – much of it is psychic debris stirred up by the Eclipse.

Though love will get tested by the Eclipse, your love life looks good for most of the month. Singles are looking for a friend as well as a lover. Romantic opportunities come at organizations and seminars – at group activities or through introductions made by friends. Spiritual compatibility becomes very important after the 21st. Venus in your own Sign after the 8th enhances your physical appearance and social magnetism. Stylish clothing or jewellery – or the wherewithal to buy these things – will come to you this month. For singles the Eclipse could be a healthy thing for love, as it causes a desire for change in marital status – this could mean a decision to marry.

Finances are strong all month, but especially after the 8th.

Pisces

)(

THE FISH

Birthdays from
19th February
to 20th March

Personality Profile

PISCES AT A GLANCE

Element – Water

Ruling Planet – Neptune
  Career Planet – Pluto
  Love Planet – Mercury
  Money Planet – Mars
  Planet of Health and Work – Sun
  Planet of Home and Family Life – Mercury
  Planet of Love Affairs, Creativity and
  Children – Moon

Colours – aqua, blue-green

Colours that promote love, romance and social
harmony – earth tones, yellow,
yellow-orange

Colours that promote earning power – red, scarlet

Gem – white diamond

Metal – tin

Scent – lotus

Quality – mutable (= flexibility)

Qualities most needed for balance – structure and the ability to handle form

Strongest virtues – psychic power, sensitivity, self-sacrifice, altruism

Deepest needs – spiritual illumination, liberation

Characteristics to avoid – escapism, keeping bad company, negative moods

Signs of greatest overall compatibility – Cancer, Scorpio

Signs of greatest overall incompatibility – Gemini, Virgo, Sagittarius

Sign most helpful to career – Sagittarius

Sign most helpful for emotional support – Gemini

Sign most helpful financially – Aries

Sign best for marriage and/or partnerships – Virgo

Sign most helpful for creative projects – Cancer

Best Sign to have fun with – Cancer

Signs most helpful in spiritual matters – Scorpio, Aquarius

Best day of the week – Thursday

Understanding the Pisces Personality

If Pisceans have one outstanding quality it is their belief in the invisible, spiritual and psychic side of things. This side of things is as real to them as the hard earth beneath their feet – so real, in fact, that they will often ignore the visible, tangible aspects of reality in order to focus on the invisible and so-called intangible ones.

Of all the Signs of the Zodiac, the intuitive and emotional faculties of the Pisces are the most highly developed. They are committed to living by their intuition and this can at times be infuriating to other people – especially those who are materially-, scientifically- or technically-orientated. If you think that money or status or worldly success are the only goals in life, then you will never understand a Pisces.

Pisceans have intellect, but to them intellect is only a means by which they can rationalize what they know intuitively. To an Aquarius or a Gemini the intellect is a tool with which to gain knowledge. To a well-developed Pisces it is a tool by which to *express* knowledge.

Pisceans feel like fish in an infinite ocean of thought and feeling. This ocean has many depths, currents and sub-currents. They long for purer waters where the denizens are good, true and beautiful, but they are sometimes pulled to the lower, murkier depths. Pisceans know that they do not generate thoughts but only tune in to thoughts that already exist; this is why they seek the purer waters. This ability to tune in to higher thoughts inspires them artistically and musically.

Since Pisces is so spiritually-orientated – though many Pisceans in the corporate world may hide this fact – we will deal with this aspect in greater detail, for otherwise it is difficult to understand the true Pisces personality.

There are four basic attitudes of the spirit. One is outright scepticism – the attitude of secular humanists. The second is an intellectual or emotional belief, where one worships a far-distant God figure – the attitude of most modern church-going people. The third is not only belief but direct personal spiritual experience – this is the attitude of some 'born-again' religious people. The fourth is actual unity with the divinity, an intermingling with the spiritual world – this is the attitude of yoga. This fourth attitude is the deepest urge of a Pisces, and a Pisces is uniquely qualified to pursue and perform this work.

Consciously or unconsciously, Pisceans seek this union with the spiritual world. The belief in a greater reality makes Pisceans very tolerant and understanding of others – perhaps even too tolerant. There are instances in their lives when they should say 'enough is enough' and be ready to defend their position and put up a fight. However, because of their qualities it takes a good deal of doing to get them into that frame of mind.

Pisceans basically want and aspire to be 'saints'. They do so in their own way and according to their own rules. Others should not try to impose their concept of saintliness on a Pisces, because he or she always tries to find it for him- or herself.

Finance

Money is generally not that important to Pisces. Of course they need it as much as anyone else, and many of them attain great wealth. But money is not generally a primary objective. Doing good, feeling good about oneself, peace of mind, the relief of pain and suffering – these are the things that matter most to a Pisces.

Pisceans earn money intuitively and instinctively. They follow their hunches rather than their logic. They tend to be generous and perhaps overly charitable. Almost any kind of misfortune is enough to move a Pisces to give. Although this is one of their greatest virtues, Pisceans should be more careful with their finances. They should try to be more choosy about the people to whom they lend money, so that they are not being taken advantage of. If they give money to charities they should follow it up to see that their contributions are put to good use. Even when Pisceans are not rich, they still like to spend money on helping others. In this case they should really be careful, however: they must learn to say no sometimes and help themselves first.

Perhaps the biggest financial stumbling block for the Pisces is general passivity – a *laissez faire* attitude. In general Pisceans like to go with the flow of events. When it comes to financial matters, especially, they need to be more aggressive. They need to make things happen, to create their own wealth. A passive attitude will only cause loss and missed opportunity. Worrying about financial security will not provide that security. Pisceans need to go after what they want tenaciously.

Career and Public Image

Pisceans like to be perceived by the public as people of spiritual or material wealth, of generosity and philanthropy. They look up to big-hearted, philanthropic types. They admire people engaged in large-scale undertakings and eventually would like to head up these big enterprises themselves. In short, they like to be connected with big organizations that are doing things in a big way.

If Pisceans are to realize their full career and professional potential they need to travel more, educate themselves more and learn more about the actual world. In other words, they need some of the unflagging optimism of the Sagittarius in order to reach the top.

Because of all their caring and generous characteristics, Pisceans often choose professions through which they can help and touch the lives of other people. That is why many Pisceans become doctors, nurses, social workers or teachers. Sometimes it takes a while before Pisceans realize what they really want to do in their professional lives, but once they find a career that lets them manifest their interests and virtues they will excel at it.

Love and Relationships

It is not surprising that someone as 'other-worldly' as the Pisces would like a partner who is practical and down to earth. Pisceans prefer a partner who is on top of all the details of life, because they dislike details. Pisceans seek this quality in both their romantic and professional partners. More than anything else this gives Pisces a feeling of being grounded, of being in touch with reality.

As expected, these kinds of relationships – though necessary – are sure to have many ups and downs. Misunderstandings will take place because the two attitudes are poles apart. If you are in love with a Pisces you will experience these fluctuations and will need a lot of patience to see things stabilize. Pisceans are moody, intuitive, affectionate and difficult to get to know. Only time and the right attitude will yield Pisceans' deepest secrets. However, when in love with a Pisces you will find that riding the waves is worth it because they are good, sensitive people who need and like to give love and affection.

When in love, Pisceans like to fantasize. For them fantasy is 90 per cent of the fun of a relationship. They tend to idealize their partner, which can be good and bad at the same time. It is bad in that it is difficult for anyone to live up to the high ideals their Piscean lover sets.

Home and Domestic Life

In their family and domestic life Pisceans have to resist the tendency to relate only by feelings and moods. It is unrealistic to expect that your partner and other family members will be as intuitive as you are. There is a need for more verbal communication between a Pisces and his or her family. A cool, unemotional exchange of ideas and opinions will benefit everyone.

Some Pisceans tend to like mobility and moving around. For them too much stability feels like a restriction on their freedom. They hate to be locked in one location for ever.

The Sign of Gemini sits on Pisces' 4th Solar House (of Home and Family) cusp. This shows that the Pisces likes and needs a home environment that promotes intellectual and mental interests. They tend to treat their neighbours as family – or extended family. Some Pisceans can have a dual attitude towards the home and family – on the one hand they like the emotional support of the family, but on the other they dislike the obligations, restrictions and duties involved with it. For Pisces, finding a balance is the key to a happy family life.

Horoscope for 2000

Major Trends

1999 was a strong financial and career year, and while this trend continues in the year 2000, some of the emphasis is shifting. By mid-February you will be pursuing intellectual interests and educational goals, and by the summer you will be focused on setting up a stable home base and growing psychologically. Writers, marketers and teachers will have a very productive year.

1999 was a very spiritual year, and the trend continues in the year 2000. Two powerful planets in your 12th House of Spirituality, including Neptune, your Ruler, indicates great change and growth in this area – this year and over the long term. More on this later.

There are an unusual number of Eclipses in the year 2000 – more than normal. And while these Eclipses create changes in the world and in those around you, they seem to leave you untouched. They merely shatter walls and obstacles that were obstructing you.

Your Houses of Power this year are the 2nd House (Money and Finance) – until 15th February; the 3rd House (Intellectual Interests, Domestic Travel, Siblings); the 4th House (Home and Family) – after 1st July; the 10th House (Career); and the 12th House (Spirituality, Charity, Ministry, Voluntary Activities).

Your paths to greatest fulfilment this year are health and work, children, creativity, amusement and fun, finance (until 15th February), intellectual interests (from 15th February to 1st July), and Home and Family (from 1st July onwards).

Health

Though your 6th House of Health is not a House of Power this year, other subtle signals indicate that you should not ignore this area. Two Eclipses occur here – a Lunar Eclipse on 21st January and a Solar Eclipse on 30th July – indicating great changes in this area. Health attitudes and health regimes change. Flaws in your present health regime or with your doctors or health plans are revealed so that you can correct them. The second Eclipse (30th July) is the more serious one, and you should take a reduced schedule during this period – for two days before and a day after. Furthermore, three major long-term planets are in stressful alignment with you from 11th August to 27th October – so your normal vitality is not what it should be. When vitality is low you become more vulnerable to various ailments.

Health is wonderful the first half of the year. But it won't hurt to get involved in a serious health discipline during this period. Build up resistance now for the latter half of the year, when your vitality is not up to par.

Those of you who have Pisces children should let them sleep more if they feel like it. Don't worry that they are becoming 'lazy'. They want to sleep because they have a need to.

Pisceans should take more naps, spend time with uplifting and positive people, and have their feet massaged on a regular basis.

A disciplined health regime now will stand in you good stead for the rest of the year and for next year, when Saturn moves into a long-term stressful alignment with you.

Now is the time to focus on essential things, to create priorities in life and to stick to them. Delegate or let go of lesser things. Think less, talk less and do less. Think of your energy the way the businessperson thinks of investments: use it where you are sure of a good return.

Wear the colours, scent, gem and metal of your Sign.

The Sun, as your Health Planet, shows that health can be enhanced by strengthening the heart. Generically, the Sun rules joy and creativity. Thus, a cultivation of happy states and of creative hobbies will also help your health. Avoid depression like the plague. Avoid depressive people as well – unless you feel strong enough to handle them. Your sensitive, empathic nature makes you vulnerable to negative conditions which are not your own. You must guard against this. How did you feel when you spoke to so-and-so at that party? Did you feel tired afterwards or uplifted? What did you feel in your body when you spoke to the seemingly kind neighbour? Did you have pains in your body? These are all clear psychic messages and you must be alert to them.

When you feel stressed, tired or depressed, 9 times out of 10 it is something you've picked up – don't identify with these feelings. Soaking in a hot tub for an hour or so is very healing and will disperse any negative mood. You respond beautifully to all therapies involving water. Jacuzzis, spas, whirlpools and hydro massage are all excellent for you.

If you maintain your energy levels and practise the above techniques you will get through the year 2000 with flying colours – and you will have learned a valuable skill as well.

There is much more to be said about water therapies for you, but as you practise, new insights will come to you.

Home and Domestic Life

For some years now you have been career-driven. The 'outer' world and outer achievement have been your main focus. Emotional and psychological issues were left on the back burner. This is about to change in 2000. You have made great strides in your career. After 1999 you are where you want to be in that department. Career goals have been basically achieved. Now is the time to start cultivating emotional harmony – to feel right about things, to find your emotional 'comfort zone' which you have so long ignored.

Come the summer, home and family issues will become a top, and happy, priority.

Jupiter, moving into your 4th House, brings better relations with family members, a new home or expansion of the present home, the fortunate sale or purchase of a home, the acquisition of second and third homes, speculative success in property, new additions to the family through birth or marriage, and upbeat moods. You are creating a happy day-to-day lifestyle this year.

Some of you may view this as a diversion from your career, but in reality it is not so. It is a temporary breather, a deepening of the emotional underpinnings that support your career. Once the day-to-day lifestyle issues are improved, your career will be able to expand again.

Jupiter is your Career Planet. Thus its move into your 4th House – opposite its normal position – indicates that many of you will be setting up home offices, working from home, pursuing career goals from home, getting involved in family-type businesses, and perhaps even making your family your career.

Now that your career is where you want it to be, many of you will be supporting the careers of family members – getting them to where they want to be.

Of course you won't be able to ignore your career alto-gether – Pluto in your 10th House won't allow you to – but you will create a better balance between family and career.

Relations with family could get sticky and burdensome from 11th August to 27th October, but this is short term. The basic relationships are healthy this year.

Siblings could move house (due to marriage or serious romance) this year. A parent could also move house. The domestic life of adult children seems to maintain the status quo.

Love and Social Life

Love issues are not particularly important this year, and I expect that the status quo will prevail. Singles will tend to remain single and married people will remain married.

Of course you will still have a social life, but your heart is not really in it. Many other issues take priority now.

The 22nd August to 23rd September is probably your most powerful and active social period this year. The 30th May to 7th August brings a hot romance which has many ups and downs, stops and gos. A very confusing situation. It's doubtful whether this will lead to anything serious – though your unique personal horoscope (based on your pre-cise date and time of birth) could modify this.

Jupiter's conjunction with Saturn in May and June brings new and powerful friends into the life – these seem involved with your career and are not romantic in nature. You meet them in your neighbourhood or through an introduction made by siblings.

Mercury is your Love Planet and its movements and aspects will indicate the day-to-day fluctuations and trends in love. When it is moving forward quickly there is great social confidence and progress. When it goes retrograde (three times this year: from 21st February – 14th March, 23rd June – 17th July, and 18th October – 8th November) your social confidence is weaker and your judgement is not as sound. Relationships seem to go backwards instead of forwards. Mercury's position and aspects will also play an unusual role in love. When it is well positioned and well aspected, love issues will go well and harmoniously. When it is poorly positioned and stressfully aspected, there will be conflicts or crises in love. But remember that Mercury is a fast-moving planet – moving through all the Signs and Houses of your Horoscope in one year. Therefore these events – for good or ill – are temporary, short-term things and not long-term trends. You should get neither too excited nor too depressed by these things. They pass quickly. Mercury's movements are covered more fully in the month-by-month forecasts, below.

Mercury's fleeting movements show that you have many and ever-changing needs and attitudes to love. You are fickle in this area. Someone who seemed to fit the bill last month might not next month – and thus you feel unfulfilled. The reverse is also true. Someone you may have spurned a month ago could look very alluring in another month. Good communication with your spouse, partner or lover can alleviate much confusion.

A parent could marry this year, though the road is not a smooth one. Adult children face crises in their marriage. Grandchildren of marriageable age are getting ready to tie the knot.

Career and Finance

Money and career are still important this year, but not as important as they were last year – as mentioned earlier.

Jupiter is still in your Money House as the year begins, expanding earnings, bringing financial opportunities and increasing the value of the assets you already own. The year 2000 is still a banner financial year, and those of you born late in the Sign of Pisces – from 15th March onwards – will feel this especially intensely.

But as the year progresses and financial goals are attained, your attention shifts elsewhere. Money per se becomes less and less important. You have enough and you don't need to focus too much on it.

Jupiter moving through your 3rd House from 15th February to 1st July brings new communication equipment, a car, and educational opportunities to you. Jupiter moving through your 4th House from 1st July onwards brings luck in property speculations, the fortunate purchase or sale of a home and profits from home-based or family businesses. Industries that cater to the home look profitable as investments during this period – but of course do the necessary research.

The career is still blazing hot as the year begins. Pay rises, promotions and increases in public esteem and status are still happening – especially for those of you born late in the Sign. But as mentioned earlier you are entering a period during which you need to balance your career with a happy home life. You need to shore up the foundations upon which your future career growth depends.

Jupiter, besides being the planet of abundance, is also your Career Planet. Thus its moves (and it does move unusually fast this year) indicate the changes in your career attitudes and how you best attain to career goals. While Jupiter is in Aries (until 15th February) you will tend to measure success in financial terms. The more money you make, the more successful you deem yourself to be. When Jupiter moves into Taurus, your 3rd House (15th February to 1st July) you will further your career through sales, marketing, advertising and, in general, getting the word out about yourself or your company. You will measure success in terms of how many people you've reached and in terms of how much you have learned. When Jupiter moves into Gemini, your 4th House, you will measure success in terms of how good or bad you feel – how good or bad your domestic life is.

Two Eclipses in your House of Work show job changes for those of you who work for others. These changes can be disruptive, but they are ultimately good, as flaws in the present situation will get corrected. Employers could see shake-ups in their staff during these Eclipse periods as well. These Eclipses occur on 21st January and 30th July, and will be discussed in the month-by-month forecasts, below.

Mars is your Money Planet, and financial ease or conflict will be shown by its movements and positions. Mars will be moving forward all year, which is a good financial signal.

Self-improvement

Last year there was great conflict between your spiritual urges and your worldly urges. The urge to be in seclusion, to meditate and get closer to the Higher Power within was competing with the equally strong urge for worldly success, name and fame. It was a seesaw battle, now one side taking precedence and now the other. This year the conflict is less stark. The spiritual side will win. Now that you've had your taste of outer success – its joys and tribulations – you are more inclined to satisfy your spiritual longings and to put this success into the correct perspective. You will notice ever-greater spiritual longings beginning in the summer. No, there is nothing wrong with you and you are not abnormal. This is all part of the Great Plan of your life. Your inner life is going to be much more exciting than your outer life this year.

Month-by-month Forecasts

January

Best Days Overall: 1st, 2nd, 10th, 11th, 19th, 20th, 28th, 29th

Most Stressful Days Overall: 3rd, 4th, 17th, 18th, 23rd, 24th, 30th, 31st

Best Days for Love: 3rd, 4th, 5th, 6th, 7th, 13th, 14th, 15th, 16th, 22nd, 23rd, 24th, 25th, 26th

Best Days for Money: 3rd, 4th, 10th, 11th, 13th, 14th, 19th, 20th, 21st, 22nd, 28th, 29th, 30th, 31st

March forward boldly towards your dreams, Pisces, as the Cosmos is powering you up beyond all imagination. The entire universe supports your independence, and your way is its way. Assert yourself with grace and create conditions as you like them – the world will adapt to you.

With 90 to 100 per cent of the planets in your Eastern sector there is no need to compromise (though there's no need to get arrogant or ugly, either). Work towards your fondest goals and love will find you. It is already chasing you and by next month will catch up with you. You will be popular not by toadying up to others but by being true to yourself and to what is really important to you.

Between 60 and 70 per cent of the planetary power is still in the upper half of your chart, indicating an emphasis on worldly success and outer activities. Maintain your focus, as important breakthroughs are happening around the 9th.

By the 12th all the planets will be in forward motion, so there is great change, forward momentum and progress in your life – goals can manifest with breathtaking rapidity now.

The most important areas of interest this month are the

career, friends, groups and organizations, and the spiritual life and charities.

The Lunar Eclipse of the 21st is kind to you and the disruptions it causes work in your favour. This Eclipse seems to affect the workplace. If you work for someone else you could change jobs around this period. This could be within your present company or with a new company. Employers probably will see a shake-up in their staff.

The Moon is also your Planet of Love Affairs, Creativity and Children. Thus the Eclipse causes some disruptions in these areas as well. But as mentioned the disruptions are good ones – happy things can be just as disruptive as unhappy ones.

Health is excellent all month, and when Mars moves into your own Sign on the 4th it will get even better. Exercise regimes go well. Your athletic ability (as well as your libido) increases. You need to guard against temper tantrums and irritation as you tend to be more forceful and demanding about getting your way. You do not suffer fools gladly. The zeal of the Lord of Hosts is upon you now, and things get done very quickly.

Love is happy this month, though not that important to you. Romantic opportunities abound at organizations, group activities, charitable functions or ministerial activities. Singles meet someone significant around the 19th–21st.

Finances are spectacular and you dress for success and in general project an image of wealth. No need to run after financial opportunities, they are chasing you ardently. But you need to ensure that a short-term financial gain doesn't jeopardize your long-term career goals. Financial opportunities need to fit in with your overall goals in life.

February

Best Days Overall: 7th, 8th, 15th, 16th, 24th, 25th

Most Stressful Days Overall: 13th, 14th, 19th, 20th, 26th, 27th, 28th

Best Days for Love: 2nd, 3rd, 6th, 11th, 12th, 15th, 16th, 19th, 20th, 22nd, 24th, 25th

Best Days for Money: 7th, 8th, 9th, 10th, 17th, 18th, 19th, 26th, 27th, 29th

The balance of planetary power is shifting to the bottom half of the Horoscope by the 20th. So your career is becoming less important than it has been. Jupiter's move into Taurus shows that your career is stabilizing – on a routine track for a while – and that you can put it on automatic pilot and focus some attention on your home and family life. Of course, with Mercury retrograde from the 21st onwards, you should be making plans and giving thought to family issues – execute your plans next month.

Between 90 and 100 per cent of the planets are in the Eastern sector of your chart. Mercury (also your Love Planet) will be retrograde from the 21st onwards. Thus, you can de-emphasize love and social activities and focus on building the life that you want. You can have things your way now and the world will adapt to you. There is great energy and independence – a clear sense of direction – that you should use to your advantage.

Between 90 and 100 per cent of the planets are still moving forward, and like last month you are in a period where you will see quick progress towards your goals and plans.

The Solar Eclipse of the 5th is very powerful for the world at large, perhaps causing earthquakes, floods and major changes in science and technology. But for you this Eclipse will be kindly. Its effects will be felt in the inner life rather than the outer life. Your dreamlife will be hyperactive – but not very reliable – so make sure you get confirmation from other sources before being guided by it. Those on a spiritual path will have major spiritual revelations leading to changes in their meditative path and in their spiritual direction. Meditation will be harder during this period, yet it is more necessary than usual.

A sudden job change is looming. Employers can see shake-ups in their staff. Many of you will change doctors, health plans or health regimes. The health of your spouse or partner is a concern, and if there are hidden flaws in the body – impurities – they are sure to come out now. Your spouse or partner could also change jobs.

Love is still chasing you, Pisces, but perhaps less ardently than before. There is some cooling in the beloved's ardour due to Mercury's retrograde. But this is temporary. The beloved is re-thinking and re-evaluating from the 21st onwards. Love will be back on track next month.

Health is excellent all month as 80 to 90 per cent of the planetary power is in good aspect to you. Still, as mentioned, you might change your health regime.

Your Money Planet (Mars) moves into the Money House on the 12th; this is a positive financial signal. You have unusual control over earnings, a take-charge attitude and a willingness to take on some risks.

March

Best Days Overall: 5th, 6th, 14th, 15th, 22nd, 23rd, 24th

Most Stressful Days Overall: 12th, 18th, 19th, 25th, 26th

Best Days for Love: 3rd, 4th, 5th, 6th, 12th, 13th, 14th, 15th, 18th, 19th, 22nd, 23rd, 24th

Best Days for Money: 1st, 7th, 8th, 9th, 10th, 18th, 19th, 27th, 28th

A happy month in a happy year. The planetary power is overwhelmingly in your Eastern sector during this period. Further, there are many planets in your own Sign of Pisces now. You are filled with energy, zeal and enthusiasm. You can have your way in life and build conditions as you desire them to be. Ninety per cent of the planets are moving forward, ensuring progress and success in your ventures.

By the 13th the planetary power will have dramatically shifted to the bottom half of your Horoscope (below the Horizon). And though career will be important this year, you can safely de-emphasize it for a while and get your emotional and family life in order. Mercury's forward motion on the 14th will help you in these endeavours.

Your most important areas of interest this month are spirituality, charity and volunteer-type activities, the body, image and personal pleasure, finance, and local travel, intellectual interests, sales and marketing projects and siblings and neighbours.

Though love is delicate right now, things will improve by the 14th. Venus moves into your own Sign on the 13th, bringing personal glamour, beauty, a sense of style and social grace to your image. The Sun in your own Sign is granting energy and strength. Mercury, your Love Planet, will start moving forward on the 14th, clarifying your love life. You are having your way in love. Love is pursuing you and your spouse, partner or beloved is going way out of his or her way to please you now. No need to go anywhere special or do anything special to find love – it is there, it is finding you.

Health is excellent all month. After the 20th you are more concerned about financial health than personal health. Investments in health-orientated companies or industries might be lucrative for Pisces investors – but of course do the necessary research. Your net worth should be increased by the time the month ends.

Your Money Planet's move into your 3rd House on the 23rd is another important financial signal. It joins two other power planets in that House – Jupiter and Saturn. Thus there is a nice financial windfall – coming either at the end of this month or early next month. This could come through your job, or from elders or parents. Sales, marketing and communications become ever more important on a financial level.

April

Best Days Overall: 1st, 2nd, 10th, 11th, 19th, 20th, 29th, 30th

Most Stressful Days Overall: 8th, 9th, 14th, 15th, 21st, 22nd

Best Days for Love: 1st, 2nd, 10th, 11th, 12th, 13th, 14th, 15th, 21st, 22nd

Best Days for Money: 4th, 5th, 6th, 7th, 14th, 15th, 24th, 25th

Almost all the planets are in the East and 90 per cent of them are moving forward. There is great (and fast-paced) personal progress and achievement now. Change happens with blinding speed. A seemingly eternal problem can change in a week. There is so much activity that a week seems like an eternity now.

Move forward towards your goals. Create conditions as you desire them to be. Act on your desires and watch how the Cosmos supports you.

The majority of planets (60 to 70 per cent) are below the Horizon of your chart, showing this to be a month of inner, psychological progress rather than outer, worldly-orientated progress. Mercury, now moving forward, is further helping you emotionally and domestically.

The North Node of the Moon makes an important shift from your 6th House of Health and Work to your 5th House of Creativity. Thus, there is great emotional fulfilment and personal happiness from creativity, children and child-related issues, and from the fun aspects of life. Life is to be enjoyed, as you will see in the coming months.

Your important areas of interest this month are spirituality and charity, the body, the image and personal pleasures, finance, sales, marketing, communication and intellectual interests, and local travel, neighbours and siblings.

Health is strong all month, but be careful of overspending on 'miracle' foods or diets. There is a tendency for you to be rash about these things. Study before you buy. The same holds true regarding investments in these industries. Don't allow financial ups and downs to affect your health. Keep these two areas of your life separate. And though this is a great financial month it is only natural that some days will be less great than others.

Love is still happy this month and you are getting your way. Love has to be physical and expressed physically for you to be satisfied – platonic love doesn't do the trick now. After the 13th, singles find love as they pursue their normal financial goals and obligations. Your lover or spouse is very supportive financially. Material gifts are romantic turn-ons. Unattached singles look for lovers who can do them some financial good.

Finances are powerful and the new Moon of the 4th is making them even more so – for often, more than money, we need ideas. These the Moon will supply as the month progresses. Important financial highs occur around the 5th and 6th. Financial opportunity comes through friends or professional organizations around the 15th–17th. Sales and marketing (like last month) are still very important for your bottom line.

May

Best Days Overall: 7th, 8th, 16th, 17th, 26th, 27th

Most Stressful Days Overall: 5th, 6th, 12th, 13th, 18th, 19th, 20th

Best Days for Love: 3rd, 4th, 12th, 13th, 14th, 22nd, 23rd, 24th, 25th

Best Days for Money: 1st, 2nd, 3rd, 4th, 5th, 12th, 13th, 14th, 15th, 21st, 22nd, 24th, 25th, 28th, 29th, 31st

Two important developments take place this month. The planets make a shift to the West and Neptune, your Ruler, goes retrograde on the 8th. Thus there is a psychological shift this month. There is less self-confidence, self-assertion and independence – but also less of a need for these things. The Cosmos is very clever. Now is the time for cultivating the good graces of others, and for road-testing your recent creations. Avoid power struggles like the plague.

The planets are still very much below the Horizon and your 4th House is a major House of Power – especially after the 20th. Thus finding and functioning from your emotional comfort zone is much more important than worldly success during this period. Finding your emotional comfort zone is also going to be more difficult during this period as you feel out of synch with the world and with the environment. There are almost no planets in your native Water element during this period – there is power in Earth (early in the month) and Air (after the 20th). Thus people around you are concerned with bottom-line practical issues, or with abstract ideas and theories. They seem insensitive to the feeling dimension – unaware of their own feelings and unaware of the feelings of others. Practicality is expressed in purely materialistic terms, and the feeling dimension is left out. Thus, to you (and other sensitive types) people seem cruel. Bear with this and be patient. Their behaviour is not malicious – it's just the astrological weather.

The important areas of interest this month are neighbours, siblings, local travel, sales, marketing, communications and the pursuit of intellectual interests, the home, Family and psychological issues, and spirituality.

With your 3rd House very powerful this month many of you are involved in advertising, marketing, buying, selling and trading. The energy of the period favours a practical approach. Stress the bottom-line, good value aspects of your product or service and you will get better results. This is no time to get visionary. Sell the steak, not the sizzle.

Health is delicate after the 20th so be sure to rest and relax more and to focus on essentials. Conserve energy for the really important things in your life.

Mercury, your Love Planet, moves forward speedily, indicating great social confidence and progress. Singles are probably dating more. Love needs and attitudes change frequently and people think of you as fickle. Love is close to home during this period.

Finances will be strong all month. Working from home boosts your bank balance.

June

Best Days Overall: 4th, 12th, 13th, 14th, 22nd, 23rd

Most Stressful Days Overall: 2nd, 8th, 9th, 15th, 16th, 29th, 30th

Best Days for Love: 2nd, 4th, 5th, 8th, 9th, 10th, 11th, 12th, 13th, 22nd, 23rd

Best Days for Money: 2nd, 3rd, 8th, 9th, 10th, 11th, 17th, 18th, 19th, 22nd, 23rd, 25th, 26th, 27th, 28th

There is short-term health stress until the 21st, so rest and relax more. Philosophical conflicts with the family, or emotional upheavals caused by differing world views, can be depleting. If your philosophy is correct it doesn't need defending, it will prove itself as the normal events of life progress.

Most of the planets are below the Horizon and your 4th House of Home and Family is an important House of Power. Your Career Planet is retrograde and there seems much temporary opposition and conflict in your career. Let career issues slide for a while and focus on the home and family. This is a month of great psychological progress. A good month for doing heavy work around the house – repairs, moving of furniture, redecorating and the like. Family gatherings are more numerous and bittersweet.

The general tone of life improves after the 21st. There is a party atmosphere now. There are more entertainment events, sporting events and parties. Life is optimistic. With 40 per cent of the planets retrograde after the 23rd you may as well enjoy yourself as nothing much is happening anyway – there's little you can do to hasten events.

Many planets in the West and the retrograde of Neptune, your Ruler, suggests a need to avoid power struggles and to focus on cultivating the good graces of others. Your way might not be the best way during this period. Good is coming through others.

Mercury's retrograde on the 23rd shows a need for more caution and patience at home and in love. Purchases for big-ticket items in the home should be done before the 23rd. The same goes for repair projects and redecorating. Love opportunities are plentiful and happy, but seem non-committal. Only time will show whether a current love affair will develop into something more – in the meantime enjoy it for what it is.

Finances will be strong and happy after the 21st. Money is earned easily and in fun types of ways. Job-seekers should focus on work that they enjoy rather than the financial aspects of potential employment.

There is so much optimism about finance that there is a tendency to overspend. Speculations seem favourable, though you shouldn't bet with more than you can afford to lose, and only under the dictates of intuition.

Always creative, during this period you are even more so. Those of you in the artistic fields have a banner month. There is good income from the sale of creative products.

There is much power in your native Water element after the 21st, and people around you – including you yourself – are more hypersensitive. Children, especially, are hypersensitive and will react to minor nuances in speech, voice tones and the body language of those around them.

July

Best Days Overall: 1st, 2nd, 10th, 11th, 20th, 21st, 29th

Most Stressful Days Overall: 5th, 6th, 12th, 13th, 26th, 27th

Best Days for Love: 1st, 2nd, 5th, 6th, 10th, 11th, 20th, 21st, 22nd, 23rd, 29th, 30th, 31st

Best Days for Money: 1st, 2nd, 6th, 7th, 10th, 11th, 14th, 15th, 20th, 21st, 22nd, 23rd, 25th, 26th, 29th

The three Eclipses that occur this month could be disturbing to sensitive types such as yourself. Your tendency to pick up vibrations from the environment can cause you to internalize outside events. The fact is that though there is much change and upheaval going on, you remain untouched. These Eclipses are basically kind to you. Feelings, dreams and visions are for the most part either psychic rapports or 'flotsam and jetsam' caused by the Eclipses. Any Eclipse tends to roil the psychic energy on the planet, and this roiling is what you are feeling.

Most of the planets are below the Horizon and Jupiter makes a major move into your 4th House of Home and Family on the 1st. Thus you can safely let career issues coast and focus instead on the family now. Family issues are very happy and there seems to be great emotional support for you and your career. A happy move is likely now. Those of you looking to sell or buy a home enjoy good fortune. It's a good time to boost your own career by supporting the careers of family members. Many of you will enjoy career success and fulfilment by working from home – in a home-based or family-orientated business. You have a unique opportunity in the coming months to integrate emotional harmony with career success – a beautiful achievement.

The Solar Eclipse of the 1st occurs in your 5th House and affects relations with children and creative projects. It could also temporarily disrupt a love affair, causing hidden flaws to surface. Avoid financial speculations during this period.

The Lunar Eclipse of the 16th occurs in your 11th House of Friends – but also affects children, love affairs and creative projects. It reinforces what is written about the Solar Eclipse of the 1st. In addition there could be disruptions with a friend or with a professional organization to which you belong. The Eclipse is kind to you, so rest assured that when the dust settles things will be better than before.

The Solar Eclipse of the 30th occurs in your 6th House of Health and Work. Job changes are happening, and conditions at the workplace are disrupted. There could also be a change in doctors and health regimes during this period.

Speculations are favourable during this period, but avoid them around the 1st and 2nd – the period of the Eclipse. Money is earned happily and easily this month. Love affairs can be stormy now, but romantic, committed love is improving. Mercury's forward motion on the 17th is restoring your social confidence and judgement.

August

Best Days Overall: 6th, 7th, 16th, 17th, 25th, 26th

PISCES

Most Stressful Days Overall: 1st, 2nd, 8th, 9th, 23rd, 24th, 29th, 30th

Best Days for Love: 1st, 2nd, 8th, 9th, 11th, 12th, 18th, 19th, 20th, 21st, 29th, 30th

Best Days for Money: 3rd, 4th, 8th, 9th, 13th, 14th, 18th, 19th, 23rd, 24th, 27th, 28th

Saturn's move into Gemini along with the presence of many planets in Virgo after the 22nd increases the health stress on you, Pisces. Rest and relax more. Wear the gem, metal, colours and scent of your Sign. Refuse to allow yourself to get overtired. Maximize energy by thinking less, talking less and focusing on the essentials in your life. Delegate work wherever possible. Have your feet massaged regularly. Health is also enhanced by brisk physical exercise and more attention to the heart. Gold (in addition to your Pisces colours and metal) is a healing colour now, and a good metal to wear.

Saturn in Gemini complicates domestic and family issues. Many of you are moving to larger quarters or expanding your present residence. But along with this you need to make better, and smarter, use of the space you already have. Merely expanding won't solve problems. Family support is bittersweet. Love is complicated by conflicts with the family. Either they don't approve of the beloved or the beloved doesn't approve of them.

This month the major challenge is balancing love, career and the family. Each is pulling you in a different direction and each seems to conflict with the other. Your job is to make them harmonize with each other.

Job-seekers see good success this month. Employers find workers relatively easily as well.

Financial health seems as important as physical health, but you must not allow the normal financial ups and downs to affect your health. You are more than just money – and infinitely more than your bank balance or the sum of your investments. Money comes through work during this period.

Having most of the planets in the West and the retrograde of your Ruler Neptune indicates that this is a social month. A month to coast and to allow your good to come through others rather than forcing things to happen. Coast, adapt, compromise, seek consensus and develop your social skills and you'll breeze through the month. Avoid power struggles wherever possible.

Love is happy and singles find abundant romantic opportunities. Love comes at the workplace, with co-workers or through introductions made by co-workers. Love happens at parties and social gatherings later in the month as well. Domestic duties, or disagreements about domestic issues, need to be overcome for love to flower as it should.

September

Best Days Overall: 7th, 8th, 17th, 18th, 25th, 26th, 30th

Most Stressful Days Overall: 5th, 6th, 19th, 20th, 25th, 26th

Best Days for Love: 1st, 10th, 11th, 19th, 20th, 25th, 26th, 29th, 30th

Best Days for Money: 1st, 5th, 6th, 10th, 11th, 14th, 15th, 16th, 17th, 19th, 20th, 25th, 26th, 27th, 28th

Though your 4th House of Home and Family is a major House of Power this month, the shift of the planets above the Horizon is accelerating. This is still a month of juggling – as best you can – the home and the career. Your Career Planet is now firmly in your 4th House, indicating a need to blend emotional harmony with outer achievement and success. This is going to lead to all kinds of experimentation. Some of you will work from home and create your own hours. Others will start up your own business and run it according to your personal preferences. Others will opt for a shorter working week. Once this balance is attained, you will have the pearl of great price, one of the ultimate achievements in life.

Most of the planets are still in the West and Neptune, your Ruler, is still retrograde. Take a low profile and avoid power struggles. Adapt to situations rather than trying to change them. Cultivate the good graces of others – though this will not be so easy with Mars going through your 7th House after the 17th.

Your important areas of interest are the home, family and psychological issues, love and romance, personal transformation, the deeper things of life, debts and their repayment, helping others to prosper, libido, religion, foreign travel and higher education, and spirituality.

You've had better health periods in your life, Pisces. Rest and relax more until the 22nd. You need to be careful after this time as well, but this is the most difficult and vulnerable period for you. Lessened vitality will force you to focus on the really important things in your life and to let more minor things go or delegate them to others. Keep the peace with friends and lovers as much as possible. Sexual moderation becomes important after the 22nd. Wear the colours, gem and scent of your Sign.

Love is active, but can get stormy when Mars moves into your House of Love on the 17th. The tendency is to become overly aggressive in love or in social situations. On the positive side this gives you great social courage and confidence, but it can also lead to power struggles with the beloved or with the object of your affection. Singles find love as they pursue their normal financial goals. Love is at the workplace, the bank, brokerage or financial planner's office. Material gifts turn you on now. You are interested in people who can further your financial goals.

Finances are stormy this month and you will have to work harder for your earnings than usual. Expenses in the home or a on foreign trip can put a dent in your financial resources. Friends and social contacts boost earnings.

October

Best Days Overall: 1st, 9th, 10th, 11th, 18th, 19th, 27th, 28th

Most Stressful Days Overall: 2nd, 3rd, 16th, 17th, 23rd, 24th, 29th, 30th

Best Days for Love: 1st, 9th, 10th, 11th, 18th, 19th, 20th, 21st, 23rd, 24th, 27th, 28th, 29th, 30th

Best Days for Money: 4th, 5th, 6th, 7th, 24th, 25th, 26th

With Saturn's retrograde back into Taurus and many planets in the Sign of Scorpio, the stresses on your health are much relieved. You will hear good news on this front.

Mars in the Sign of Virgo is an excellent financial indicator. It makes you more cautious, value-conscious and careful about how you spend your money. This is a good period for shopping (before the 18th) as your judgement will be good. It's also a good time for sorting out your accounts and handling financial minutiae.

Mars in Virgo shows that financial goals should be pursued through social means – at parties, through friends and gatherings. The social graces bring earnings. Good friends are like money in the bank. Prospective lovers need to be supportive of your financial goals in order to interest you. Your present spouse or lover also seems supportive. A business partnership is likely. Consummate all social arrangements or partnerships before the 18th – when Mercury starts to retrograde.

Many planets in the Western sector of the chart further reinforces the need to achieve goals by social means. The good graces of others are vital this month.

The retrograde of two important planets plus most of the planetary power above the Horizon shows that it is safe and advisable to let home and family issues slide for a while and to focus on your career and outer ambitions. Venus' move into your 10th House of Career on the 19th brings success and the favour of those above you in status.

Job-seekers enjoy incredible luck until the 23rd. Afterwards, job-seeking seems more difficult.

Much power in the 9th House makes this a happy month. The mind is expanded. The 'how to' of things is revealed. Happy educational opportunities come. You meet teachers and mentors effortlessly. There are happy opportunities for foreign travel. Love can find you while you are in a foreign land, or at a church or university function. Perhaps you fall in love with your professor or vice versa. Religious illumination and experience enhance your love life. There is much optimism and joviality in your life.

November

Best Days Overall: 6th, 7th, 15th, 23rd, 24th

Most Stressful Days Overall: 13th, 19th, 20th, 26th, 27th

Best Days for Love: 6th, 7th, 8th, 9th, 15th, 16th, 19th, 20th, 23rd, 24th, 28th, 29th

Best Days for Money: 2nd, 3rd, 4th, 8th, 9th, 12th, 13th, 21st, 22nd, 30th

The Grand Trine in the element of Air (after the 4th) is a mixed blessing for you, Pisces. On the one hand it sharpens your mental faculties and increases your communication skills; on the other, you are surrounded by people who want to gab about nothing in particular. Being a secretive type, this grates upon you. But if you know that this is the astrological weather you will handle it better.

Health is excellent until the 22nd, but afterwards rest and relax more. Health stress is considerable after the 22nd, and you must do everything possible to conserve and maximize energy. Take nothing too much to heart, and focus on the art of the possible.

By the 22nd the planetary power will be dominant in the East. Neptune, your Ruler, is firmly forward. You are much more independent and self-reliant – more able to control your destiny – than in previous months. Neptune in Aquarius and receiving beautiful aspects shows a new sense of personal freedom as well. Shape your future as you will.

The planets are still mostly above the Horizon and your 10th House of Career becomes powerful after the 22nd. Let emotional and family issues slide for a while and focus on your outer ambitions. A new and happy job offer comes after the 22nd. Career gets boosted the old-fashioned way – through work and productivity – and not through politics.

Though your vitality is not what it should be, your personal appearance shines and you are very attractive to others. Mars, leaving your House of Love on the 4th, is a positive love signal as power conflicts with the beloved begin to abate. Either they are settled or there is less of an urge towards these struggles. The forward motion of your Love Planet on the 8th also helps. Love opportunities arise at religious or academic events or parties. Your personal spiritual path could create a temporary conflict with the beloved. You look for educated, refined types but then get into philosophical arguments with them. Spiritual compatibility with the beloved doesn't come easily now and must be consciously worked out.

Finances become super-charged after the 4th as Mars receives beautiful aspects from most of the planets. Money comes to you as you help others to prosper. Channel extra cash into paying off debt. Borrow only if you can make more from the cash than the interest expense. Investors will flock to good ideas and projects now.

December

Best Days Overall: 3rd, 4th, 12th, 13th, 20th, 21st, 22nd, 30th, 31st

Most Stressful Days Overall: 10th, 11th, 16th, 17th, 23rd, 24th

Best Days for Love: 6th, 7th, 10th, 11th, 14th, 15th, 16th, 17th, 18th, 19th, 24th, 25th, 28th, 29th

Best Days for Money: 1st, 2nd, 6th, 7th, 10th, 11th, 18th, 19th, 28th, 30th, 31st

Most of the planets above the Horizon and much power in your 10th House makes this an important career month. Handle home and family issues with dispatch but get right back to your major focus – your career. The Sun moving through your House of Career shows that old-fashioned hard work and productivity boost your career – and will produce luck and expansion. Mercury in your Career House from the 3rd to the 23rd shows that spouses, lovers and family members are supporting your career and that you are supporting theirs. There is much socializing with bosses and those above you in status during this period. And, for singles, an office romance is likely.

Though love and social activities are prominent and happy during this period, many planets in the East show that you are more your own person these days. You have the will, the power and the wherewithal to have things your way and to create your life as you desire it to be. It's not necessary to adapt to unpleasant situations.

The Solar Eclipse of the 25th deals kindly with you, Pisces. Though it could produce a job change and a testing of the marriage, the end result will be good and the disruptions in your life will be minimum. Flaws in the home could be revealed so that they can be corrected, and many of you might move house. A family member or spouse redefines their personality and changes their image.

Venus travels near Neptune after the 8th, bringing nice, stylish clothing or jewellery to you and otherwise enhancing your image. You are very attractive to others this month. Early in the month you want someone who can further your career. Later on you will want a friend and comrade. Early in the month you are interested in your lover's status; later you want an equal.

Mars (your Financial Planet) in your 8th House for most of the month indicates a focus on helping others to prosper. There is a need to pay off debt; spare cash should be channelled for that purpose. Money comes from your spouse or lover. When Mars moves into Scorpio on the 23rd your financial judgement becomes deep and sound. Investments made during this period will be shrewd ones. Your financial urges become intense and one-pointed – perhaps fanatical. This fanaticism could conflict with your high spiritual ideals. Financial goals will be achieved easily.

Rest and relax more until the 21st.